THE TEACHING AND TEACHINGS OF TEMPLE BUDDHISM IN CONTEMPORARY JAPAN

THE TEACHING AND TEACHINGS OF TEMPLE BUDDHISM IN CONTEMPORARY JAPAN

Stephen G. Covell

UNIVERSITY OF HAWAIʻI PRESS
HONOLULU

Paperback edition 2025
Printed in the United States of America

First printed, 2024

Library of Congress Cataloging-in-Publication Data

Names: Covell, Stephen Grover, author.
Title: The teaching and teachings of Temple Buddhism in contemporary Japan / Stephen G. Covell.
Description: Honolulu : University of Hawaiʻi Press, [2024] | Includes bibliographical references and index.
Identifiers: LCCN 2024002847 (print) | LCCN 2024002848 (ebook) | ISBN 9780824897574 (hardback) | ISBN
9780824898717 (epub) | ISBN 9780824898724 (kindle edition) | ISBN 9780824898700 (pdf)
Subjects: LCSH: Buddhist education—Japan. | Buddhism—Study and teaching—Japan.
Classification: LCC BQ162.J3 C68 2024 (print) | LCC BQ162.J3 (ebook) | DDC 294.3/750952—dc23/eng/20240510
LC record available at https://lccn.loc.gov/2024002847
LC ebook record available at https://lccn.loc.gov/2024002848

ISBN 9780824898878 (paperback)

Cover: Lessons at Gannōji Temple, Nagoya. Photograph by Enshin Sakurai.

University of Hawaiʻi Press books are printed on acid-free paper and meet the guidelines for permanence and durability of the Council on Library Resources.

This book is dedicated to my mother, Dr. Ruth Covell (1936–2022). She supported me through thick and thin, even if she did think folks in the humanities took their sweet time getting things done.

CONTENTS

ACKNOWLEDGMENTS

I could never have managed to finish this book without the help of many people. Shimazono Susumu helped to guide some of the early research when I worked with him on a postdoc many years ago. My colleagues in the Midwest Japan Seminar read drafts of two of the chapters and gave me valuable feedback and encouragement. Initial phases of the research were made possible by a Fulbright Fellowship. The faculty and staff at Taishō University were always helpful and kindly put up with my questions and requests over the years. I should especially thank Saitō Enshin and Shioiri Hōdō for their help with materials and advice. Finally, I must also thank my fellow faculty who kindly did not complain when I took a year off from over ten years of serving as department chair to write up the last few chapters. Most of all, I would like to thank my family for all their support and endless patience.

1

BUDDHISM IS WHAT BUDDHISM DOES

If it were only about walking, the postman would be far greater. Our job is worshipping as we walk.

—Hagami, *Kaihōgyō no kokoro*

Early on in my research on Temple Buddhism in Japan I became fascinated by what is taught at Buddhist institutions. How do they communicate Buddhist teachings, and what teachings are communicated? It quickly became apparent that what I was seeing at Buddhist training temples and Buddhist universities was not limited to courses and workshops on classical doctrine and the writings of early masters. Something more digestible, more readily understood by priests in training as well as by the public, was being taught. Indeed, these more accessible outward-facing teachings appeared to be the dominant form of Buddhist teachings in Japan. This book is an exploration of what is taught by Buddhists at Buddhist educational institutions and by a group of leading Buddhist practitioners. This examination also highlights how those teachings are communicated.

Before venturing further into an examination of the teaching and teachings of Temple Buddhism today, it may be helpful to understand what drove me in this direction for my research. The title of this chapter—"Buddhism Is What Buddhism Does"—has its roots in two sources stemming from two time periods in my academic life. First was an event that shaped how I view the object of study. Many, many years ago, when I was working on my master's degree at the University of Hawaiʻi, my adviser scolded a student in class, a Buddhist nun, when she made the bold claim that Tendai Buddhism was not really Buddhism. My adviser commented to the effect that if someone claims to be Buddhist, we should assume that they are Buddhist, and that if such a person claims their teaching is Buddhism, then we should view it as Buddhism. Certainly in the case of Tendai, were we to say it should no longer be considered Buddhism, almost the entirety of Buddhism in East Asia would disappear with it. The point is, for scholars to enter sectarian debate over what is and is not really Buddhism boxes us in and shutters from our view the contexts and contours of Buddhism as it is practiced. We bring enough of our preconceptions and biases to the table already; we would do best to set aside the question of what qualifies as "real" Buddhism. After a decade of running a Religion Department and having this conversation with many faculty inside and outside my department, I am more convinced than ever that as academics we should do as my adviser said and neither discount nor redefine from on high the claims made by practitioners. This is not to say that we cannot unpack sectarian histories, seek out the roots of belief systems, and splay open lineage charts, but in doing so we should not be involved in picking winners in the "who or what is really Buddhism" debate. In a similar way, David McMahan writes,

> Let us re-ask the question, then. Is the contemporary articulation of interdependence an unalloyed rendition of canonical and classical understandings? Harris and Blum are generally correct in saying that it is not. It is something unique to this age—a hybrid construction that is based on Asian and Western sources, synthesizing them into a novel conception. So one might be tempted to argue that it is "inauthentic." But this would be to grant a static, essentialized meaning to canonical texts, to the normative interpretation of one school or another, or to a particular moment in the history of Asian forms of Buddhism. The historian of religion, qua historian, should not merely recapitulate sectarian or even canonical rhetorics of authenticity but examine what practitioners *do* with the texts and other elements of the tradition.[1]

It is my contention that, minimally, when a self-declared Buddhist, as a member of an institution that identifies itself as Buddhist, proclaims certain writings, utterances, or practices to be Buddhist teachings, then we have to understand them as Buddhism. That does not preclude investigating their sources, whether those be in Buddhist or Confucian texts or something altogether different, but it *is* a problem when we as scholars declare them "not Buddhist." To do so is, on the one hand, to participate in sectarian debates—in which case we must ask ourselves, what is our stake in those debates? And, on the other hand, such an exercise in delineating who has the authority to speak on Buddhism within the academy can only serve to silence voices and create false divisions and categories. If we insist on denying that something is Buddhism while ignoring claims of Buddhist practitioners that it *is* Buddhism, then we are no more than Buddhist theologians tied to defending our own understanding of Buddhism; we are no longer scholars observing ongoing developments in religious history.

The second event that shaped my views on this subject is one that made me question how authority to speak on Buddhism is contested within Buddhist studies. Years ago there was a conference sponsored by the Bukkyō Dendō Kyōkai (仏教伝道教会) that Buddhist studies scholars from a variety of backgrounds attended. At that conference, the majority of the papers focused on practices and people that had rarely received such attention. At the close of the conference, this question was asked: Are these marginal practices and practitioners? In other words, are they practices and practitioners seen as outside the mainstream and therefore understudied? Or have these people and practices been marginalized by the elites of their times and, at least as importantly, have contemporary researchers marginalized them by the way they view the field and conduct their work? I am interested here in the latter question.

The basic source of the problem within academia—namely, the silo effect of fields of study—has been covered from a variety of directions from as early as thirty years ago by Bernard Faure, Griffith Foulk, Louis Gomez, Bob Sharf, and others. These have been summarized in the work Mark Rowe and I did for the *Japanese Journal of Religious Studies* almost two decades ago, revisited by Jørn Borup (*Japanese Rinzai Zen Buddhism*), and hammered on again by Rowe in 2012 (*Bonds of the Dead*). Nevertheless, their remarkable resilience makes me think the conversation is not over. As an administrator I deal with this on a regular basis. The silo effect has an impact not just on how we approach the object of study but also on funding, and visions of higher education that can shape our field as well.

Since the silo effect has been covered elsewhere, here I approach this issue briefly through an angle perhaps a little different than others. First is the question of language. The long history of philology at the center of Buddhist studies impacts how we understand who has the scholarly authority to discuss Buddhism. Do you read Sanskrit or Pali? No? Then not too long ago your grasp of Buddhism would have been questioned by fellow academics. The same goes for classical Chinese. Indeed, often your access to the study of Buddhism is limited based on your mastery of certain languages, because programs base entrance on prospective students' skills in classical Buddhist languages.

The question of mastery of language, especially of classical languages, belies a deeper problem, one especially strong among religious elites but also within Buddhist studies, which is the valuation of old over new. As an example of what I mean, on one of my research trips to Japan I found that very few copies remain of many of the contemporary newsletters, minutes from denominational meetings, or video footage from old TV interviews. This kind of material was not considered central to the denomination and was wholly overlooked by scholars. This was in stark contrast to the manner in which treatises on classical texts by scholar-priests at Buddhist universities or the dharma talks of leading, long-dead priests were treated. Now imagine that you are at an ancient temple. The head priest—himself a leading Buddhist studies scholar—and his son and a couple of temple lay members are sorting through boxes of material in the aging storehouse. As you stand by watching, they pull out a dust-covered box, open it up, and begin rummaging through the documents inside. There, shoved into the box, you see sermons from past priests, essays from leading lay members, and materials from headquarters about priestly promotions—a veritable gold mine of information. All of this pulled from just one box in the old temple storeroom. Before you can pipe up and say, "Wow, that looks interesting," the priest lifts the box, carries it outside, and dumps it on the growing pile of garbage burning in the firepit outside the temple. I know for most of you, as for me, this would be a heartbreaking moment. Just imagine the amazing material lost. Whole dissertations have been written on far less material from the Nara (710–794), Heian (794–1185), or Kamakura (1185–1333) periods. Nevertheless, in this case it is a pile of contemporary newsletters, sect communiqué, and other documents that, to the priest and, until recently, to many scholars, are seen as having little value. They are not, after all, key historical documents, or are they?

This division of labor—separating historians, Buddhologists, and anthropologists—which at its heart appears to favor the past over the present within Buddhist studies, brings us back to the first issue: how we define the object of study, Buddhism/Buddhists. As just mentioned, there has been a tendency within traditional Buddhology to sort out what is "Buddhist" from what is not based on an inherent bias for age. This approach places Buddhism as an artifact from the past to be unearthed and read back into life, and struggles to see Buddhism as an ongoing, changing religion. This is something McMahan discusses in some depth in his work on modern Buddhism. One area where this is still seen is the way the study of contemporary Buddhist lay movements has not been understood to be a part of Buddhist studies proper but instead has been assigned to the realm of religious studies or anthropology and the study of new religious movements (NRMs).

In addition to the language capabilities of the researcher and the age of the material, a third area of bias relates to the physical site of the creation and maintenance of the teachings. The denominational training centers, head temples, and, perhaps more recently, research institutes at Buddhist universities are turned to when looking to understand the teachings of Buddhism. I would argue that the center is much more diffuse. Work on the contemporary production of Buddhist teachings being done by Victoria Montrose, John Nelson, Jolyon Thomas, Mark Rowe, myself, and others points to a far more negotiated process in which a single, central physical site of production cannot be readily identified. For example, working on the present, a period awash in data, allows us to see how denominational doctrinal centers interact—or at times fail to interact—with local priests as those priests attempt to understand the teachings they have been taught in their training and make those teachings accord to the needs of their local constituency and blend with local tradition.

When I first dove into the topic of the teachings of contemporary Temple Buddhism, my goal was to find out what Buddhists were teaching in Japan today. By understanding what was being taught on the ground, I hoped to learn what self-declared Buddhists and Buddhist institutions in contemporary Japan understood Buddhism to be. There are many ways in which teachings are created and understood and many more in which they are disseminated, just as there are a great variety of people we might call Temple Buddhism teachers. One thing for certain is that in trying to understand Buddhist teachings, we must look at Buddhist education, including Buddhist universities, Buddhist secondary and primary education, Buddhist kindergartens, and Buddhist seminaries and training programs. Buddhist education is a thread that winds through Japanese religion and society and is itself woven together from government education policy, the interests of denominational headquarters, local temple needs, critical family and community issues, proselytizing interests of Buddhist institutions, and various Buddhist understandings of practice and doctrine, among others. For these reasons the next three chapters focus on various aspects of Buddhist education.

We will see in the chapters that follow that what is taught, how it is taught, and where and to whom it is taught are all influenced by regulations, laws, and institutional practices and biases. Especially when considering the outward, public-facing teachings, those taught not just to priests but also to the laity at a variety of venues (kindergartens, colleges, books, outreach programs, etc.), we see that contemporary Temple Buddhism teachings represent a blending of traditions, some of which have become cultural norms whose religious roots are lost to most people.

For the purposes of this study, Temple Buddhism in contemporary Japan is what Buddhists say and do. It is multifaceted and always in flux, and it is created in and re-created through interaction with other traditions both secular (as we can see in Buddhist education) and religious (as we can see in the interaction between Temple Buddhism and Buddhist lay movements). In the following chapters, I will discuss four examples of the teachings of contemporary Temple Buddhism: the teachings found at Buddhist kindergartens, the teaching of Buddhism at Buddhist colleges, the teachings of Buddhist educators concerned about moral education, and the teaching of a group of elite ascetic practitioners. I will argue that what is taught, despite not always reflecting classical doctrine or regularly citing specific sutra, represents the outward/public-facing teachings of Buddhism in contemporary Japan and, measured by the number of people it potentially reaches, is the predominant form disseminated. I hope that the examples I present show what is taught as Temple Buddhism today, how teaching is conducted, and what factors have shaped the teachings and teaching of Buddhism throughout the modern and contemporary periods. In so doing, I seek to move us toward reconsidering how we approach studying Buddhism and how we go about deciding where the center and periphery, mainstream and marginal, lie in the realm of the production and distribution of Buddhist teachings.

Throughout the following chapters we will see a strong interest in a renewal of the education system on the part of members of the Temple Buddhism community. They, like many others in Japan, see Japan as having grown in material wealth at the expense of spiritual wealth. Many also see Japan as in moral decline, something they believe diminishes Japan's global status. We will also see that Buddhist educators and leading practitioners alike believe that the Japanese people have within their cultural heritage the roots of Buddhist teachings and that education can draw out that heritage and return the Japanese people to a firm moral grounding.

Furthermore, we will learn in the following chapters that Buddhist leaders in early childhood education, primary and secondary education, and higher education, along with leading Buddhist ascetic practitioners, espouse a similar set of teachings. These teachings include interdependence, which is a core Buddhist teaching. Here we find it is used in part to emphasize one's connection to family, the ancestors, and the broader community. Other teachings we will encounter repeatedly include sincerity, gratitude, empathy, self-reliance, persistence, perseverance, and compassion. We will also learn how an emphasis on faith and reverential awe in a higher power are important teachings. Individual chapters will bring to light the practices that are believed to lead to the embodiment of these teachings. Practices that we will often see include using role models to learn proper manners and behavior, greetings, and service. Greetings, for example, when done with persistence, are understood to be transformative, leading one to understand interdependence, empathy, and sincerity. The fact that all of this sounds very much like the worldview of the new religious movements in Japan, and especially the Buddhist lay movements studied by Helen Hardacre, Shimazono Susumu, and others, will be discussed.

Chapter 2 concerns Buddhist early childhood education. Although rarely (if ever) regarded as a site for the production and dissemination of Buddhist teachings, Buddhist early childhood education facilities are generally run by priests, staffed by teachers who received their teaching licenses at Buddhist colleges, and attended by large numbers of people. For many Japanese they are the first place and, until death, one of the only places where they interact with a Buddhist institution. As with other educational facilities that will be examined in the following chapters, kindergartens and their related networks are responsible for the oversight and dissemination of Buddhist teachings that reach a vast audience. Buddhist early childhood education allows a view into the complex system of interactions that serves to create Buddhism today. The Buddhist teachings of Buddhist early childhood education are about thankfulness, interdependence, and knowing Buddhas and deities as present in this world. They are taught through repetition, practical application, and sentiment education, which involves the use of nonverbal cues.

From early childhood education we move on, in chapter 3, to Buddhist colleges. This chapter examines what is taught at Buddhist universities and how what is taught has been shaped by laws and regulations governing higher education through the modern period as well as by regulations and programs that target religious institutions. We see a shift over time from training for the priesthood, to education designed for the priesthood, to education designed to reach a lay audience. This chapter explores these changes and looks at the ways Buddhist colleges and universities seek to reach audiences beyond their traditional constituency of Buddhist priests in training. While priests studying at Buddhist colleges and universities learn classical doctrine and sectarian history, it is apparent that they are learning to integrate that knowledge into contemporary areas such as social outreach. It is also clear that these institutions seek to inculcate at least a modicum of understanding in basic Buddhist concepts along with an appreciation for Temple Buddhism in their non-priesthood-bound students.

Chapter 4 moves the conversation away from Buddhist higher education and looks at how Buddhist educators view and engage in debates regarding moral education. After exploring the modern history of moral education, with a special emphasis on heart/mind (*kokoro*) education, this chapter investigates the teachings of two Buddhist educators. It then examines approaches taken by Buddhist secondary education institutions to promote moral education. One key finding is that what is taught as Buddhism tends to reflect what we saw in the earlier chapter on Buddhist early childhood education. Manners, thankfulness, reverential awe for something beyond human power, and returning a debt of gratitude to one's parents, ancestors, and society are all key teachings at Buddhist secondary schools, just as they are at Buddhist early childhood education facilities.

Chapter 5 brings us out of K–12 and college education, which may seem far from the center of Buddhist authority, and asks us to consider the teachings of contemporary practitioners of Buddhist asceticism, in this case the practitioners of the *kaihōgyō* (回峰行). This chapter, which was previously published in a shorter version, was partly what inspired me to explore what was taught as Buddhism in Buddhist education. I wanted to find out whether the teachings these elite monks espoused represented something unique to them, or whether they were taught more broadly within Temple Buddhism. It is placed at the end of this book as a way to reflect on the contemporary public-facing teachings of Temple Buddhism and to show that what we have seen in Buddhist kindergartens, high schools, and colleges is very similar to what is taught by some of the most elite practitioners of Buddhism in Japan today. These practitioners represent to some the Buddhist ideal type. They are seen by the faithful as living Buddhas. They undergo extreme practices that take many years to complete, and they preach to large audiences both in person and through the written word. We find the same basic teachings that we have found in previous chapters such as gratitude, sincerity, and belief in something beyond human power. This indicates that the outward, public-facing teachings of Buddhist educational institutions are not unique to those institutions but are shared by the most elite practitioners and in this way represent mainstream Buddhist thought and practice in Japan today.

This is by no means a comprehensive study of the contemporary teaching and teachings of Temple Buddhism. This book focuses on the teachings as expressed by elite practitioners, denominational leaders, and Buddhist educators. To be a truly comprehensive work, this book should include analysis of the dharma talks of Buddhist priests from a variety of locales and a variety of backgrounds (temple sons, priests from a lay background, temple wives). Encouraging work in that area is currently being done by Jessica Starling, Tim Graf, Nathon Michon, and others. In addition to the myriad differing voices of local priests, to be truly complete, I should also include a study of denominational propagation associations and the institutions within Temple Buddhism denominations that are charged with keeping the orthodoxy. No doubt a thorough study of priestly training at national and regional training temples would also be crucial. I hope that others will dive into these areas to further add to the picture. The material presented here is a broad overview. It is a sampling of the teachings, and how and why those teachings are communicated as they are, that will hopefully inspire others to investigate the areas I just identified above to learn more about how Buddhist teachings are created and re-created in contemporary Japan and what that process says about how we as scholars approach Buddhism as a subject of research and teaching.

2

BUDDHISM FOR CHILDREN?

Buddhist Early Childhood Education in Japan

> I am certain that the three years spent in *yōchien* before entering elementary school are the most important years between when one is born and when one dies for shaping one's heart.
>
> —Nakano Kindergarten

In terms of doctrinal orthodoxy, Buddhist preschools, kindergartens, and daycares are not generally viewed as being anything more than marginal to the "real" Buddhism of the elite monastic training centers. Yet they are most often run by priests and are regularly staffed by teachers who earn their teaching licenses at Buddhist colleges. Every denomination hosts training workshops, and most have kindergarten associations that provide seminars, sample lesson plans, and the like. Buddhist preschools, kindergartens, and daycares are not small operations. They reach a large number of people and represent one of the first and—until death and a funeral—one of the only places where laity interacts regularly with a Buddhist institution. Buddhist preschools, kindergartens, and daycares at their peak comprised up to a quarter of all such facilities in Japan. Around 90 percent of all Japanese citizens now attend at least two years of kindergarten or daycare.[1]

The exact number of Buddhist facilities is hard to determine. On its home page the Japan Buddhist Nursery and Kindergarten Association (Nihon Bukkyō Hoiku Kyōkai, 仏教保育教会, hereafter NBHK) claims 1,163 daycares and kindergartens as members, or roughly 8 percent of all facilities in Japan.[2] Although this is the main organization for Buddhist facilities, not all schools are members. According to the Buddhist scholar Mochida Eiichi's numbers from the late 1970s, there were approximately 4,200 Buddhist daycares and kindergartens that represented roughly 28 percent of all such facilities.[3] It is likely that the actual percentage of Buddhist schools is currently between 8 percent and 20 percent of the total. An equally intriguing number is enrollment. One small Buddhist daycare provider wrote in 2005 that since opening in 1955 his daycare had graduated over 7,000 children.[4] While that number on its own is not large, this is one of but many such facilities. The impact of teaching in kindergartens, at least in terms of numbers of people potentially exposed to Buddhist teachings, is tremendous. Kindergartens and their related associations, college certification programs, and the like represent a network of sites responsible for the oversight and dissemination of Buddhist teachings that reach a vast audience on a regular basis. This network overlaps with other sites of production, including denominational centers responsible for maintaining orthodoxy, preaching associations, regional denominational networks, and secular early childhood education networks. As such, Buddhist early childhood education and care illuminates the complex system of interactions that have created Buddhism today. Be that as it may, Buddhist early childhood education and care facilities tend to be mentioned in research on Temple Buddhism only as an institutional development designed either to compete with similar developments in Christianity or as money-making ventures. They are never discussed as sites for the production and dissemination of Buddhist teachings.

This is one reason that Buddhist early childhood education and care facilities (hereafter ECEC) are interesting to examine. Most books on Buddhism and the events of the Meiji period (1868–1912)—including Buddhist responses to the persecution of Buddhism, and Buddhist reactions to the influx of Christian missionaries—tend to at least footnote the advent of Buddhist daycare facilities and kindergartens. Research on the postwar period also tends to note that Buddhist groups became involved in ECEC in increasing numbers following World War II, and it was these assertions that initially led me to study Buddhist ECEC. If Buddhists pursued education to address a variety of issues in the modern period as an important part of their practice, perhaps these endeavors warrant more than a footnote or a statistic in a chart.

I also became interested in the topic through research into Buddhist propagation. Christian groups have long used education to gain converts and to spread the teachings of Christianity. I wanted to examine whether Buddhist education is also tied to spreading the teachings of Buddhism. In this chapter, I begin with a history of ECEC in Japan to put Buddhist education into context. Then I provide an outline of Buddhist ECEC, and finally I focus on what is taught as Buddhism in Buddhist ECEC in Japan.

I define the term "early childhood education and care" as the education and care of children under six.[5] There are several terms in Japanese that encompass this definition. In particular, this chapter focuses on *hoikuen* (保育園, nursery/daycare) and *yōchien* (幼稚園, preschool/kindergarten).[6] In recent years, with the growing demand for more educational preparation at daycares and longer hours at kindergartens to meet family working schedules, the services offered at these two types of childcare facilities have grown very similar.[7] The manner in which the Japanese government administers them hints at the major historical difference: *yōchien* are governed by the Ministry of Education, and *hoikuen* are governed by the Ministry of Welfare.[8] As we will see, the history of Buddhist early childhood education draws from and runs parallel to Buddhist welfare activities in childcare.

EARLY CHILDHOOD EDUCATION AND CARE IN MODERN JAPAN

Modern early childhood education made its debut in Japan during the Meiji period (1868–1912). Although the image of Meiji Japan most often presented is one of a country playing a frenzied game of catch-up to the West, an examination of early childhood education shows that Japan was developing right alongside its Western counterparts. The first *yōchien*—a public school attached to Tokyo Women's Higher Normal School 東京女子高等師範学校, now Ochanomizu University お茶の水女子大学—opened in Japan in 1876.[9] The importance of this early effort can be seen in the presence of the empress and empress dowager at its opening.[10] The kindergarten movement itself was only a few decades old in Europe at that point and, in the United States, was still just getting underway. The first US kindergarten appeared only sixteen years before the first one in Japan.[11]

The kindergarten movement was founded by Friedrich Froebel (1782–1852) in Germany. What separated his approach from previous views of early childhood education was his rejection of the idea that children are inherently sinful. Based on this radical new idea, he developed an age-based curriculum.[12] His ideas slowly spread throughout Europe, and by the early 1860s they were making some headway in the United States. Within a few years, these ideas would find their way into Japanese education. According to Joy Hendry, "It is hardly surprising that the Japanese took greatly to their hearts the teachings of Froebel, who saw man's nature as good, and the bad side of child behaviour as due to a disturbed relationship between 'the true, original nature of a child and the distorted world of his environment.'"[13] Froebel's views meshed well with indigenous views of childhood and human development.

In her history of the kindergarten movement in Japan, Roberta Wollons describes two main lines within the development of early childhood education: public and Christian. As we will see, a third major line—Buddhist—develops later. Wollons persuasively argues that the fundamental values of the kindergarten movement, particularly the development of individual capacities, meshed well with the new Meiji government's educational goals as outlined in the 1872 Gakusei (学制, Education Order).[14] The Gakusei emphasized personal cultivation of talent and prosperity. Four goals were set forth: "(1) to eliminate feudalistic barriers and open educational opportunities to all citizens, (2) to consider the individual's success in life and enlightenment as the goals of study and education, (3) to emphasize the three Rs and other practical studies (e.g., medicine and engineering), and (4) to leave the cost of education to individuals."[15] The Gakusei called specifically for the establishment of *yōchi shōgakko* (幼稚小学校) for the education of children up to the age of six. While the school system did not end up developing exactly as laid out by the Gakusei (largely due to funding shortfalls),[16] 5 *yōchien* (1 national, 3 public, and 1 private) had opened by 1880. By 1925 there were 957 (2 national, 347 public, and 608 private); by 1940 there were 2,079; and by 1965 there were 8,391.[17] In 1971 there were 11,180, and in 2013 there were 13,170.[18]

The initial handful of *yōchien* catered to the children of the elite. This situation changed as interest in early childhood education spread and as the number of people trained as teachers grew. Christian missionaries played an early and dominant role in the development of *yōchien* and were influenced heavily by Froebel, a devout Christian.[19] Wollons and Nishida Yukiyo describe the most famous case.[20] In 1889 Glory Kindergarten was established in the port city of Kobe and served as a training center. The founder, Annie Lyon Howe, became an influential figure in the Japanese early childhood education movement. In some ways, Howe's very success led to a diminishing role for Christian facilities. As the number of graduates from her training center increased, Japanese instructors took control of the teaching and dissemination of early childhood education and began to shift the curriculum to reflect Japanese values and to move away from Christian education.[21] In particular, the Meiji government's emphasis on moral education, as articulated in the 1899 Imperial Rescript on Education (教育勅語, Kyōiku Chokugo), came to be reflected in the teaching emphasis at *yōchien*.[22] The Meiji government also came to stress early childhood education as preparation for further schooling, an idea that went against Froebel's view that education should focus on the child's development in stages.[23] The desire to connect early childhood education with elementary school preparation continues today with directives from the Ministry of Education, Culture, Sports, Science, and Technology (文部科学省, hereafter MEXT) that encourage just such a connection. Such directives now, as in the past, shape the type of educational experience that can be had at a *yōchien* or *hoikuen*.[24]

While *yōchien* were developing for children of the affluent, early childcare efforts came to be focused on poor and abandoned children. Care for children in poor or working neighborhoods and for abandoned children expanded in the late Meiji.[25] By the late 1800s, industrialization brought many women into the workforce, which led to a new trend in child-focused welfare activities. The need for female labor in the factories of a modernizing Japan created a concomitant demand for childcare facilities (most often referred to as *takujijo,* 託児所). A short while later, the Russo-Japanese War (1904–1905) further increased the demand for childcare facilities as production ramped up and men were called away to fight. The industrial expansion that occurred around the time of World War I yet again put stress on childcare facilities. This is also when growing public and government demands for increased regulation of the childcare business began to be heard.[26] Following the end of World War II, there was a marked increase in childcare facilities. This was especially due to the growth of the Japanese economy and the corresponding shift in work patterns and family structures. These changes necessitated more care options outside the home for young children.

BUDDHIST EARLY CHILDHOOD EDUCATION AND CARE

The above history gives us the backdrop against which to observe the growth of Buddhist ECEC. Buddhist developments, as we shall see, tend to mirror those that occurred in society at large. Buddhists entered the realm of modern early childhood education after Christian missionaries but eventually came to play a dominant role. For many within Buddhist education, entering the realm of ECEC was and is seen as an opportunity to make a difference in the lives of many. As one educator wrote,

> It certainly feels that a negative image of [Temple Buddhism] as largely concerned with funerals is being advanced today. It is true that a lot of funerals and memorial services are held these days. Be that as it may, I am certain that the three years spent in *yōchien* before entering elementary school are the most important years between when one is born and when one dies for shaping one's heart. And I want to carefully communicate the Buddha's teaching [in these formative years].[27]

Buddhist education is often linked to *terakoya* (寺子屋), schools that offered basic education to commoners throughout the Tokugawa period (1603–1868). According to education scholars Okano Kaori and Tsuchiya Motonori, these schools had a "three Rs" curriculum and, unlike most other educational institutions of the time, admitted women.[28] They also served as platforms for the teaching of popular moral values such as those taught by the founder of the Shingaku movement, Ishida Baigan (石田梅巌, 1685–1774).[29] Although *terakoya* have their roots in temples going back to early Buddhist welfare activities in the Kamakura period (1185–1333), by the Tokugawa period *terakoya* were no longer associated exclusively or even primarily with Buddhist temples. The term simply indicated local schooling efforts aimed at commoners.[30]

Buddhists today often point even further back into history when describing their efforts to care for children. A commonly used example is that of a renowned nun, Hōkin-ni (法均尼, or Wake no Hiromushi, 和気広虫, 730–799), the elder sister of the court official Wake no Kyomaro (和気清麻呂, 733–799) who in 765 took in eighty-three abandoned children. Her efforts are seen as the early roots of modern Buddhist childcare.[31] The reference to the eighth-century efforts of a lone nun is best read as an apologetic, because there is little direct connection between these early activities and their modern counterparts. This is much like Buddhist references to Shitennoji (四天王寺), a late sixth-century temple complex designed, in part, to provide care for the poor by providing medicine and other services. Buddhists use Shitennoji as evidence of welfare activity that far outdates that of Christian missionaries in Japan and thus "proves" that modern Buddhist efforts were not simply a response to the Christians.

Buddhists became involved in childcare in the Meiji period after heeding the Meiji government's call for increasing educational opportunities for the poor.[32] Buddhist efforts in this arena were also likely driven by a desire to demonstrate the value of Buddhism to the Japanese people and thereby overcome negative critiques launched under the banner of *haibutsu kishaku* (廃仏毀釈, Destroy Buddhism and Throw Out the Buddha), a movement to dismantle Buddhist institutions in the late 1800s.[33] Research by Japanese scholars on Buddhist childcare is also often couched in terms of countering Christian efforts. As the preeminent scholar of Japanese Buddhism and social welfare Yoshida Kyūichi points out, however, this was not simply a tit-for-tat game of catch-up; rather, it reflected the sincere worries of many Buddhists that Christian education would undermine Japanese values—a view that continues to arise in some quarters of Temple Buddhism today.[34] Buddhist views of Christian education were, in that sense, sympathetic to the government's views as well. According to Nishida Yukiyo, a scholar of early childhood education in Japan, the 1899 Ministry of Education Private School Order (私立学校令, Shiritsu Gakkōrei) "was apparently an attempt by the Ministry of Education to control Christian missionary schools."[35] And as Isoyama Fukumasa, a scholar of Buddhist education, notes, the Ministry of Education's Order No. 12 (訓令第１２ 号, Kunrei Daijūnigō) promulgated in 1900 disallowed religious education in public and private schools. According to Isoyama, the target of this order was Christian schools, because their teaching centered around *jiyūshugi* (自由主義, liberalism), which was not seen as compatible with the government's educational goals.[36] Isoyama writes that although the 1900 ban on religious education effectively meant that Buddhists also had to cease religious education, the Buddhists at that time saw their primary educational activities as training priests, so they did not fight the order to any great extent.[37] This view of Christian (now lumped together as Western) education continues today. For example, the scholar of education Mochida Eiichi argues that Buddhist education can help to overcome the Western emphasis on the individual by de-emphasizing the self and, in that way, support an identity found within the connections of a group.[38] An example of the view that the Western/Christian worldview is egocentric is found in the 2009 remarks of a Japanese politician reported in a *Japan Times* article under the headline "Ozawa Lashes Out with Scathing Remarks on Christianity": Ichirō Ozawa, then-secretary-general of the Democratic Party of Japan, called Christianity "an exclusive, self-righteous religion."[39]

Initial Buddhist efforts were directed at the children of the poor and at other at-risk children. These efforts often were part of other activities taking place at the same institutions and reflected a broad approach to welfare activities.[40] In addition to care for abandoned children, Buddhists endeavored to provide *kanka kyōiku* (感化教育, lit. "influence education," an education designed to influence the emotional nature of the pupil, generally used to describe the education of miscreant youth). The first such Buddhist institution was Chiba

Kanka'in (千葉感化院), which was founded in 1886 in reaction to an increase in youth crime.[41] In the following decade, Buddhists became involved in work caring for youth in the rapidly developing slums in major cities. Yoshida provides ample evidence that there were calls for Buddhist involvement from a variety of quarters, including the mass media and from within Buddhist denominations. As with Christian and public facilities, the emphasis on care for the children of the poor began to shift to an emphasis on providing daycare facilities for women working in factories and, later, with the Russo-Japanese War, on providing daycare for children whose fathers were away at war or killed in action. In 1904, for example, Tsukiji Honganji (築地本願寺, in Tokyo) opened the Dekasegi Gunjin Yōjihoikujo (出稼軍人幼児保育所, Childcare Facility for Soldiers Away from Home), which was aimed at, as its name suggests, the children of deployed soldiers.[42]

The first Buddhist ECEC facility was Kyōai Yōchien (共愛幼稚園) at Kōtokuji (光徳寺) in Himeji, which opened in 1897. It was followed in 1901 by Ashiri Yōchien (足利幼稚園) in Ashiriyama and Tokiwa Yōchien 常葉幼稚園 in Kyoto, and in 1902 by Asakusa Honganji's (浅草本願寺) Tokufū Yōchien (徳風幼稚園) in Tokyo.[43] According to the *Dictionary of Buddhist Social Welfare,* by 1929 there were 531 Buddhist *takujijo* and 243 *yōchien.*[44] These numbers are slightly different than the data presented by Saitō Akitoshi for 1930. The scholar of Buddhist education Saitō says there were 289 Buddhist *yōchien* and 459 *takujijo.* The Pure Land (Jōdo shū) and True Pure Land (Jōdo Shinshū) denominations were the most active, with a total of 185 *yōchien* and 238 *takujijo* between them.[45] Following World War II, the number of Buddhist early childhood education facilities expanded rapidly. In 1968 there were 2,482 *hoikuen* and 1,656 *yōchien.*[46]

As the level of activity increased, Buddhists involved in early childhood education formed the Nihon Bukkyō Hoikukai (日本仏教保育会, hereafter NBHK) in 1929. (By way of comparison, the Christian Kindergarten Union of Japan formed in 1906.)[47] This association provided a forum for discussing everything from curriculum to government policy. Its first national conference was held in 1931 in Tokyo, and the first postwar national conference was in 1950. The five points listed for the 1931 conference give us some idea of the issues the organization believed were of paramount importance: (1) determining the best methods for a thorough Buddhist early childhood education, (2) determining how best to spread Buddhist early childhood education, (3) determining how best to train Buddhist early childhood education teachers, (4) assessing the financial impact on a temple of running an early childhood education facility, and (5) understanding how best to promote the development of such facilities at all temples.[48] This organization still exists today and acts as the central organization for Buddhist ECEC. It publishes two monthly magazines/journals (*Bukkyō Hoiku* 仏教保育and *Bukkyō Hoiku Curriculum* 仏教保育カリキュラム), children's books for use in class, and books on Buddhist education. It also sponsors research, surveys, seminars, and workshops.

The above discussion deals primarily with activities taking place in the cities. There is also a history of Buddhist childcare in rural areas. Isoyama traces Buddhist *kisetsu hoikujo* (季節保育所, seasonal childcare facilities) to the Taishō period. The first of these opened in 1926 at a temple in Mie Prefecture where the temple wife took on the duties of caregiver so mothers could work in the fields during planting and harvesting seasons. These seasonal facilities grew in importance as Japan's occupation of Manchuria in the 1930s deepened and women's labor in the fields became vital. During this period, Buddhist efforts dovetailed with government calls for supporting the nation and the troops.[49]

BUDDHIST ECEC AFTER WORLD WAR II

Isoyama hypothesizes that as a result of Buddhist efforts to work with government demands, Buddhist facilities did not undergo the same level of persecution or suppression that Christian facilities did during the period leading up to and through World War II. And because of that experience, Buddhist educators did not deliberate extensively on the meaning of, and possibilities for, Buddhist education's role within public education in a state in which religion and education were expected to remain separate.[50] This, he surmises, left them unprepared for the changes that followed World War II.

After Japan's defeat in World War II and the promulgation of the Fundamental Law on Education (教育基本法, Kyōiku Kihonhō) in 1947 and the Constitution in 1951, the way religious educational institutions were treated changed. The Constitution and the new law left some ambiguity as to how religious educational institutions were to be treated. Article 20 of the Constitution clearly separates church and state, but Article 9 of the Fundamental Law on Education states that religion must be respected.[51] This dual mandate to separate church and state and yet to respect religion has led to some confusion regarding the way Buddhist ECEC should be treated by the government. On the one hand, they are public institutions in that they provide a public service and meet local public needs. On the other hand, they are religious institutions, therefore the state is bound by the Constitution to avoid directly supporting them.

As it stands, today there is limited state funding for Buddhist ECEC. That funding, when available, is less than that provided for publicly run institutions and has come to place Buddhist efforts at a competitive disadvantage.[52] According to a 1985 article in *Gekkan Jūshoku* (月刊住職), a trade journal for Buddhist temples, *yōchien* had to be registered as Educational Juridical Persons (学校法人, *gakkō hōjin*) in order to receive state support. The average annual income per student at that time was 250,000–300,000 yen. State support added an additional 67,000 yen, making for a substantial funding gap between facilities that qualified for support and those that did not. The authors of the *Gekkan Jūshoku* article point out, however, that Buddhist *yōchien* that failed to register as Educational Juridical Persons suffered not only from a funding gap but also from a negative perception: schools that are registered as educational institutions appeared to consumers (parents) to be better than those that did not.[53]

A new category of "Registered ECEC Centers" (認定こども園, *nintei kodomoen*) introduced in 2006 brought new worries. According to an article in *Chūgai Nippō* (中外日報), the new system, which came into full effect by 2016, entailed changes in funding that created new challenges and opportunities for Buddhist institutions. The new system also involved a requirement that all applicants be accepted (barring certain allowable exceptions). Buddhist childcare facilities questioned whether this would infringe on their religious freedom.[54]

One critique of Buddhist ECEC in postwar Japan is that Buddhists increased their activities in this field to make up for funding lost to postwar land reform and a diminishing lay member base. In an extended article published in *Gekkan Jūshoku* in 1977, one Jōdoshū priest makes it clear that this is precisely why he started his facility for foster children: "It's embarrassing, but to be honest the reason I opened this childcare facility was to make a living." He writes that the postwar land reformation had seen all his lands confiscated and that he had a wife and children to support. The temple lay members did not want his wife to work outside the temple, so he had to think of a way to support his family and maintain the temple that would also benefit society and would gain the support of temple lay members. A friend who was also a temple priest told him that he did not need any experience to open a facility and that if he opened one he would receive support from the national and prefectural governments. He admits that once he opened the facility, he realized both how much work it truly was and the important role it could play in children's lives.[55]

Although opening childcare facilities could prove fiscally advantageous for some, Buddhist facilities often were at a disadvantage from the beginning, assuming they did not incorporate separately from the temple. An examination of the realities of operating such facilities shows that while income generation may very well be one factor in seeking to open a facility, it cannot be the primary factor. Watanabe Masumi outlines six components of opening and running a successful facility: (1) there must be local demand; (2) the temple must have property that can be utilized; (3) there must be funding on hand for buildings, supplies, and so on; (4) the head priest, even if not in charge of operations, must enthusiastically support them; (5) there must be someone in charge who is dedicated to early childhood education; and (6) the temple lay members, the denomination, and the priest's family must be supportive of the project. Lining up all six factors can be very difficult, which means that a facility cannot be easily launched solely as a money-making operation for the temple.[56] The critique of *yōchien* and *hoikuen* as money-making operations also overlooks the way Buddhist educators define their own roles. Literature produced by organizations such as the NBHK and denominational ECEC associations, as well as by individual priests, points to a sincere desire on the part of Buddhists to provide an educational experience for the children that is imbued with a Buddhist character.

Item 6 in the above list points us to one important aspect of the practice of Buddhist ECEC. Today, as for centuries, temples serve as the nexus of activity in local communities. However, the temple community, composed primarily of temple lay membership, is not always contiguous with the local community. Any new endeavor at a typical temple centering on lay members at minimum must receive the blessings of those members. This is because care for their families' ritual needs (primarily ancestor veneration) represents the religious basis for the temple, and because lay members represent the financial foundation of the temple. Satō Benshō argues that ECEC facilities offer temples a chance to integrate into the local community beyond their lay member base.[57] Mochida argues that such facilities offer temples a chance to create a new communal society.[58] Indeed, for schools to survive they must draw on children from beyond their temple member base. If successful, Buddhist educators believe these facilities can serve as a means of spreading the teachings of Buddhism to a broader audience while increasing the temple's local relevance.[59]

One cannot discuss the role of the temple as a community center or the role of educational facilities as income sources and proselytizing venues for temples without discussing Japan's aging society. Buddhist early childhood educational facilities are facing a challenge from the other end of the age spectrum. The dramatic rise in the number of elderly in Japan has drawn the attention of Buddhist organizations. The desire among many Buddhists to reach out to the elderly community has put elder care into direct competition with childcare for scarce resources. Combined with the decreasing birthrate in Japan, we are likely to see the increasing impact of demographics on Buddhist ECEC in the future.[60]

Human resources are the key to the success of spiritual care at temples, just as they are for the childcare offered at temples. Buddhist facilities have found that if they are to compete with other institutions and meet government regulations, they must hire trained teachers and care providers who may not be devout Buddhists.[61] According to Mochida, these teachers often do not see their work at Buddhist institutions as any different from work at public or other private institutions.[62] Therefore, some within Buddhist education argue that the education and care experience offered at Buddhist institutions is in danger of losing its Buddhist nature. In a related matter, it appears many Buddhist institutions have moved toward a status as educational juridical persons (教育法人, *kyōiku hōjin*) to reap the financial and status benefits associated with incorporation and, in so doing, have become separate legal entities from their parent religious juridical person (the temple). This, too, is seen as a move that could lead to a weakening of their Buddhist nature.

As a counterargument to worries about the possible dilution of the Buddhist nature of Buddhist ECEC facilities, Buddhist educators often promote the roles of ECEC facilities as community centers and preaching platforms. They argue that Buddhist education has a critical role to play in local society and, more broadly, in modern Japanese education. For example, in the January 2005 issue of *Zenbutsu* (全仏), the magazine of the Japan Buddhist Federation (全日本仏教会, Zen Nihon Bukkyōkai), the editors comment that Japanese education is in a dilapidated state and is therefore a serious social problem. They make clear that at least part of the blame should be placed on the way religious education is viewed in Japan. They argue that moral education in Japan is weak because it is taught without reference to the foundation of morals, which, in their eyes, is religion.[63] Buddhist ECEC facilities are offered as a potential remedy. They are not seen as separate from public education, or the education of the public. Indeed, by offering a values-based education they are understood to be acting in the public good by shoring up the moral foundations of Japan. One online site for people seeking work in daycares and people looking for help with daycare lists the merits of Buddhist ECEC as the following: learning values such as thankfulness, learning morals, learning basic religious rituals, being in touch with culture, and avoiding facilities related to "cults" and "New Religions."[64]

At the same time, there is an argument within Buddhist education that Buddhist ECEC must consider issues in modern education. Because of factors such as teacher education and the rights of children, the dissemination of the teachings cannot be the sole basis for education. In other words, from this perspective a modern education should be offered. Buddhist ECEC cannot exist just to pass on the Buddhist teachings. Nevertheless, most Buddhist educators stress that Buddhist education must have a distinctly Buddhist character, including the overt goal of spreading the teachings. Mochida argues that if Buddhists lose sight of Buddhism within their educational practices, Buddhist institutions become indistinguishable from other public and private facilities. Education, he continues, must be more than just about the transmission of technical information; it must be about understanding human existence and about how to live together in society. According to Mochida, these are two topics that Buddhism is eminently suited to communicate.[65]

We see within Buddhist ECEC today a debate over the purpose of such education. While income generation is clearly part of the picture in some cases, it is not the whole picture. Teaching morals is seen as important, but whether that means education is to be based on the idea of spreading the Buddhist teachings over and above offering a modern education is debated. And in all of this, government regulation and demands continue to play a role in how ECEC facilities operate.

THE TEACHING AND TEACHINGS OF BUDDHIST EARLY CHILDHOOD EDUCATION AND CARE

Before picking up the thread of what is taught, I wish to draw our attention to the teachers of Buddhist ECEC today. In particular, I will highlight the role of Buddhist universities and the NBHK in teacher training.

The NBHK webpage lists thirty-four institutions of higher education offering teacher training for Buddhist ECEC on its webpage. Most of these are Buddhist universities and junior colleges. NBHK was directly involved in teacher training early on. Established in 1935, the first facility for training Buddhist childcare workers in the Tokyo area was the Bukkyō Hoiku Kyōkai Hobo Yōseijo (仏教保育教会養成所, Buddhist Nursery and Kindergarten Association Caregiver Training Facility) at what is today Hōsen College (宝仙大学). In order to remain financially viable, certificate programs for teachers at Buddhist colleges must cater to a broader audience than simply lay members of the parent denomination. The programs recruit people from the general populace who are not necessarily seeking employment at Buddhist facilities. An examination of the websites of each of these programs shows that few go out of their way to promote their Buddhist character. Comments from alumni as part of program advertising on several university websites centered on things like job placement and skills. None mentioned anything about Buddhism.[66]

Training programs at Buddhist universities and junior colleges must teach the required curriculum for accreditation. Their online presence is designed to show prospective students that they will get the training they need to acquire the necessary licensure. Nevertheless, some schools emphasize their Buddhist character as a selling point. For example, Tsurumi Junior College (鶴見大学短期大学部) lists five points about its training. A Buddhist education that "instills a sense of empathetic caring" is listed as number 4.[67] Most schools have one or two courses on Buddhism as part of their required curriculum. For example, Tsurumi requires a course on "Buddhist *hoiku,*" and Kachō Junior College (華頂短期大学) requires a two-course sequence titled "Humanity and Buddhism," as do Seiwa Gakuen College (聖和学園短期大学) and Jin'ai Women's College (仁愛女子短期大学).[68] Universities and colleges that describe themselves as Buddhist tend to clarify what that means, regardless of denomination, by saying they are based on *Bukkyō seishin* (仏教精神, Buddhist spirit). Some define this spirit directly, others indirectly. Kyoto Women's University (京都女子大学) says that its educational ideals are based on a Buddhist spirit in compliance with Shinran (親鸞, 1173–1263, the founder of Jōdo Shinshū) and that it seeks to nurture sincere people possessed of a heart/mind that sees all life as equal.[69] Osaka Ohtani University (大阪大谷大学) states that "there are a wide variety of meanings in the term Mahayana Buddhist Spirit but, since the opening of the university, it has been understood to mean returning the debt of gratitude [報恩感謝, *hōon kansha*]."[70]

The practice of training teachers focuses primarily on instruction in modern early childhood education theory and technique. This emphasis is in large part due to government regulations regarding teacher licensing and the accreditation of institutions offering teaching degrees. This lends strength to arguments that Buddhist ECEC today are less likely to focus on spreading the Buddhist teachings because the human resources they draw on lack a thorough training in the teachings of Buddhism. Nevertheless, most programs require at least one course on Buddhism, so it is clear there is still some attempt to train future teachers in basic Buddhist ideals. The editors of a volume produced by the NBHK write that "even if someone does not have a deep understanding of the Buddhist teachings, if his or her actions are in accord with them then we can say that person is a Buddhist."[71] Moreover, according to Hayashi Akiko and Joseph Tobin's research on Japanese preschools, the core values taught and the primary teaching method used in Japanese ECEC, *mimamori* (見守り,"supporting children's social-emotional development by holding back and watching without intervening"),[72] are learned through on-the-job mentoring and are not part of teacher training programs. As such, it can be argued that teachers at Buddhist institutions, just like teachers at secular institutions, learn to communicate core values while on the job.[73]

Teacher training is an ongoing practice. The NBHK offers regular seminars, conferences, and publications to aid teachers in bringing Buddhism into the curriculum. According to NBHK's 2012 annual report, the NBHK offered or supported at least forty-six events ranging from their annual national gathering to regional workshops and seminars.[74] At NBHK conferences and seminars, teachers discuss pedagogy and Buddhist ideals. They also have the chance to meditate, do ritual cleaning, and copy sutras. Guest speakers at the national conference tend to be education professionals who are not Buddhist educators, but they also include well-known priests who frequently are called on to give dharma talks and explain basic teachings. The content of their talks varies little from the books they write for popular audiences or from the sermons they might give at their home temples.

The NBHK defines Buddhist ECEC as that which uses materials and methods based on the Buddhist spirit and seeks the perfection of human character.[75] The work of the NBHK is mirrored in the various ECEC associations of the different denominations. Denomination-level meetings include annual summer retreats focused on hands-on training that incorporates Buddhist ideals. If the frequency with which NBHK material appears on the webpages of Buddhist ECEC facilities can be seen as a gauge of its influence, then it appears that the NBHK plays a significant role in shaping how *hoikuen* and *yōchien* frame their Buddhist character.

The NBHK is also active in lobbying the Japanese government on issues related to ECEC. They are joined in this by the Japan Buddhist Federation and the leadership of many Temple Buddhism denominations. As has been noted, Buddhist interests at times intersect with those of the state. One area where this can be seen is the call for increased religious education or religious sentiment education (宗教情操教育, *shūkyō jōsō kyōiku*) as a means to put Japan back on track as a morally grounded nation (I discuss this further in chapter 4). Calls to reform the education system include those from within the government, such as the 2003 Central Council for Education's (中央教育審議会, Chūō Kyōiku

Shingikai) stated goal of "educating Japanese who are strong, rich in heart and able to break open the 21st Century."[76] The council sought to create an education system that nurtures independent individuals who are healthy and rich in heart, have a sense of their identity as Japanese, and work toward being a part of society. These goals appear directly or indirectly in many of the educational goal statements at Buddhist kindergartens.

Regarding Article 9 of the Fundamental Law on Education, the Central Council for Education stated in 2002 that the clause regarding no support for sectarian education must stay but acknowledges that "there are many who hold the opinion that general education about religion is very important."[77] The Japan Buddhist Federation, in a 2005 open letter to the Central Council for Education, supported the general outline of the revisions sought and noted that Buddhist teachings such as symbiosis (共生, *kyōsei*) are at the heart of Japanese culture and identity and that one weakness of Japanese education is that it downplays religious education.[78] When the Fundamental Law on Education was revised in 2006, a line was added to the effect that students should have a general knowledge of religion.[79]

Just how Buddhist education should fit into modern public education is debated within Japanese Buddhist education circles. Buddhist educators make clear their view that the system as it stands is flawed in its application in Japan.[80] Buddhist educator Miyasaka Yūkō, for example, draws on his teacher Mochida to offer six points about Buddhist education that he believes makes it a more appropriate basis for Japanese education than Christianity, which is understood as fundamental to Western education. These points give us some sense of how Buddhist educators approach their teaching: (1) the Buddhist teachings can be accommodated to the times, (2) Buddhism has no absolute deity and is about the perfection of humans, (3) Buddhism takes a realistic view of human life and seeks to relieve suffering from that perspective, (4) Buddhism is rational and based on practice, (5) Buddhism is about equality, and (6) Buddhism stresses friendship and togetherness.[81] Item 2 above is similar to an argument made in *Kodomo no kokoro sodateyō* (子供の心育てよう, *Let's Develop Children's Hearts and Minds*), a book on the education of children sponsored by the NBHK: "[Buddhism] also has another meaning. It means the teaching that you can become a Buddha. In the case of Christianity, it does not matter how believers practice, they cannot become Christ or God."[82] Arguments such as those made by Miyasaka and the NBHK are clearly drawing on Buddhist views as they developed in the modern period and are directed at usurping the Christian/Western view (as Mochida and others see it) and replacing it with a "modern," "rational," yet "traditional" Japanese value system.

At the heart of the Buddhist critique of the current education system is that it teaches individual over social identity, and selfishness over selflessness. Buddhist education, with its emphasis on the related teachings of no-self (無我, *muga*), symbiosis (*kyōsei*), and compassion (慈悲, *jihi*), is offered as an antidote. In her study of kindergartens, Joy Hendry finds that parents hope that kindergartens (both public and private) will help their children overcome selfishness (わがまま, *wagamama*) and become gentle and obedient (素直, *sunao*).[83] Buddhist schools make a point of teaching no-self, symbiosis, and compassion to address just those issues. The NBHK provides materials for this purpose in, among other places, its webpage section titled "Kodomo ni wakaru tokumoku (子供にわかる徳目)" or "Virtues Children Can Understand." This section is also published in their curriculum journal. One example given is that of "*jiri rita* (自利利他)," or "To Benefit Self and Others." The author of this example suggests using the picture book produced by NBHK called *The Monkey Bridge*. This book tells the story of a mother monkey who can save herself but instead suffers so that her children can be saved, and in the process inspires a king to work to benefit all his people. The story teaches that having saved yourself, you must continue to benefit others.[84] Holloway, in her study of early childhood education in Japan, found that helping students develop consideration for others and compassion were fundamental parts of the curriculum and teaching at the Buddhist kindergarten she observed.[85]

Other key teaching goals in early childhood education in Japan include developing empathy (思いやり, *omoiyari*), kindness (親切, *shinsetsu*), health (元気, *genki*), and perseverance (頑張る, *ganbaru* / 忍耐, *nintai*).[86] As we shall see, these are the common goals of Buddhist early childhood education as well. What differs is *how* these goals are taught at Buddhist institutions as opposed to secular institutions. The key distinction is the emphasis on religious sentiment education found at Buddhist schools.

The NBHK offers the Three Treasures—the Buddha, the Dharma, and the Sangha—as one model for Buddhist early childhood education and care.[87] First, the Buddha is said to stand for education that respects life. The Buddha is related to the term *jishin fusetsu* (慈心不殺), "to give rise to compassion and to not kill," and is linked to the child-friendly term and desired character trait "to be bright" (明るく, *akaruku*). Second, the Dharma is said to stand for education that seeks out that which is correct and ceaselessly proceeds forward. The Dharma is related to the term *butsudō jōju* (仏道成就), or "perfecting the Buddhist path," and is linked to the term "to be right/correct" (正しく, *tadashiku*). Finally, the sangha is held to stand for education that creates good members of society. The sangha is related to the term *shōgyō shōjin* (正業精進), "to do good acts and practice/promote purity," and is linked to the term "to get along well with others" (仲よく, *nakayoku*). The terms "bright," "right," and "get along well" put difficult Buddhist concepts into conceptually simple terms that can appeal both to children and parents. They make clear the desired character traits to be developed through the *yōchien* or *hoikuen* experience, and they draw a direct line between these traits and authoritative Buddhist teachings.

The NBHK produces a calendar with a theme for each month that is designed to communicate these ideals at Buddhist facilities. The suggested themes are as follows:[88]

April: *Gasshō monbō* (合掌聞法) Place your hands together and listen carefully

Form your hands in prayer (*gasshō*) and pay respect to the Three Treasures (Buddha, Dharma, Sangha). In addition to taking care of yourself and respecting others, let's find the precious meaning of these teachings.

May: *Jikai wagō* (持戒和合) Maintain the precepts in harmony and unity

Keeping your promises is the first step in social life. This is the basis for maintaining group order. Life here at the *yōchien/hoikuen* is your first big step into social life, so let's have fun.

June: *Seimei sonchō* (生命尊重) Respect life

Recognizing the importance of your own life while recognizing the importance of the lives of others and all other forms of life has a major effect on children's sentiments.

July: *Fuse hōshi* (布施奉仕) Practice giving and service

Being kind to others comes around to you as well. Setting aside the advantages and disadvantages to oneself, in every situation hidden acts of kindness will brighten society.

August: *Jiri rita* (自利利他) Benefit self and others

You should know that having someone do something that you can do yourself is embarrassing. Even if it is not work that was assigned to you, let's keep trying to do all that we can do.

September: *Hōon kansha* (報恩感謝) Return the debt of gratitude

On your own you cannot do anything about how society works. At the same time, without the blessings of nature—clothing, food, and shelter—you could not live even one day. Let's foster a heart of humility that brings us closer to society and nature.

October: *Dōji kyōryoku* (同事協力) See things from the same perspective and cooperate

If there is something you cannot do on your own, it can be done by two people. If two cannot do it, then many can. Let's understand that if everyone helps each other, there is nothing that cannot be accomplished.

November: *Shōjin doryoku* (精進努力) Diligence and effort

No matter how good of an act you attempt, if you break down partway through you won't be able to finish it. It is important to practice from childhood seeing everything you do through to the end.

December: *Ninniku jikyū* (忍辱持久) Lasting perseverance

You can enrich your life through knowing the teachings of the Buddha and striving to get even a little closer to the teachings.

January: *Wagen aigō* (和顔愛語) Speak with empathy

Regardless of how cold you are, or how difficult things are, or how sad you might be, it simply won't do to put on a pathetic face. No matter what is going on, always wear a bright smile and try your best to get along well with others.

February: *Zenjō seijyaku* (禅定静寂) Be calm and focused

Things rarely go just the way you think they will. Before you act, think things through thoroughly, don't get caught up in all the hubbub going on around you, and live your life with your feet firmly planted on the ground.

March: *Chie kibō* (智慧希望) Wisdom and hope

Always keep hope in your heart, aim for a bright day tomorrow, learn well, work well, play well, and strive to make a happy society for all people.[89]

The Three Treasures model reflected in the monthly themes above is implemented in classrooms through a variety of means. I had the opportunity to visit several ECEC facilities. One school that I visited emphasized having the children embody the terms. This idea of learning the teachings through the body, by doing rather than studying, is common within Japanese religion, particularly Buddhism.[90] During the visit, as children practiced concepts such as "getting along well" through cheerfully exchanging greetings, school leaders encouraged them to keep in mind the compassion of the Buddha. Compassion and consideration for others was put into practice at a school observed by Holloway as well, where "they emphasized this message in the weekly prayer service at the temple . . . [and] also provided relevant practical experiences such as caring for the preschool's plants and animals."[91] The NBHK recommends care for animals, such as rabbits, as a way to learn to respect life and to understand how difficult raising even one life can be. The NBHK also advocates growing vegetables so that children can learn to give thanks for the food they eat.[92]

The practice of compassion is linked in writings to the teachings of interdependence and perseverance. For example, properly exchanging greetings is a way to express one's connection to others and a way for others to gauge how one is feeling. Making daily pledges to the Buddha is another method of reinforcing these key terms. One example of how such teachings are offered at a Buddhist school is this verse that children recite together:

We vow to cherish all things, living and not.
We vow to try our hardest to the end.

We vow to think things through.
We vow to promote the good.
We vow that, even if we fight, we will play well together.
We vow that after we play, we will pick up.
Buddha, please look after us.[93]

One can see in this verse ideals that are also found at secular kindergartens, such as respecting life, persevering, and getting along well with others. Yet here they are phrased in terms of a promise and prayer to the Buddha. Because they are enveloped in a vow to the Buddha, the teachings become associated with Buddhism. Keeping the pledge and pledging anew each day creates a routine and teaches the children the value of seeing something through to the end as well as establishing a sense of connectedness to the Buddha. The Buddha, often called "Nono sama" by children,[94] is always watching them, thus they should be sure to always act properly—even when their teachers or parents are not present. The presence of and interaction with the Buddha and deities is an important aspect of Buddhist teachings today at Buddhist preschools and daycares, just as it is at the most elite training centers.

The teachings and practices above can be found on the home pages of many Buddhist ECEC, where they are often listed under the heading of "educational goals."[95] It can be argued that these are "dumbing Buddhism down" to the point that it is no longer Buddhism, as some Western Buddhologists let me know when this material was presented at a conference. But such a critique steals away the agency of those living Buddhism today. The teachings are understood by those teaching them as expressing the "Buddhist spirit" in ways that open the teachings to those who cannot understand the more difficult concepts to which the terms "bright," "right," and "get along well with" are pegged. In some ways these key terms are like the ever-popular *omamori* (お守り, amulets and talismans) that can be found for sale at temples all across Japan.[96] The outside is inscribed with an easy-to-understand wished-for outcome, the benefits of which are clear and tangible (safe childbirth, safe driving, and so on), and the inside holds indecipherable Sanskrit seed syllables or a sutra in classical Chinese. Buddhologists of the past would likely spend most of their time unwrapping the *omamori* and trying to decipher the writings hidden inside when they really should be asking about how and why people create and interact with the *omamori*. Buddhologists and sectarian authorities alike have tended to look down on *omamori* as not "real" Buddhism even though they are the face of Buddhism at many temples. They have similarly looked past Buddhist ECEC facilities despite, or possibly because of, their ubiquity and their simplified public-facing teachings.

Another often overlooked form of teaching that is central to Buddhism and Buddhist ECEC facilities is sentiment education, which is discussed in more detail in chapter 4. Children, it is believed, cannot learn complicated Buddhist teachings through textual study but must instead be taught through *Bukkyō jōso kyōiku* (仏教情操教育, Buddhist sentiment education). Buddhist ECEC use prayer, ceremonies, material culture, and daily routines to create an atmosphere of Buddhist teachings that, it is believed, allow children to naturally come to embody the teachings. An NBHK publication states, "Through participating in rituals one can without effort naturally cultivate feelings of Buddhist sentiment."[97] This is something many facilities make direct reference to on their websites. A Buddhist worldview is cultivated through routine and atmosphere. In truth, this varies little from the ways in which Buddhist temples approach the public in other venues. Pilgrimages, for example, offer an opportunity to draw people to the temple, where they will experience the temple atmosphere such as the grounds and the architecture. Annual festivals and rituals often are looked at in a similar light. They represent opportunities to interact with the laity in terms that are meaningful to the laity.

In addition to its monthly themes calendar, the NBHK provides a calendar of events and ceremonies along with curricular goals for each event on its website. This calendar is repeated in localized fashion on the websites of many schools. Ceremonies include the Buddha's birthday and the birthday of the denomination's founder, as well as such things as a celebration of the Buddha's enlightenment. Other events are held in common with secular schools, such as the entrance ceremony, but in the Buddhist schools this ceremony is taken as a chance to teach a Buddhist lesson such as venerating the Buddha, or compassion.

In much the same way that events can work to engender the sought-after religious sentiment, creating the right physical ambiance is understood by Buddhist educators as another key method for Buddhist sentiment education. Here the important thing is not only what is said but also the physical environment in which education occurs. Buddhist schools are often on or nearby temple grounds. Buddhist statuary, artworks, and even the simple presence of priests combine to create an atmosphere that is qualitatively different than that found in secular schools. The NBHK writes, "The most important part of the environment for a Buddhist daycare is to be able to feel that the Buddha is close to you, and the Buddha is watching over you. . . . The grounds should have statues of the baby Buddha or Jizo Bodhisattva and the like so that not just the children and their parents but anyone who visits feels the desire to raise their hands in prayer or to bow their head."[98]

Many schools stress that not just the Buddhist environment but also the natural environment is critical to cultivating religious sentiment. This close attention to the natural environment is also found in the guidelines for *yōchien* education produced by MEXT. In the postwar period, the government's focus has shifted over time from an emphasis on observing nature to plant the seeds of scientific inquiry, to including observing nature in order to generate a feeling of awe and a respect for life.[99] Buddhist educators emphasize ideas about peace of mind and natural cycles of change, as well as the concept that all nature is Buddha nature. The head of Wakakusa Hoikuen (若草幼稚園) writes, "In Buddhism there is a teaching that mountains, rivers, grass, and trees are all Buddha nature. Not just humans, but all living things including mountains, rivers, grass, and trees, all are the Buddha's heart; in short [the Buddha's heart] is the building block of life. When I am at the kindergarten I feel this fact all the time."[100] He then goes on to describe the bounty of natural phenomena at the facilities he operates. This mirrors the arguments made by temples during the Kyoto tax dispute of the 1980s, in which Buddhists claimed that visitors to their temples were engaged in religious acts, whether they were conscious of it or not. They argued that simply entering the temple grounds and being exposed to the temple environment was undergoing a form of religious teaching. The grounds, the sublime ambiance they create, and the peace of mind that is said to be found there are themselves the Buddha's teachings.[101]

Finally, there is daily practice. Children are taught, for example, to say "*itadakimasu*" (a phrase expressing thanks said before meals) and "*arigato*" (thank you) in their daily lives. They are also taught to exchange greetings while doing *gasshō* (pressing the palms of their hands together in prayer). Their teachers explain to them that the reason for doing this is that we are all connected to each other through *en* (karmic bonds) and that we are equal because we are all the children of the Buddha (or that we all share Buddha nature).[102] Holding their hands together in *gasshō* manifests respect for the other. One *yōchien* in Hokkaido expressed these ideas on its website in the following prayer called "Life":

> I received my life from my father and mother
> My father and mother received their life from their father and
> mother
> Life has its beginnings in the ancestors and in their ancestors
> From generation, to generation, to generation life continues
> And now there is me
> On my birthday I express gratitude from my heart and
> I say "thank you" to my father and mother
> Within life there is movement
> Living is movement
> Children are the encouragement for the future
> The elderly are the limitless spring of the knowledge of life
> All life, simply existing, deserves respect
> Living deserves respect
> For this life of mine, I take the life of rice
> I take the life of fish
> I take the life of vegetables
> This is my true self
> I put my hands together out of gratefulness to thank this life
> "Itadakimasu"
> *Gasshō.*[103]

While such practice is found front and center in Buddhist education, Hendry draws our attention to the significant position that *aisatsu* (挨拶, greetings) have in all Japanese early childhood education. As she notes, the importance of greetings goes beyond simply showing proper manners; they "serve to demonstrate and emphasize a number of basic categories and values of the society at large. The child is made aware of its own identity in its unique ability to reply to its personal name, but it is reminded of the relationship it has with other people to whom certain phrases are appropriately used in certain situations."[104] Buddhist facilities ground these basic cultural values within a Buddhist context. Children are taught that they exist within or because of relationships in a cycle of interdependence.

The practice of mealtime rituals, including saying "*itadakimasu*" before meals and "*gochisōsama deshita*" (thank you for the meal) afterward, is common at Buddhist and secular schools. One of Holloway's Buddhist informants offers the following:

> Japanese put their hands together in prayer before eating a meal. They take doing so for granted. . . . A sense of gratitude is what we should consider most important. But today's Japanese people tend to forget the importance of this activity, which is the foundation of life. . . . Children should extend their gratitude and then have a meal. Also they should extend their gratitude to their parents. They acquire this as a habit and this is most important.[105]

As with greetings, Buddhist educators are more likely to explicitly draw the connection between mealtime rituals and teachings about karmic bonds.

Just as in secular schools, children in Buddhist schools are taught to be obedient and to get along well with the other children. However, these lessons are imbued with a Buddhist character by linking them to such teachings as NBHK's "bright," "right," and "get along well." The most frequently recurring teachings found listed as educational goals or key points on webpages of Buddhist facilities are: nurturing a heart/mind of thankfulness, learning right from wrong, respecting all things, empathy, and perseverance.

Thankfulness is often linked to the teaching of no-self and is explained through reference to parents and ancestors to whom we are indebted for our lives. Thankfulness has been the theme of more than one NBHK summer seminar. In the classroom, mealtimes are often used to teach that we must be thankful not just for the food but also for our parents who made the food (or the staff at the facility who did), for the farmers, and for the animals and plants whose life sustains our own. The Q&A section of Kōrin Yōchien's (光輪幼稚園) website includes the question "How are manners taught?" The response gives insight into how the teaching of thankfulness is practiced: "We always say thank you. In a society of one, thankfulness cannot arise. The children are able to say thank you when they understand that they live in a society made up of everyone. It is from there that communication begins. Greetings [*aisatsu*] and thankfulness are crucial."[106] In short, it is believed that children learn to naturally give thanks to those around them as they become aware of the interconnected nature of society and see themselves as part of something larger. The head of Minori Yōchien (みのり幼稚園) in Yanagawa writes, "The [Buddhist] teachings of wisdom and compassion are sublimated into the term *hōon kansha* [to give thanks and return the favor/gift]. When one comes to understand the mystery, miracle, and gift of life, a heart of gratitude is born, and one bows one's head returning the favor to all those who have supported one's life."[107]

Many Buddhist kindergartens note in their materials that people in Japan today clamor for *kokoro no kyōiku* (心の教育, heart/mind education) as an antidote to what is perceived as the moral malaise into which contemporary Japanese have fallen. This is discussed in detail in chapter 4. The strong emphasis on learning right from wrong found in Buddhist schools is aimed directly at this. School leaders point out that learning proper moral behavior has been the core of Buddhist education throughout history, implying a comparative advantage over secular schools and their perceived failings. Empathy and perseverance are likewise linked to Buddhist ideals; again, though, these are couched not in difficult philosophical language but in terms of how we are all interconnected or how we need to see things through no matter how hard they may seem now.

There has long been a sincere effort to put forth a Buddhist-based education within Japanese Temple Buddhism. The goal of this effort is to help children embody and learn basic Buddhist ideals. There is debate within the Buddhist educational community as to how best to accomplish this goal and the extent to which the goal can be reached in harmony with modern educational goals and techniques. Buddhist early childhood education is not alone in its desire to teach "traditional" Japanese values. As Hayashi and Tobin note, whereas much of secondary education in Japan has come under severe pressure for change, ECEC have remained, and indeed appear to be expected to remain, bastions of "core cultural values." "To ameliorate the negative impacts of social change, Japanese preschools have a mandate to pass on to young children the values, perspectives, and social skills that are believed to be at risk in the contemporary, hyper-modern society."[108] If anything, this pressure on ECEC to carry forward that which is perceived as core to Japanese identity places Buddhist schools, with their claims of a lasting history of such teaching, at a competitive advantage. Holloway claims that "this strategy has paid off" for the Buddhist facility she observed because it has seen robust enrollment despite an ever-decreasing pool of children to recruit from.[109]

Buddhists are currently grappling with the question "What is Buddhist about the educational goals put forward?" After all, obedience, health, and getting along well with others are also strongly pronounced in secular education.

The five guidelines set by the Ministry of Education in the late 1980s would seem to demonstrate that the main goals and teachings of Buddhist education differ little from secular education:

> (1) To foster the basic habits of daily life and the attitudes needed for a healthy, safe, happy life and to build the foundation for a sound mind and body; (2) To foster affection and trust toward others and to cultivate/foster attitudes of autonomy and cooperation and the awakening of morality; (3) To foster interest and concern about nature and other things close at hand and to cultivate the awakening of a wealth of feelings and the power to think about these things; (4) To foster, in daily life, interest and concern about language and to cultivate enjoyment in talking and listening and a sense of language; and (5) To foster a richness of emotion through diverse experiences and to foster creativity.[110]

As we have seen, however, despite many similarities to secular education, what is taught in Buddhist schools tends to be couched in terms of a Buddhist worldview. Jørn Borup, in his work on modern Rinzai Zen, notes that Zen institutions explicitly teach about family and harmony, for example, as denominational teachings. He states that Buddhist teachings of no-self and interdependence would "have a different resonance" if not tied to these broader "cultural" concepts.[111] I would take the argument one step further and state that since the denominations teach these concepts not just within a Buddhist framework but as Buddhism, then we must understand them as being Buddhist. We may nod to their origins in Confucianism, but at this point they are part of Temple Buddhism. It might also be argued, of course, that many of the so-called cultural values have themselves originated over time from the intermixing of religious values in Japan, including Buddhist values. Holloway, in her work on preschool in Japan, makes just such an argument:

> While they may represent a minority, preschools with religious organizations are very interesting because they set in relief certain cultural models that are represented—often in diluted form—in nonreligious preschools as well. It is simply inevitable that religious beliefs that have existed in a society for well over a thousand years—in the case of Shinto and Buddhism—will have permeated people's thinking about the nature of children and their care, and thus manifest in nonreligious as well as religious organizations.[112]

The editors of an NBHK-sponsored volume on early childhood education make the same argument, claiming that over time, Buddhism became the foundation of Japanese culture. They argue that classical forms of literature, art, theater, architecture, and dance were all heavily influenced by Buddhism and continue to influence Japanese culture. Furthermore, they write that practices such as tea ceremony, flower arrangement, and calligraphy, which continue today (and indeed are often taught at temples), are all informed by Buddhism.[113]

Given all the above, the use of categories that are fixed in time and distinct such as "Buddhism" or "Confucianism" is shown to be of little help in understanding how values are understood and communicated in the lived world. The content of these categories must be understood as in flux. What was considered Buddhism one hundred years ago may not be understood as Buddhism today. That does not mean it is any less Buddhist. Buddhism is what Buddhists and Buddhist institutions, including Buddhist preschools and daycares, say it is.

3

BUDDHIST COLLEGES AND UNIVERSITIES

> In today's world it just won't suffice to train priests in sectarian studies—they must study more broadly if they are going to be able to lead temple lay members in today's high education achievement society.
>
> —Okamoto, "Kore kara no daigaku no kyōiku to shūmon deshi yōsei ni tsuite"

When I first traveled to Japan to conduct research on contemporary Temple Buddhism in the early 1990s, I was lucky enough to be affiliated with Taishō University, a trans-sectarian Buddhist university located in Tokyo. At the time, my focus was on broadly understanding issues in contemporary practice. I audited a variety of courses—from the practical, such as "Buddhism and the Religious Corporations Law," to those on practice, like "Buddhist Liturgical Chanting." I also held a research assistant position at Taishō's Institute for the Comprehensive Study of Buddhism (総合仏教研究所, Sōgō Bukkyō Kenkyūjo), where I could interact with and learn from leading Japanese scholars of Buddhism. It was not until later, however, that I realized I should have been not just studying *at* Taishō; I should have been studying Taishō itself. It is at schools like Taishō that ongoing changes to the teaching and teachings of Buddhism can be observed firsthand.

Buddhist education in Japan has changed significantly over the last two hundred years. Today there are sixty-five institutions of higher education registered as members in the Council of Buddhist Universities (仏教系大学会議, Bukkyōkeidaigaku Kaigi). These institutions include two-year and four-year colleges, seminaries with small enrollments, and comprehensive universities with over 30,000 students. Exploring the changes to Buddhist higher education in the modern period significantly enhances our understanding of the teaching and teachings of Buddhism in Japan today. Nevertheless, a comprehensive history of Buddhist higher education is not possible in one chapter. For that reason, what follows is a selective introduction. This chapter offers an overview of the history of modern Buddhist higher education. In addition to the historical background, we will also explore issues in contemporary curricula, both in Buddhist studies programs and in broader educational offerings. With this approach, we will gain a better overall picture of Buddhist higher education, the issues it faces, and the issues it raises for our understanding of the teaching and teachings of Temple Buddhism in Japan.

LOOKING BACK TO THE FOUNDERS

A review of university self-evaluation reports, the home pages of Buddhist institutions, and the writings of Buddhist educators makes clear that each denomination has a story to tell about how central the education of the priesthood, the laity, or the education of the nation as a whole was to its founder. And they often emphasize the unique and pivotal role the founder is imagined to have played in the formation of Japanese educational ideals and practices. For example, in the 1995 self-evaluation report for Kōyasan University (高野山大学), a Shingon institution located on Mt. Kōya, the authors draw a clear line between their contemporary educational ideals and those of Kūkai (空海, 774–835), the founder of Japanese Shingon Buddhism. They write that Kūkai sought to spread the teachings of esoteric Buddhism and that his goal was the salvation of all sentient beings.[1] He understood, they state, that human development was the path to salvation and that education was fundamental to human development.[2] For these reasons, Kūkai established an educational institution that catered to both the priesthood and the laity. In the same way, members of the Tendai denomination often cite Saichō's (最澄, the founder of Japanese Tendai, 767–822) foundational text, the *Sangegakushōshiki* (山家学生式), in which Saichō discusses the importance of education for priests and the nation. The *Sangegakushōshiki* is also referenced in nearly every history of Buddhist education in Japan as a foundational text.

PREMODERN EDUCATION

Contemporary Buddhist education is often linked, if only as a matter of ideology, to these distant founders and their philosophies of education. However, the roots of Buddhist education in the beginning of the modern period can be more readily traced to the *dangisho* (談義所, lecture or sermon hall), *gakuryō* (学寮, seminary), and *kangakuin* (勧学院, study academies), especially as they developed in the Edo period (1603–1868).[3] Initially these institutions were for a select few within the priesthood. According to Saitō, early institutions such as the *kangakuin* at the Buddhist centers of Mt. Hiei, Tōdaiji, Kofukuji, Enkakuji, Gokurakuji, or at Mt. Kōya took only a dozen students at a time.[4] Eventually, *dangisho* and *gakuryō* spread throughout Japan. By the beginning of the early modern period, there were dozens of these institutions related to the various denominations of Temple Buddhism, especially Tendai, Shingon, and Jōdo.[5]

Most *dangisho* were in the Kanto region, but there were others in Kyoto, Kyushu, and elsewhere. Tendai, for example, had as many as sixty *dangisho* by the end of the sixteenth century.[6]

As each denomination adjusted its system of educating priests during the early modern and the beginning of the modern periods, they repurposed the sites and often the curriculum of the *dangisho* and *kangakuin* to meet changing demands. These demands were the result of Japan's rapid modernization, in which Buddhism was disparaged and attacked for its links to the old regime and for being a failed foreign experiment. For example, the Higashi Honganji branch of the Jōdo denomination set up its Gohōjō (護法場) in 1868, and in 1873 the Tendai denomination restructured its Kangakukōin (勧学講院), which had served as the center of the eight *danrin* (previously called *dangisho*) in the Kanto area,[7] as the Tendaishū Daigakurin (天台宗大学林, Tendai Great Learning Academy). In 1868, the Jōdo denomination created a new facility for training priests at Zōjoji called the Kōgakujo (興学所), renamed Kangakujo (勧学所) in 1870.[8] In the same year, also at Zōjoji, Kansōgakuin (貫綜学院), a facility for studying so-called other teachings (Christianity/foreign teachings) and general education, was established.[9] With the creation of the Great Teaching Academy (大教院, Daikyōin) for the Doctrinal Instructor system (see below) in 1873, these facilities eventually merged.[10] These various facilities provided the foundation for future developments in Buddhist education. Today Buddhist universities continue to trace their roots to these premodern institutions.

THE MEIJI PERIOD DOCTRINAL INSTRUCTOR SYSTEM

The modern period was marked by a sweeping transformation of Japanese institutions of governance and education. The Meiji government engaged in a number of efforts to radically transform Japan throughout the late nineteenth and early twentieth centuries. One such effort was the short-lived National Doctrinal Instructor (教導職, Kyōdōshoku) system, which began in 1872.[11] The goal of this system was nothing less than creating a moral citizenry dedicated to the nation and the emperor. This was to be accomplished primarily through the training of instructors in a new unified national ideology. These instructors would then educate citizens across the country in a propagation/education system centered on teaching academies (教院, *kyōin*). As James Edward Ketelaar points out, "The creation of the position of Instructor was a thinly veiled attempt by the state to create, in fact, a de facto state priesthood."[12] The National Doctrinal Instructor system played a transformative role in Buddhist education. Buddhist schools (*danrin, kangakuin,* etc.), which were already in the process of adapting to the pressures of Japan's increased contact with the West by adding *gaigaku* (外学, literally outside studies but here referring to studies other than sectarian and Buddhist studies, in particular Western studies),[13] found themselves in the position of having to align with a state-directed campaign that promoted its own set of teachings and was based in a new system of teaching academies.

Doctrinal Instructors taught the Three Great Teachings: "(1) respect for the gods, love of country; (2) making clear the principles of Heaven and the Way of Man; (3) reverence to the emperor and obedience to the will of the court."[14] There was no explicit banning of Buddhist, Christian, or Shinto institutions. Nevertheless, because propagation of any sort could only be done by Doctrinal Instructors, the Doctrinal Instructor system had the potential to subsume all religions into a state religion.

In the beginning, Buddhist reaction to the system varied from cautiously supportive to playing an instrumental role in its creation. Leaders within Temple Buddhism saw participation in the system as a way to get into the good graces of the new government and thereby curb attacks on Buddhism and reclaim land lost under the new government's policies. In fact, Buddhist priests came to represent one of the largest groups of instructors. Buddhist priests had a long history of preaching and were considered some of the best instructors in the new system. Buddhist priests also had a long history of preaching in defense of the state, albeit promoting Buddhism as the ideology best fit to protect the state.[15] Before the system came to an end, Buddhist priests comprised 80 percent of instructors.[16]

As time moved on, the Doctrinal Instructor system became clearly identified with Shinto and the undermining of Buddhist preaching and practice. Leaders within Temple Buddhism, led by the Jōdo Shin denomination (which had the largest number of instructors), called for Buddhist withdrawal from the Doctrinal Instructor system. This withdrawal forced the government to reconsider the system and led to a shift in how it was administered. The system moved from strict state control to a more dispersed format in which individual denominations effectively controlled the instructors' education.

The institutional aspects of the Doctrinal Instructor system played a significant role in shaping the development of the modern Buddhist education system. The Doctrinal Instructor system was part of the Great Teaching Promulgation Campaign (大教宣布運動, Taikyō senpu undō) and was built around a system of teaching academies. The headquarters was the Great Teaching Academy (大教院, Daikyōin) in Tokyo, which came to be located at Zōjōji (増上寺), a temple of the Jōdo denomination that had been the memorial temple for the Tokugawa family. A Middle Teaching Academy (中教院, Chūkyōin) was located in each prefecture, usually at the most prominent Shinto shrine. The Middle Teaching Academies were largely in charge of testing and ranking of the instructors. Small Teaching Academies (小教院, Shōkyōin) were located in towns and villages throughout Japan and very often were located in temples and shrines.[17]

The Great Teaching Academy at Zōjōji was initially created at the request of Buddhist leaders in a petition to the government in 1872 and was established in 1873. But Shinto priests, who found themselves in a position of power in the new government, rapidly took control. Eventually Buddhism, which at the time was under attack as foreign and corrupt, could not be used in teaching the Three Great Teachings, and propagation efforts became deeply influenced by Shinto.[18] As we saw above, Buddhists pushed back, and in 1875 the Great Teaching Academy at Zōjōji was shuttered.[19] In 1877 the Ministry of Doctrine was closed down and the Doctrinal Instructor system was moved under the control of the Home Ministry's Bureau of Shrines and Temples. The system officially ended in 1884.[20]

Despite its failure to last, this system went on to provide the structural outline for Buddhist bureaucratic and educational institutions. Each denomination set up its own Great Teaching Academy following the end of the state's Great Teaching Academy in 1875 and also tended to follow the now-established pattern of a Middle Teaching Academy heading each prefecture and Lesser Teaching Academies at the local level.[21] For example, the Tendai Great Teaching Academy was established at Sensōji (浅草寺, a major temple in Tokyo).[22] In 1880 the Tendai Great Teaching Academy was abolished, and Sensōji became the administrative headquarters of the Tendai denomination. Enryakuji (延暦寺) on Mt. Hiei then became the head temple of the denomination. The Middle Teaching Academies in each prefecture became denomination administrative offices (宗務長, *shūmuchō*). At the time that these changes were made, new guidelines for the denomination created a Daigakurin (Great Learning Academy) as well as a Chūgakurin (Middle Learning Academy) at Enyrakuji and a Chūgakurin in Tokyo (Kangakukōin was renamed) and designated temples across the country as Shōgakurin (Lesser Learning Academy).[23]

Another example of the quick reordering of education facilities is that of the Shingon denomination. The Shingon denomination in this early period is especially interesting in that it was an uneasy amalgamation of several branches that were together only because of the state's "one school, one leader" (一宗一管長, *isshū ichi kanchō*) mandate, in which the branches of various denominations were required to unite under a unified administration.[24] Shingon established its Great Teaching Academy (Daikyōin) at Shinpukuji (真福寺) in Tokyo and began opening Middle and Lesser Teaching Academies in each prefecture. In 1876, when a brief shift in the rules regarding "one sect, one leader" occurred, branches of Shingon began setting up their own academies. In 1877 a Great Learning Academy (Daigakurin) was set up on Mt. Kōya at Kangakuin. The Shingon Chizan Branch set up Chizan Mongakurin (智山門学林) in the same year. The Buzan branch created its own academies as well. Shortly after this the government reaffirmed the "one sect, one leader" rule in 1879.[25] This led to a restructuring of the various Shingon academies. A Great Teaching Academy was created at Tōji (東寺). Middle Learning Academies were set up in each prefecture, and local administrative headquarters were made Lesser Learning Academies (*shōgakurin*).[26] As the scholar Hayashi Makoto notes, this was a period in which numerous Buddhist academies were created; for example, between 1886 and 1888, in addition to Shingon's Great Learning Academies, Rinzai Zen founded Hanazono Gakuin Kōtōbu (花園学院高等部), and Jōdo established Jōdoshūgakuhonkō (浄土宗学本校).[27]

In the end, the Doctrinal Instructor system left its mark on Buddhist institutions by emphasizing the Great, Middle, and Lesser Academy structure. As we shall see, the system also shifted the role of the priest to that of teaching professional—a job that had specific educational requirements and rankings that could be identified and assessed. The educational content at these various denomination-managed academies was essentially the same as it had been in the late Edo period. However, it also reflected the curriculum at the Great Teaching Academy that was established at Zōjoji as part of the Doctrinal Instructor system. That curriculum had been composed of eight fields of education, including studies of Shinto, Confucianism, and Western history and the English language.[28]

ORDER NO. 12: BANNING RELIGION IN THE SCHOOLS

In addition to its efforts to create a moral citizenry via the Doctrinal Instructor system, the Meiji government pushed through a complete reformation of the education system that included compulsory education and a national curriculum that was heavily influenced by Western educational models. As time passed, however, Japan's relationship with the West shifted. The treaties forced upon Japan as the country opened up to the world in the mid-nineteenth century included provisions to allow Westerners to move out from the restricted living areas they had been corralled into for centuries and take up residence throughout Japan. At the same time, schools spearheaded by Christian missionaries fast became seen as some of the best schools because they offered access to Western (modern) education. As the decades wore on and education system reforms began to take hold, the government came to see Christian schools as posing a potential threat to efforts to bring the nation together under a unified ideology.

In 1890 the Imperial Rescript on Education was promulgated and set forth a clear agenda for Japanese education to inculcate a set of emperor-centric values based primarily on Confucianism. In 1899 Order No. 12 was put forward to curb education in values that the government deemed as running counter to those of the state as expressed in the Imperial Rescript on Education. The order read as follows: "It is necessary from the standpoint of the school administration to make general education stand outside religion. Therefore, the government and public schools, and the schools under the application of provisions of the laws and ordinances relating to the curriculum shall not be permitted to conduct religious education or to observe any religious ceremony even outside the regular course."[29] The order was issued to supplement the Private School Ordinance, which was issued in the same year. A clause within the Private

School Ordinance regarding the removal of religion and religious ceremony from education had been stripped out prior to its passing.[30] On the surface, Order No. 12 was aimed at removing the threat of Christianity. But its primary target was the concept of liberalism that was seen as underpinning the Western education promoted at Christian schools. Liberalism had been gaining in popularity and was believed to be a threat to the unified state ideology propagated by the Japanese government.

Technically, the ban on religion at school was directed not at just one religion but at all religious activity. Its impact on Christian schools was severe, and one might assume that it would have an equally deleterious effect on Buddhist schools. But Buddhist leaders expressed little if any complaint against the order. Buddhists did only the bare minimum necessary to change their curriculum or practices to comply with the order. The scholar of Buddhist education Ejima Naotoshi notes that some Buddhist schools added General Studies to their curriculum but otherwise did not change.[31] One of the main reasons for this was that at the time Buddhist schools were almost wholly focused on the education of priests, unlike their Christian counterparts, which aimed at the teaching, and possible conversion, of regular citizens. Students who graduated from schools not in compliance with government regulations could not advance on to higher education institutions, as their degrees would not be recognized. For example, few families would want to send their children to a noncompliant Christian elementary school if it meant their child could not then advance on to a public middle school. In the case of Buddhist schools, since they were focused on the education of priests, there was little need to advance outside the priestly education system, so there was little impetus to conform to Order No. 12.

The Buddhist studies scholar Hayashi Makoto draws our attention to the fact that, at least initially, Buddhist schools fell under the jurisdiction of the Home Ministry's Bureau of Shrines and Temples and therefore were not under the jurisdiction of the Ministry of Education.[32] When they later incorporated under the University Ordinance (大学令, 1918), they came under the purview of the Ministry of Education and its Order No. 12. Regardless, education at Buddhist schools was not based on the Western ideals of liberalism, which were the true target of Order No. 12, so they were generally ignored. If anything, education at Buddhist schools was in tune with government efforts to teach loyalty to the state. For example, in his speech at the opening of Taishō University in 1926, Sawayanagi Masatarō (澤柳政太郎, 1865–1927), the founding president, said that faculty and students should know right from wrong and have the courage to not take even one step toward evil or that which is unreasonable. They must overcome the selfishness of the modern world and never forget to benefit others. Selfish individualism was and remains today a critique often leveled at the West. In short, Sawayanagi argued that character education at Taishō University was to be based on religious feeling (宗教的雰囲気, *shūkyōteki fuinki*), repentance, concern for others, truth and wisdom, and the courage to avoid evil, rather than selfishness and bias. In other words, it was an explicit rejection of Western liberalism and individualism;[33] it was not a threat to state ideology.

Initially Buddhist educators did not raise concerns about Order No. 12. By the 1920s, however, Buddhist educators like Sawayanagi—along with other educators across the country—began to argue for a more open role for religion in education. They saw religion as offering the foundation for moral behavior that could temper the rapid social changes occurring as Japan industrialized and Westernized. Experiments in democracy led the period to become known as the "Taishō Democracy." Movements during this period, such as those for women's rights, were perceived by many conservatives as possible threats to family structures. The increasing number of New Religions, which could directly compete with traditional religions and their values, that arose during this period of great social upheaval also represented a challenge for those who held conservative views.

For many, traditional established religion was seen as an indispensable part of moral education. As a result, few argued against state ideology; rather, they argued for using religion in schools in support of it. At the National Association for Teacher's College Presidents in 1927, Andō Masazumi (安藤正純, 1876–1955), a Nishi-Honganji branch Jōdo Shin priest and member of the House of Representatives, said, "With the elimination of religion, education has devolved to formalism. It has lost the ability to impart beautiful ideals and burning passion." He continued, "One reason for the failure of moral education at school is the ignoring of religion. . . . [Without a foundation in religious education] the people are weak in the face of superstition and false teachings."[34] As we will see in chapter 4, this sentiment is shared by others.

In a series of statements and legal drafts between 1929 and 1935, the government responded to clarify Order No. 12. Sectarian education was strictly forbidden, but religious sentiment education was acceptable and, indeed, encouraged if it did not go against the aims of the Imperial Rescript on Education. A vice minister of education wrote in 1935, "A right faith should be respected but at the same time superstitions which injure the public order and good manners should be destroyed by all means."[35] In 1945, shortly after the end of World War II, Ministry of Education Instruction No. 8 clarified that religious education could be carried out in private schools, thereby opening up the possibility for Buddhists and others to openly teach religion and conduct religious ceremonies.[36]

THE PROFESSIONAL COLLEGE ORDINANCE

The Meiji period witnessed a constant barrage of new laws and codes regarding education. In 1872 the Fundamental Law on Education was issued, establishing a modern national education system, and in 1879 it was abolished and replaced by the Education Ordinance (教育令, Kyōikurei). The system was based on the US model of education (elementary school, middle and high schools, university) and the French model of centralized administration. In 1886 the Elementary School, Middle School, Normal School, and Imperial University Ordinances were issued. In 1890 the Imperial Rescript on Education was promulgated. And in 1899 the revised Middle School Ordinance, the Professional College Ordinance, Private School Ordinance, and others were put forth.

The early Meiji changes to the Japanese education system began to bear fruit, leading to a growing demand for institutions of higher education for the graduates of the modern middle school system. This eventually led to the Professional College Ordinance (専門学校令, Senmon gakkō rei) in 1903.[37] The Professional College Ordinance continued the emphasis on a modern academic curriculum found in the middle school system. For Buddhist and other religious schools that sought status as a professional college, this ordinance forced a shift toward the academic study of religion and away from the traditional sectarian studies model.[38] Despite the changes to the curriculum that registering as a professional college could lead to, the benefits for the denominations, including state recognition, were enough to encourage a rapid expansion of Buddhist professional colleges. Buddhist leaders were engaged in an effort to reshape Buddhist institutions in order to overcome critiques made against Buddhism as backward and not useful to a modern state. The creation of Buddhist professional colleges was one avenue for expressing a willingness to work with the state and to demonstrate participation in modern education.

Efforts to work within the system could both help to prove the willingness of Buddhist institutions to work with the state and provide an education that would allow priests to more effectively operate within the modern state. In 1903 Jōdoshū Kōtō Gakuin (浄土宗高等学院) became the first denominational school to become recognized under the new law. It was quickly followed by Sōtōshū Daigakurin (曹洞宗大学林), Shinshū Kangakuin (真宗勧学院), Tendaishū Daigaku (天台宗大学), Nichirenshū Daigakurin (日蓮宗大学林), and Shinshū Daigaku (真宗大学) in 1904; Kogi Shingonshū Rengō Kōtōchūgakkō (古義真言宗連合高等中学校) and Bukkyō Daigaku (佛教大学) in 1905; Takakura Daigakuryō (高倉大学寮) in 1907; Hanazono Gakuin (花園学院) and Buzan Daigaku (豊山大学) in 1908; Shingonshū Rengō Kōyasan Daigaku (真言宗連合高野山大学) in 1909; and Shinshū Gakuin (真宗学院) in 1912.

In addition to requirements for a curriculum based on advanced academic studies, the Professional College Ordinance and Ministry of Education Order No. 14 (also issued in 1903) placed requirements on the qualifications of entering students. Schools that became professional colleges could accept only students who had graduated from a recognized middle school, women's high school, or the equivalent. And Ministry of Education Order No. 13 required that instructors have academic degrees and be graduates from an imperial university or national university, or the equivalent (among other things, this appears to have included those who went abroad to study and returned to Japan to teach).[39] This meant that students entering a Buddhist professional college would have grounding in the modern education system and that their instructors would have been exposed to and trained in the academic study of Buddhism.

In short, to acquire the advanced education needed to teach at the professional colleges, Buddhist priests technically had to attend public universities. The Imperial University (today the University of Tokyo) established a chair in Sanskrit studies in 1901, a program in Indian philosophy in the Philosophy Department in 1904, a chair in the science of religion 1905, and a chair in Indian philosophy in 1917.[40] The center for the modern academic study of Buddhism thus became a public university and not a Buddhist school, thereby changing the landscape of Buddhist learning. Buddhist denominations sent top young priests to study abroad or at the Imperial University, and they brought what they learned back to the Buddhist professional colleges and Universities where they taught.[41] Stone gives the example of Watanabe Kaikyoku (渡辺海旭, 1872–1933), a Jōdo denomination priest who studied in Germany and returned to Japan to teach at Shūkyō Daigaku (宗教大学, a Jōdo denomination school that later merged with other institutions to form Taishō University) and Tōyō Daigaku (東洋大学, a nondenominational Buddhist college originally named Tetsugakukan, 哲学館, that was founded by Inoue Enryō, 井上円了).[42]

Leading Buddhist intellectuals of the early twentieth century saw the Western academic approach to the study of Buddhism as offering a way to reform aspects of Temple Buddhism. The education of Buddhist priests inevitably changed under the combined influences of education laws that required training within the modern education system to teach at an accredited professional college and the shift toward Western approaches to the study of religion found therein. The training of Buddhist priests, by default, would be altered by the modern education system and would be further separated from the previous *danrin* system.[43] Nevertheless, the basic curriculum and the training for priests at Buddhist institutions still maintained close ties to the *danrin* system until the University Ordinance (大学令, Daigakurei) of 1918.

BIRTH OF THE MODERN UNIVERSITY

The University Ordinance of 1918 brought about another sea change in Buddhist education in Japan, this time on a scale far outstripping that of the Professional College Ordinance. Much as the Professional College Ordinance emphasized advanced academic education, so, too, did the University Ordinance, which added an emphasis on academic research (as opposed to sectarian research). It did not allow for religious education, including training in ceremony, ritual, and so on. As Ejima notes, the focus was on "objective, scientific research."[44]

There were three conditions that proved particularly disruptive for Buddhist universities. First, they could not use the name of a specific denomination or religion in the name of the university. And second, they would not be recognized under the regulation if they consisted of only one faculty, which meant they could no longer exist with just a Faculty of Buddhist Studies.[45] This meant that those institutions that wanted to continue to be clearly identified by name and curricular content as solely Buddhist, and also be a state-recognized school, had to remain or become professional colleges. These changes were also reflected in the universities' mission statements. These changes, though sometimes subtle, had a lasting impact, shifting the mission of Buddhist universities away from sectarian training of priests and toward a broader mission of offering higher education imbued with a Buddhist spirit.

A third condition that changed the course of Buddhist education was that incorporating under the University Ordinance meant that religious ritual, propagation of sectarian teachings, or otherwise engaging in religious activities was forbidden. In addition to changing the name of the school as required by the new ordinance, names of departments began to change to reflect the new (or at least revised) content. Departments of Zen Studies and Pure Land Studies came to replace the previous Department of Sectarian Studies.[46] Hayashi concludes, "Religious education involving prayer, preaching, and mission work was prohibited, but conducting academic research on religion was permitted by the Ministry of Education. Many religiously affiliated universities, when establishing courses and subjects associated with religions, gave them the title 'Religious Studies' and with that a veil of academic objectivity."[47] Sectarian universities also began to accept students other than priests and those seeking to become priests. Especially after the end of World War II, this practice expanded greatly to cater to the postwar baby boomers. This forced a move away from only training priests and toward a curriculum, even in Buddhist studies, that was focused not on the practice of religion but on the academic study of religion.[48]

Some denominations moved swiftly to create a university, while others took much longer. In all cases, the debate about how to integrate Buddhism and General Studies, priests and laity, continued for decades. The Buddhist studies scholar Fujii Masao explains one of the chief concerns for Buddhist institutions as they debated incorporating under the new ordinance.

> One example of a problem that occurred when Buddhist universities were being established was the word *sōgaku*. Would *sōryō no gaku* (clerical education) gel with the concept of a modern University? Until now we've based ourselves on monastic education (*sōdōkyōiku*), what exactly will we teach at the university? Faced with this, people then had to ask what exactly is meant by higher education. If academia is about looking at phenomena objectively, well, then, monastic education is extremely subjective. Therefore, it was thought that *sōgaku* wouldn't fit in with the modern university system.[49]

It took six years from the issuance of the ordinance and considerable debate for the Nichiren denomination to establish Risshō University (立正大学).[50] Likewise, when debating whether or not to transform Buzanha Daigakurin

(豊山派大学林) into a university under the new ordinance, some Shingon denomination Buzan Branch leaders brought up a variety of reasons not to make the move. It was argued, for example, that the mixing of secular students with priests could create problems for the priests and their education. There was also the question of how to imbue the regular curriculum with Buddhist values. Finally, there existed practical arguments about funding for the new facilities that would be needed to accommodate secular students.[51]

Saitō gives the example of the Sōtō denomination deliberations over what their new university should look like. He cites a 1921 Sōtōshū document that argues for the need to educate priests and members of the laity. The document lists four points that clearly show strategic thinking regarding the education of the laity. First, the education of priests should be at the same or higher level as that found at the Imperial University. Second, secular children should be accepted and provided an education that serves to nurture them as Buddhist faithful. Third, future educators should be taught based on Buddhist ideals. And, fourth, those with the most influence on people's thought, such as the managers of newspapers and magazines, should be the target of their secular recruiting efforts.[52] In short, accepting lay students and shifting away from educating only priests should happen only if the lay students were taught Buddhist values and were in a position to influence society after their graduation. In order to comply with the University Ordinance, schools that wanted to become accredited universities but still maintain a Buddhist mission had to reconfigure themselves as centers for the propagation of Buddhist values to the laity.[53]

Universities incorporating under the new system also faced a fourth hurdle, one that would end up creating distance between the university and the home denomination. Universities had to be overseen by a foundation (財団法人, *zaidanhōjin*) and therefore could not be directly administered by the denomination. Of course, the board of the foundation could be stacked with denomination officials and people friendly to the denomination. Nevertheless, in some cases this stipulation eventually led to a divergence in the interests of the foundation and the denomination.[54] Conflicts testing the limits of that separation occurred. For example, in 1923 the Honganji Branch of the Jōdo Shin denomination stripped a professor at Ryūkoku University (龍谷大学), Nonomura Naotarō (野々村直太郎), of his priesthood because of his stance on basic Pure Land teachings concerning rebirth. Nonomura was heavily influenced by modern religious studies and modern Western academic studies of Buddhism, which situated Buddhism in the early Pali and Sanskrit texts. Nonomura viewed the Pure Land teachings on the afterlife as incongruous with Indian Buddhism. Furthermore, he wrote that the Pure Land teachings helped to support Japanese feudalism. These stances were in direct conflict with traditional Pure Land doctrinal studies and infuriated those working in that field as well as the conservative leadership of the denomination.[55] The problem of his priestly status was compounded by the fact that Ryūkoku University, where he taught, required all instructors to be priests. When his priesthood was stripped away, the denomination also expected him to be fired from his professorship. But because Ryūkoku was registered under the new University Ordinance, its faculty could not be hired or fired at the whim of the denomination. Nonomura's dismissal led to a fierce debate over not only modern academic studies of Buddhism at a Buddhist university but also academic freedom more generally.[56]

Aside from questions of how Buddhism could be taught, and what was taught as Buddhism as well as to whom and by whom it could be taught, the University Ordinance also created more mundane hurdles for Buddhist educators. Linked to the requirement to set up a foundation to administer the university was a stipulation that a certain level of funding had to be raised prior to incorporation to demonstrate the viability of the proposed university. This proved to be a significant barrier for many smaller denominations that wanted to take advantage of the prestige and recognition that came with creating a university but could not easily raise the large sums required.[57]

CHANGES TO DENOMINATION BYLAWS

As we have seen, legal changes led to significant adjustments in Buddhist educational institutions. These adjustments also came to be reflected in denomination bylaws, which were updated frequently to reflect the changing nature of the legal structures for religious and educational institutions. Changes in bylaws, in turn, demonstrate a shift in how the role of priests and the training of priests were viewed. In the modern period, priests no longer enjoyed a special status within society that was demarcated by legal codes. The Meiji family registry law (1872) removed the special status priests had enjoyed under the Tokugawa regime. Instead, "priest" was simply one among many job titles.[58]

This change came to be reflected in the bylaws of various denominations that began to define priests as *kyōshi* (教師, teachers, i.e., a job title, not a class), and this, in turn, came to mandate a priestly education system based on the idea of learning (学習, *gakushū*) as opposed to training (修行, *shugyō*).[59] An 1895 communication from the Home Ministry required that Shinto and Buddhist *kyōshi* have at least a middle school or equivalent education.[60] Buddhist denominations had to rewrite their bylaws regarding priestly ranking to take these government regulations into account. Throughout the modern period, updates to bylaws continued to reflect later laws and orders regarding education. Saitō gives the example of the Sōtō denomination bylaws concerning priestly ranking circa 1930 as a way of understanding this shift from an emphasis on traditional training in a temple to education in a school. The following are listed as qualifying for the first rank as a priest:

> (1) One who has graduated from Komazawa University and has completed a six-month retreat at *ryōhonzan* (両本山, the main training temples) either

> during or after graduation. (2) One who has graduated from the Indian Philosophy or Religious Studies Department, or something recognized as similar, at an imperial university or a university under the University Ordinance or from Komazawa University Professional College, Department of Buddhism (Komazawa diagaku senmonbu bukkyō gakka, 駒澤大学専門部仏教学科), and has completed a one-year retreat at *ryōhonzan* either during or after graduation. (3) Someone who has graduated from Komazawa University Professional College, Primary Department, Special Department or Preparatory Department, or a professional college or university preparatory school recognized as the equivalent or better and has completed a two-year retreat at *ryōhonzon* either during or after graduation.[61]

As can be seen, the more classroom education one had, and the perceived quality of that education (i.e., at the denomination's university, or professional college, etc., and specializing in Buddhism or not), the less time one had to spend at the main training temples. This emphasis on education continues today. For example, in contemporary Tendai, there are several ways to climb the ranks as a *kyōshi*. Tendai requires success both in practice and in learning in order to advance in priestly rank. Educational achievement plays a significant role. To be promoted to the rank of *dairisshi* (大律師), for example, a priest needs to have completed *shidōkegyō* (四度加行, the basic practice regime in which esoteric ritual is first learned) and either *tōdanjukai* (登壇受戒) or *nyūdankanjō* (入壇灌頂) for the practice portion,[62] as well as one of the following educational achievements: major in Buddhist studies at a university recognized under the Fundamental Education Law and take at least twenty credits in Tendai studies; graduate from a junior college recognized under the Fundamental Education Law and take at least twenty credits in Tendai studies; graduate from Eizan Gakuin (叡山学院, Tendai's seminary on Mt. Hiei) Primary Department and take at least thirty-six credits in Tendai studies; or graduate from Taishō University's Buddhist professional college and take at least twenty credits in Tendai studies.[63] From this list it is clear that not only does education make a difference, but the relative quality of that education is also weighted.

In the end, we see the back-and-forth waves of influence on the training of Buddhist priests. State legal structures impact sectarian education. Sectarian institutions change bylaws in response to legal changes. These changes in turn reinforce the external demands and push the training model for priests even further away from traditional temple retreats and toward classroom education.[64]

ALL FOR ONE AND ONE FOR . . .

During the Meiji period some Temple Buddhism leaders attempted to create educational institutions that transcended denominational or at least branch boundaries. An early example is the Sōkō (総黌) at Tōji (東寺) established in

1880.[65] At the time, Shingon and all other denominations of Buddhism were under the state's one sect, one leader order that forced different branches of each denomination under one umbrella. The Sōkō resulted in part from this effort by the state. It combined the *gakurin* of three branches of Shingon. Because of its trans-Shingon nature, the school at Tōji tended to blur the difference between the competing branches of Shingon. Graduates of the Sōkō could become abbots of important temples. The top students from the various branch *gakurin* were selected to attend the Sōkō.[66] Shaku Unshō (釈雲照1827–1909), a leading proponent of the precept revival movement that was influential in Buddhist circles at the time, heavily influenced the curriculum. Because of this, the curriculum emphasized precepts and moral education.[67] In large part due to the forced nature of the project, the Sōkō did not last long. It was renamed Jisōgodenjo (事相講伝所) under the 1886 bylaws for the Shingon denomination, and shortly afterward, according to Abe Kishi, for all intents and purposes it came to an end.[68]

Buddhist leaders briefly sought strength through solidarity because of the many legal changes and the social disruptions of the Meiji Restoration. For example, in 1869 leaders from multiple denominations formed the Shoshūdōtokurenmei (諸宗道徳連盟, Trans-Sectarian Shared Virtue Association), or Renmei. The Renmei listed eight "slogans": King's Law and Buddha's Law Cannot Be Separated, Destroy and Reject the Study of False Teachings, Study Your Own Denomination, Make the Three Teachings the Pillars of Your Training, Wash Away the Old Fashion from within Your Denomination, Keep Up Schools Developed under the New Guidelines, Promote (the Development of) Human Resources in the Denominations, and Educate the Citizens of All Prefectures.[69] Among the eight slogans we can see an emphasis on Buddhist education and propagation. In light of the many and varied attacks on Buddhism in the early Meiji period, Buddhist leaders recognized the need to train the priesthood in ways that would highlight Buddhism's service to the state. The Renmei encouraged each denomination to reform its education system. It also went one step further with the establishment of the Trans-Sectarian Comprehensive Education Academy (諸宗総黌, Shoshū Sōkō) in 1870.[70] And in the same year, a trans-sectarian dorm was established at Kōshūji (興宗寺) in Kyoto. This project was designed at least in part as a model for individual denominations as they reconsidered their own educational institutions.

THE TRANS-SECTARIAN UNIVERSITY MOVEMENT

The desire to create a trans-sectarian educational institution seen in the creation of the Shoshūdōtokurenmei and its school continued into the Taishō period. Many Buddhist denominations were involved in talks to create a trans-sectarian university under the University Ordinance of 1918, including Tendai, Kogi Shingon, Jōdo, Shinshū Takadaha, Bukojiha, Honmonhōkkeha, the Chizan and

Buzan branches of Shingon, and others. A trans-sectarian institution would have practical benefits, such as sharing costs, but for many it also represented a way to transform Buddhist education, and with it the teachings of Buddhism, by overcoming sectarian differences and "returning" to shared Buddhist teachings. The movement to create a trans-sectarian university gained speed even as a number of denominations were fast creating their own universities by turning their professional colleges into universities under the 1918 University Ordinance.

A number of denominations were already in the process of creating their own universities or had already created universities. In 1923, Tendai, Jōdo, and the Buzan branch of Shingon came together to create the Committee to Prepare for the Creation of Taishō University (大正大学設立準備会, Taishōdaigaku setsuritsu junbikai). That same year Tendaishū University (天台宗大学, a professional college) and Buzan University (豊山大学, a professional college) consolidated on the campus of Shūkyō University (also a professional college) in preparation for becoming Taishō University. In 1926 the bylaws for Taishō University were created.[71]

What was the process for creating Taishō University? In 1922, representatives from the Tendai, Nichiren, Sōtō, Jōdo, and Kogi Shingon denominations as well as the Buzan and Chinzan branches of the Shingi Shingon denomination met in Tokyo to officially form the Committee for Surveying the Education of Each Denomination (各宗教育調査会, Kakushū kyōiku chōsakai). They met throughout the year and in November created the Plan to Establish the Alliance of Buddhist Denominations (仏教各宗連合設立思案, Bukkyō kakushū rengō setsuritsu shian). The preface to the plan spells out the reasons that members believed a trans-sectarian university was necessary. The authors noted that each denomination had its own financial difficulties and local issues and that each denomination was struggling with propagation and education. Furthermore, they wrote that while individually they might be struggling, united they could overcome individual weaknesses. It was also argued that forming a trans-sectarian school would not just help to overcome the economic difficulties of individual denominations but would also serve to enrich the content of their teachings and enhance and promote Buddhism overall (275–276).

Sawayanagi Masatarō, who would go on to become the first president of the trans-sectarian university, argued that sectarianism led to a weakening of Buddhist teachings. He also argued that Buddhists, perhaps in part due to their divisive sectarianism, were losing ground to Christianity. Creating a trans-sectarian platform for reaffirming the social role and influence of Buddhism was another argument for pushing forward with the university (272).

In 1923 representatives from all denominations except Jōdo Shin, which had already established two universities under the new law, met and agreed to work toward the establishment of a trans-sectarian university. Following their meeting they each took the issue back to their respective denomination Diets, where, following deliberation, the project was approved (278). However, in

August 1923 a massive earthquake stuck the Kantō region of Japan. The earthquake forced a delay in the plans to build the new university.

Jōdo, Shingon Buzan branch, and Tendai agreed to forge ahead and created the foundation required by law to finance the university. Each denomination contributed 500,000 yen to the foundation to meet the minimum investment required by law and agreed to temporarily use the facilities of Shūkyō University (285).[72] While everything proceeded quickly, there were several issues that had to be addressed. First, because of the earthquake the government required reinforced concrete buildings. This meant the construction of a new main school building and the additional expense related to construction. The law also required a significant investment in books in foreign languages. A total of four thousand German, French, and English books had to be acquired. Second, there was the issue of getting the right staff in place in a short period of time (305). These hurdles were overcome, and in 1925 the students from Tendaishū University, Buzan University, and Shūkkyō University were matriculated in the newly formed Taishō University. In 1926, the first new students were admitted.

BUDDHIST STUDIES CURRICULA

Up to now we have seen the way legal and sociopolitical challenges shaped the development of Buddhist institutions of higher education. As many Buddhist institutions of higher education moved from what were essentially seminaries to become comprehensive universities, there was an impact on what they taught. Likewise, allowing the enrollment of laypeople also changed the focus and content of instruction. Throughout the Meiji and into the Taishō and Shōwa (1926–1989) periods, the changes came fast and furious, often requiring complete curricular and institutional overhauls before the previous changes could even be fully implemented.

Curricular changes were not new to the modern period. In the case of the Tendai denomination, for example, a major curricular shift occurred in its *dangijo* during the Edo period. Tendai teaching academies moved away from the oral transmission (口伝, *kuden*) teachings of the past, which stressed practices such as *kanshin* (観心, a form of meditation and self-reflection), and were tied instead to practice as it had developed in Japan in the Heian period and the Chinese Tiantai teachings emphasized by the then-popular Anraku branch (84).

In Tendai as in other denominations, the late Edo and early Meiji periods saw yet another shift in the teachings at the *danrin* and *daigakurin* that were replacing the *dangijo.* In the case of Tendai this shift included a switch to studying the Japanese founders, a return to studying *kuden* (Japanese oral transmission), and a renewed emphasis on esoteric Buddhism and Mahayana precepts. Chinese classics were included in the curriculum, as was a new emphasis on Western learning (Western history, philosophy, and ethics). At the middle school level, English, math, Japanese, and geography were added (117). Other denominations made similar moves in the beginning of the Meiji period. For example, the Nishihonganji branch of the Jōdo Shin denomination created its Daigakurin in 1868 and there taught the same sectarian content as before but added National Learning (国学, Kokugaku), Confucianism, and other subjects designed to combat Christianity. The Higashi Honganji branch of the Jōdo Shin denomination created its Gohōjō (護法場), and the Jōdo denomination created Kōgakujo (興学所, later named 勧学所, Kangakujo) in the same year, and each followed a similar curricular pattern.[73] The Nichiren denomination's Daidanrin (大檀林) added General Studies, including English, math, and physics, to its curriculum in 1886.[74] What we see in these early changes to curriculum is a continued interest in teaching sectarian basics but also the desire to equip the priesthood with the knowledge needed to effectively interact with and combat Western ideals, especially Christianity. These changes also reflected a desire to change the view of Buddhism, brought about by the anti-Buddhist movement, that dominated the early Meiji period.

These early curricular changes were taking place alongside massive changes in Japanese education that included compulsory education, the creation of public Elementary and Middle schools, as well as the development of the Imperial University and other national universities. Buddhist educational institutions had to start including subjects that had not previously been part of basic priestly education. Math, English, Western philosophy and ethics, and so on were slowly added into the various Buddhist academies. This increased curricular burden led to the need to condense and simplify the content of the Buddhist instruction taking place, which in turn led to the need to develop textbooks. Early textbooks reflected the sectarian studies of the past but in a form more readily communicated in the truncated course hours needed to allow for the expanded curriculum. The textbooks reflect a shift in the education of priests. As Miura Shū discusses in an insightful essay, priestly education moves during the Meiji period from a program of training to one of learning.[75] Learning follows a set curriculum using textbooks (as opposed to sacred texts) and focuses on classroom education as opposed to embodied learning found in ritual training and debate.

This basic curriculum, reflecting a two-part pattern of sectarian studies and "Other Studies," continued even as the institutions changed from sectarian academies to professional training colleges under the 1903 Professional College Ordinance. For some institutions, including what came to be called General Studies was a logistical burden but one that had to be met to provide a competitive, modern education. For example, in the case of Buzan branch of the Shingon denomination, the Bunzanha Daigakurin, was established in 1901 and included two departments: a Principal Department and a General Studies Department. They did not have the staff or the facilities to teach the General Studies curriculum, however, and students were required to take those courses at Tokyo Professional College (東京専門学校, Tokyo Senmon Gakkō, which later became Waseda University), Testugakukan, or Kokugakuin.[76] Small Buddhist institutions such as the Buzan branch struggled to offer the curriculum they felt was needed. Enrollment numbers and fiscal viability also impacted curricular development at these schools. For example, the Buzan branch chose to open its middle school to the public because young priests could not provide the enrollment numbers they needed.[77] This necessitated a modern curriculum in line with that offered in public schools, which meant that the young priests learning there were getting a significantly different education than the previous generation had gotten.

The addition of General Studies was debated fiercely in most denominations. Branches of the Jōdo Shin denomination were some of the earliest adopters. Both the Ōtani and Honganji branches sent leading young priests abroad at the beginning of the Meiji period to study Western education. Shortly after those priests returned to Japan, the branches added or restructured their General Studies programs. In other denominations, debate over General Studies continued much longer. Journals of the Shingon denomination chart an ongoing debate over the value of adding General Studies and other aspects of Western curricula found at the Imperial University (e.g., requiring a graduation thesis).[78] The Buddhism scholar Abe Kishi includes the arguments made by Sawayanagi Masatarō against General Education for priests. Sawayanagi argued that until age seventeen most people do not think much about their future, and they do not know their own strengths, so General Studies is useful for expanding their horizons. After that, learning specialized studies at a professional college or a university is no different than General Studies—it's just studying and conducting research in those areas in more depth. For such people General Studies at college is especially necessary if they have not had it beforehand, enabling them to move into their areas of specialization. But priests, Sawayanagi argued, have already firmly committed to their future and so do not need General Studies for entering a sectarian school. He further maintained that those who argued for the inclusion of General Studies at sectarian schools make the claim that it is helpful for propagation. But he pressed the counterpoint that if education is for saving people, mastering morals and being an exemplar for society is far more useful. Sawayanagi adds that when laypeople ask priests about the Buddhist teachings, they do so not for knowledge but for faith. So if priests follow worldly affairs (i.e., spend time in General Studies), it will not benefit society.[79] In the end, his arguments did not win out. General Studies made their way into the Shingon curriculum and later became a critical part of the institution he would lead (Taishō University).

As discussed above, the University Ordinance of 1918 had a significant impact on Buddhist higher education. Following the guidelines of the ordinance, as institutions incorporated as universities, generally evolving from a professional college, they added multiple departments.[80] The addition of departments led to an ever-increasing number of possible elective courses, which in turn impacted the curriculum for priests in training. On a very mundane note, the credit hour totals needed for the programs in the new university system, which included General Studies, electives, and languages, decreased the number of core Buddhism courses priests in training could take.[81]

The University Ordinance had the further effect of removing ritual training from the curriculum. Under the Professional College Ordinance, institutions could offer practical courses in how to conduct rituals or how to proselytize because they were exempted from Ordinance No. 12. Under the University Ordinance such courses were prohibited.[82] This led to increasing bifurcation of roles: the training temples became the center for ritual training, and universities sites of study.

During the Taishō period, universities also began establishing research departments for qualified graduates to continue their studies. A variety of scholarly organizations and journals began to appear in these years, reflecting the new focus on the historical and philological approaches to the study of Buddhism.[83] It was also during this time that language courses were added to the curriculum for priests following the Western Buddhist studies focus on philology. Miura argues this is when sectarian studies (宗乗, *shūjō*) truly transformed into academic sectarian studies (宗学, *shūgaku*).[84]

The situation at Buddhist universities changed dramatically in the postwar period. In particular, there was a massive influx of secular students. In the Taishō and early Shōwa periods Buddhist universities opened their programs to the laity. That move had already influenced the curriculum. With the boom in students, postwar Buddhist educational leaders were forced to question the purpose of Buddhist universities: Was their primary goal the education of the next generation of priests, or was it to educate the general public while instilling a sense of Buddhist values?

THE FATE OF BUDDHIST STUDIES AT BUDDHIST UNIVERSITIES

Buddhist institutions of higher education began as places to train and educate young men to become priests.[85] With the advent of the modern education system, in which, as we have seen, universities were barred from engaging in religious education until after World War II, priestly training came to take place predominantly at denomination training centers. Even as training in ritual and ceremony shifted out of Buddhist higher education, education in the study of Buddhism remained the pillar of Buddhist higher education. Buddhist universities were centered on their Buddhist studies faculties. As noted previously, many universities expanded and began to offer education in other areas, which in some cases left the Buddhist studies faculties in the minority. Yet even in cases where the Buddhist studies faculty played a diminished role, it still remained and served, if nothing else, as a reminder of the founding ideals of the institution.

When, in 1993, Taishō University eliminated its Buddhist studies faculty and folded its programs into other faculty, it was big news in the world of Buddhist education in Japan.

The fate of the Buddhist studies faculty was part of a larger reorganization that aimed not only to restructure the core mission of Buddhist education at Taishō but also to increase enrollment. Fujii noted,

> We then switched from a yearlong system to the semester system and also changed our curriculum so that we could offer courses from nine in the morning until nine at night. These changes now compose one of the main foundations of our university. We also changed the actual times of courses during the day. All this was done to meet the needs of our students. A lot of them tend to sleep in, so we decided to focus our energies on the evening. In fact, the number of students taking the entrance exam for Taishō doubled because of this.[86]

Buddhist studies at Taishō was not eliminated; rather, it moved into the new Faculty of Human Studies (人間学部, Ningen Gakubu). The move was part of an effort to draw more students to Taishō and also to re-envision the education of priests in light of an ever-changing society. A 1991 revision to the Standards for the Establishment of Universities (Daigaku setchi kijun, 大学設置基準) that made curricular changes easier encouraged universities to experiment with their curricula. At that time, two faculties at Taishō, Buddhist Studies and Literature, were reorganized into the faculty of Human Studies (which would include a Buddhist studies program) and Literature.[87] Fujii explains the shift as follows:

> Ultimately, if it's a Buddhist institution, you have to take those founding principles and convey them to the entire university. Unfortunately, this ideal tends to become very vague [in practice] and somehow diffuse. What we thought of (at Taishō) was this: The chief concern of Buddhism is the human being. Therefore, we ended up with our Human Studies Faculty. That's why Taishō's Buddhist Studies Faculty disappeared and the Human Studies Faculty rose in its place. We wanted to be founded on the principles of humanity and really consider the many aspects of human interaction.[88]

Okamoto Gijō, head of Jōdoshū kyōgaku kyoku (浄土宗教学局, Jōdo Denomination Division of Doctrine) and at the time in charge of sectarian education at Taishō, writes, "When the Buddhist Studies Faculty was subsumed into the Human Studies Faculty part of the reasoning was that a revolution in thinking on the part of the denominations was needed regarding how priests are educated."[89] He continues, "In today's world it just won't suffice to train priests in sectarian studies—they must study more broadly if they are going to be able to lead temple lay members in today's high education achievement society." That, he writes, was one of the reasons for creating the Human Studies Faculty.[90] In a similar fashion, but pointing to both the education of student priests and regular students, then–associate professor Tada Kōshō explained in a 1991 report on the proposed changes presented at the Sixth International Buddhist Studies Conference that the goal of combining the Buddhist Studies Faculty with the Social Studies and Social Welfare Departments from the Faculty of Literature to create the Human Studies Faculty was to allow for the training of people who could contribute to the welfare of society by providing for the education of the "total person" (as opposed to the more segmented education that could be found in an isolated Buddhist Studies Faculty).[91] Regarding the education of priests specifically, Tada notes that Buddhist studies education needed to be modernized. The form of education provided up to that point had fit the needs of priests as they went out into society, but the needs of society had changed dramatically. It was hoped that through the creation of an interdisciplinary faculty, new developments in Buddhism would emerge and students would be equipped with a broad training that would allow them to become practitioners who benefit others—a basic Mahayana Buddhist ideal here interpreted to mean someone who will seek new ways to benefit society.[92]

COUNTING (ON) TEMPLE CHILDREN

The quality of the education that priests received at Taishō was crucial, but an almost equally important issue was enrollment. Okamoto states that in the past all temple children, not just the successor to the temple head priest position, would attend Taishō. Lately, however, only the temple son designated to take over from his father ended up going to Taishō. The other children went to colleges of their choosing, since they did not need to use the Taishō degree toward priestly ranking.[93] Dropping enrollment numbers related to the children of temples also served to highlight another issue related to this key constituency. As Buddhist studies scholar Komine Ichi'in notes, "With the exception of those who enter the priesthood from a lay background, in today's Japanese Buddhism the family is the temple family. Whereas in the past you entered the priesthood out of an awakening to pursue the path, today it is more of taking on the family business. Life at the temple is also life at home. Your master is your father and you cannot see him as anything other than your father."[94] This creates an issue for education at the university because, according to then–assistant professor of Buddhist studies Koyama Tenyū and others, the view that the priesthood is a job in "the family business" leads many student priests to focus on just getting the bare minimum number of credits needed for priestly ranking.[95] Fujii concurs noting that earning a degree in Buddhist studies is often seen as the easy path for those training to become a priest, since the different denominations all have regulations about credit hours and ranking as a priest.[96]

Prewar shifts in Buddhist education that led to changes in how education was viewed have come full circle. So too have Meiji period legal changes that allowed clerical marriage and the concomitant changes in Buddhist institutional structures that followed. This has led some students from temple families today to see their college education as nothing more than earning the necessary degree needed to take over the family business.[97] Taishō's leadership believed that restructuring the curriculum could serve as a way of igniting an interest in Buddhism for temple children and thereby move them away from seeing the priesthood in terms of simply a job in the family business. By making the priesthood more attractive to regular students, the leadership also hoped that the educational experience of temple and lay students would be enhanced and thus that enrollment—and, with it, finances—would stabilize.

CHANGE IS CONSTANT

Restructuring the various faculties and departments led to ongoing changes in the curriculum. Koyama details the Buddhist offerings in the Buddhist Studies Department. When he refers to "course" below, he is referring to the Japanese *ko-su,* which is not just one course, as the term is generally understood in the United States, but a track in which students take a set of classes over their four years at university. In other words, within the Buddhist Studies Department and the major in Buddhism a student can opt for one of three tracks (e.g., Buddhist Culture):

> Let me talk about the changes that happened in our Buddhist Studies Department. These changes began about five years after I joined the faculty at Taishō. We currently have a general Buddhist studies program, and within this program we have four different sections for teaching the specific doctrines of each school as represented at Taishō: . . . The number of students in the program, however, is on the decline, and we decided to come up with ways to increase these numbers. Originally, Buddhist studies meant intellectual and doctrinal history, but this approach by itself doesn't really meet the needs of our students. Therefore, we thought that by having a program on Buddhist culture and another for hands-on Buddhism, and this is an odd way of putting it, even if a student isn't into book learning, they can study how to create Buddhist iconography or, say, experience going on a pilgrimage. This is why we now have separate programs for Buddhist culture and hands-on immersion. The first graduates of this program will be this year [2004]. We now have a fairly defined system as to what classes students take in the intellectual history program,

> the hands-on program, and the Buddhist culture program. About 40 students enter the Buddhist Studies Department annually. The Buddhist Culture course has exceeded our expectations and is the most popular. The hands-on course has the fewest students. Out of these 40 students, 15 to 20 or more will enter the Buddhist Culture course; the intellectual history section is next, and the hands-on course is last, with about seven or eight students entering. Why is the hands-on program last? This is somewhat of a problem related to internal institutional matters, but all of the professors in the hands-on program are priests, so students tend to think, "How exciting. Sutra copying." It would be nice if we could point out that we offer courses in Buddhist painting and they would think something like, "Buddhist painting! I've heard that a really renowned artist teaches at Taishō!" . . . Unfortunately, there are also budgetary constraints, which means we have to use professors who are already at Taishō.[98]
>
> As can be seen, every effort was made to create tracks within Buddhist studies that might appeal to students. Shiori Hōdō, who teaches at Taishō, writes that finding ways to engage students in Buddhist studies and to reach the two audiences—students from a lay background with an interest in Buddhism and students from temple families who were in the program because they had to be—led to curricular challenges.[99]

When the Buddhist Studies Faculty was moved into the Human Studies Faculty, three tracks (Thought, Culture, Practice), along with sectarian studies for each denomination, were created within the Buddhist Studies Department. Various curricular efforts continued over the years that were designed to ignite a passion for Buddhism in temple children, and to draw more lay students into the study of Buddhism. There was a fear, Shiori says, that regular students would see temple kids as they are in college (by which he means acting like typical college students, or at least not very "priest-like" early on in their college career) and that it would only serve to further damage their view of Buddhism: "They could actually leave Taishō hating Buddhism."[100]

Faculty and staff had to consider what the needs of these two constituencies were and then how they might integrate them in a track that could help to overcome the divide between lay and temple children and benefit the work of both groups. Shiori writes, "Temple children want their priest's license. They need to study ceremony and sectarian studies and, as the foundation for sectarian studies, they need classical Chinese and trans-sectarian Buddhism (*tsūbukkyō*). What is more, they are often here because their parents pushed them to go to Taishō, so motivation can be a real problem." On the other hand, he continues, "regular [lay] students [in the Buddhist Studies Department] have a deep interest in Buddhist thought and culture and wish to study it in depth; they came to Taishō because they have an interest in the practical study of Buddhism. Of course, there are some regular students who don't really know what they want to do and others who are seeking to become priests themselves."[101]

One effort to integrate lay and temple students is the Summer Buddhist Study Program. The program is open to all students and consists of two types: the Hieizan Bukkyō Kenshū (open to men and women) and Joshi Bukkyō Kenshū (for women only, and with three sites rotated annually—Hasedera, Chishakuin, and Chionji). Each year forty students attend the Hieizan Bukkyō Kenshū. Many are from the Buddhist Studies Department, but students from other programs also attend. The majority are women.[102]

The summer program, however, is limited in scope. A more thorough attempt at bridging the lay/temple divide while also serving to ignite a passion for Buddhism is seen in the Next Community Course (NCC). Developed in 2005, the NCC also represented a way to forefront Buddhism a decade after the Buddhist Studies Faculty had been subsumed into the Human Studies Faculty.

Reflecting worries on the part of Buddhist leaders about the next generation of priests, and the lasting postwar debate about the values of the youth, Shiori writes that there was an interest in raising student social awareness. It was felt that "in order to make manifest the keywords of this age—symbiosis, coexistence, and social engagement—a curriculum which allows students to master social service know-how and thinking was necessary."[103] Toward this end, in 2005 Taishō developed the NCC, which cut across the Buddhist Studies Department, the social welfare studies major, the counseling psychology major, and the human sciences major. The NCC had as its purpose integrating Taishō with the local community and providing training and fieldwork opportunities for students that would enable them to contribute to society.[104] It created four tracks—NCC Buddhism, NCC Social Welfare, NCC Psychology, and NCC Education—and was based on providing students with training in theory and practice in its three pillars: "symbiosis," "values," and "management." It was an ambitious project that required students to enroll in the program within their primary major and required faculty often to team-teach the core classes in the NCC.

The NCC Buddhism program provides a window onto those involved in Buddhist studies at Taishō who were looking ahead to the forms Temple Buddhism in Japan might take in the future and foreshadows later developments at Taishō, such as the Buddhist Social Responsibility project (see below in this chapter). NCC Buddhism was envisioned as a track that would appeal to students from temple families enrolled in the sectarian studies program. The goal was to introduce the students to social studies, social welfare studies, and psychology to equip them with the theoretical and methodological background necessary to consider how Buddhism might react to and shape communities of the future. The program was seen as a way to shift the focus of the practical

Buddhism course from *jiri* (自利) practices, or those designed to benefit self, to *rita* (利他) practices, or those that benefit others. Traditionally, these two types of practices are seen as working hand in hand. The practitioner first engages in practices that benefit self and prepare him or her to turn toward saving others. In contemporary Japanese Buddhism there is a growing movement to turn Buddhism outward and find ways to benefit society that move beyond traditional practices and roles.

In the end it would appear that the NCC program may have served as a model for later efforts to provide training and awareness through a socially engaged education, but the program failed to survive on its own. Enrollment in the program was less than hoped, likely because it was something added to the students' workload and also because of the difficulty in creating course content and delivery that could draw students to the program.

REINCARNATION OF THE BUDDHIST FACULTY

Efforts such as the NCC program, developing and adjusting different tracks within the Buddhist studies major, and others to attract more students to the study of Buddhism and to reform the education of priests continued. As enrollment remained an issue at Taishō (as it was across the country due to dropping birth rates, see below for more), university leadership looked again to major changes across campus. In 2009 a new university master plan was created that called for a return to the founding ideals of the university. The founding ideals are described as "the actualization of wisdom and compassion based on Mahayana Buddhist thought."[105] The authors of Taishō University's 2014 accreditation report write that "great hope and expectations were placed on Buddhism" by contemporary society, as it faced myriad problems.[106]

Because of this renewed interest in explicitly promoting Buddhism, it was felt that the Buddhist Studies Faculty should be reinstituted. The Buddhist Studies Department was moved out of the Human Studies Faculty and into the newly reformed Buddhist Studies Faculty in 2010. Along with the re-creation of the Buddhist Studies Faculty, Buddhist ideals were re-emphasized across faculty, as part of their mission if not in actual practice. According to the accreditation report, the Buddhist Studies Faculty and its one department are to make manifest the wisdom and compassion of Shakyamuni's teaching, the Human Studies Faculty and its five departments have as their mission inquiry into compassion and acceptance, the Faculty of Literature and its one department seek to obtain wisdom, while the Faculty of Communication and its one department seek to comprehensively do all this in modern society.[107]

Part of the reasoning behind getting the Buddhist Studies Faculty back in place and promoting a renewed commitment to the Buddhist nature of the university was the belief that Buddhism had a role to play in contemporary Japanese society. The course offerings, the course tracks, and even the faculty continued to shift as leadership sought to position Taishō as an institution engaged with its community that trained students to initiate positive change. The most recent nod in this direction was the creation of the Faculty of Regional Development, which aims at "developing leaders who will contribute to regional development."[108] Although not explicitly espousing Buddhist ideals, the new program complements the emphasis on engagement. It is not by accident that the Buddhist Social Responsibility Center (see below in this chapter for more) came to be housed in Taishō's new Institute for Regional Development.

BUDDHISM ACROSS THE CURRICULUM: INSTILLING BUDDHIST VALUES

The history of Buddhist universities and the development of their curricula is only part of the story. As we have seen, Buddhist universities transformed from what were essentially seminaries into comprehensive four-year institutions offering a variety of degrees to students who were not on a path to priesthood. A professor of Buddhist studies at Komazawa University, Ishii Seijun, stated, "Honestly, we are a comprehensive institution that also happens to train priests. Out of about sixteen thousand students, one thousand or so are in Buddhist studies."[109] Regarding the shift in the student body from primarily Buddhist priests and the children of Buddhist priests, Professor Emeritus of Religious Studies Fujii Masao at Taishō University comments, "It's questionable at this point as to whether you can even refer to Taishō as a Buddhist university."[110] Time and again leaders in Buddhist education come back to the same question: "What are the founding ideals of the university and how, if at all, are they made manifest today?"

According to its home page, the Nichiren-based Risshō University has the following three founding ideals, which are based on the sixteenth president's modern interpretation of a vow made by Nichiren: (1) Seek truth and show sincerity, (2) Value justice and reject evil, (3) Desire peace and serve humankind.[111] The 2013 Accreditation Report for the Rinzai Zen based Hanazono University lists its founding ideals as the following: "to create strong and gentle character through training of the heart and mind based on a foundation of Zen thought. In short, the founding ideal is to train character based on a Zen-type Buddhist spirit."[112]

The founding ideals of Taishō University are listed as "the actualization of wisdom and compassion based on Mahayana Buddhist thought."[113] This is explained as follows: "Wisdom is to carry on the knowledge and wisdom accumulated by our forbearers within the long history of the teachings of Shakyamuni and further to give rise to new knowledge and wisdom—in short to obtain the strength to live. The actualization of compassion is to give rise to that knowledge and wisdom in others (to benefit others, *rita*). In short, it is the actualization of a heart/mind that gives life."[114] These ideals are in turn tied to the university's statement of purpose, which is "to develop human resources that understand humanity comprehensively and contribute to the welfare of humanity based on Buddhist spirit."[115] These ideals are expressed further in the new educational vision statement for Taishō, which is seen as a form of vow not unlike the Bodhisattva vow that is a fundamental part of Buddhist practice in Japan: "Just like the bodhisattva, faculty, staff, and students set a concrete goal, in short the educational vision is the vow of people steadily moving towards their goal."[116] This vision that functions as vow has four aspects. First is compassion (慈悲, *jihi*), which means "to become one who has a heart/mind (*kokoro*) of deep affection towards all living things." Second is to be a light unto oneself (自燈明, *jitōmyō*), which is "to become one who can rely on her/himself and inquire into truth." Third is the Middle Path (中道, *chūdō*), or "to become one who can live a proper life and give rise to a heart/mind that cannot be led astray." And fourth is symbiosis (*kyōsei*), which is "to become one who can work with others to achieve a goal and live in harmony."[117] Unlike the Bodhisattva vows, which are repeated in ceremonies, it is unclear how many students at Taishō are aware of the university vision beyond possibly having seen it on the university website. Be that as it may, the vision does appear to inform, at least in part, how administrators and faculty go about developing programs. The new vision is an expression of Taishō's efforts to re-emphasize the school's Buddhist nature.

How do Buddhist universities put the lofty goals of their founding ideals into practice? One route seen above is to transform them into vision and mission statements like Taishō University. However, as the scholar Nara Yasuaki notes, "One question that arises is, do you teach basic religious or Buddhist studies or do you teach about a Buddhist/religious way of life by embedding those values in other courses?"[118] As we shall see, Buddhist universities have tried a little bit of everything—from embedding Buddhist ideals in their mission statements, to offering Buddhist studies courses, to imbuing the university environment with a religious feeling through regular religious services, artworks, and speakers.

Most Buddhist universities today have at least one required course in the General Studies program that is either specifically on Buddhism or serves to introduce Buddhist ideals. Some appeal to the interests of students and parents for job-related skills. When asked about why they require a religious studies course for all students, the then–head of Aichi Gakuin University (愛知学院大学) said, "If you do not understand religion, as a person of the world, you cannot speak on an equal level with people from other nations."[119] But most emphasize inculcating a basic knowledge of religion in order to prepare students to live in a world where they will likely encounter a variety of ideologies, some of which could be harmful, and to be able to make informed decisions about those ideologies. Nara writes, "It goes without saying that the purpose of religious education at this school [Komazawa] includes teaching about Buddhism, Zen, the teachings of the Sōtō denomination and the characteristics and meaning of belief from the standpoint of a religious studies tradition. But, more than anything else, it is about teaching each student the proper awareness of and attitude toward religion, and to provide the foundation of a religious view of humanity and society from the standpoint of freedom."[120]

One might think that implementing a required course on religious or Buddhist studies for all students at a Buddhist university would be a simple matter, yet requiring such a course met more and more resistance as the universities grew in size and came to teach primarily students who were not training as priests, who often had no interest in Buddhism, and who in some cases did not even realize the school they were attending was Buddhist. Resistance also increased because many, if not most, faculty were no longer priests. Isshi Seijun noted in 2004, "Many departments put up a great deal of resistance to our Buddhist principles. . . . The Social Sciences Department put up a huge fight. But the department that wouldn't require students to take zazen was the law faculty. Zazen is required course for all departments." Because of the stiff resistance across campus to a required course on zazen, the length of the course was cut back: "Up until 10 years ago, we required two years of zazen. We called this the 'Religious Studies' course. First-year students would take an introduction to Buddhism and second-year students a course on zazen. We now call this course 'Buddhism and Humanity,' and it has been reduced to a one-year program that is mandatory for all students at Komazawa. The Buddhist Studies Department's position is that we will not allow this course to be diminished any further."[121] At smaller universities such as Kōyasan University, requiring students to take courses on Buddhism is easier and is advertised as part of the appeal of the university. At Kōyasan University, in 2000, the curriculum required all students to take "An Introduction to Esoteric Buddhism" and "An Introduction to the Thought of Kūkai."[122]

This battle over forcing all students to take a course many may not want is ongoing. Taishō University's Kashiwagi Masahiro is rather blunt in his assessment of just how many Buddhism or religious studies courses could be required of all students: "Despite receiving funding support from the denominations, most income for the university comes from regular students, so the administration must see to the needs of our source of income."[123]

Given the difficulty of pushing students to take more than a minimal number of courses on Buddhism, educators are forced to find ways to express Buddhist ideals in a more generalized format that can be taught in any number of courses. The scholar Komatsu Makiko, writing on religious education, states, "What is important for the youth of Japan today is to know the limited nature of human life and to return to a point where they experience a sense of reverential awe [畏敬, *ikei*] at something that is beyond human knowledge. Not only teaching that life is important or about the importance of living on one's own power, but teaching in a way that balances those views with [teaching about] the limited nature of human life."[124]

Kashiwagi is optimistic about this broader approach. He writes that mixing regular students with students training to become priests can have a positive effect on both. Priests in training, almost all of whom grow up in temples, are introduced to people and experiences outside temple life, while regular students are introduced to young Buddhist priests and will hopefully gain an affinity for Buddhism through that interaction.[125] This leads us to the other method for teaching Buddhism at a Buddhist university: sentiment education. Most Buddhist universities still require at least one Buddhism or religious studies course, but administrators are aware that they cannot force much more than that into the already crowded course schedules of their students. That leaves leaders to seek to imbue the atmosphere on campus with a Buddhist feeling through regular Buddhist ceremonies and speeches or lectures on Buddhism by faculty and/or requiring some level of participation in Buddhist events on campus. At Kōyasan University, according to the 2000 curriculum, students are required to attend the monthly Buddhist service a total of at least fifteen times during their four-year program. They are also welcome to participate in regular sutra chanting and Buddhist services on campus. Most larger schools do not require attendance at Buddhist ceremonies, but they provide many opportunities for students to participate.[126]

EXTRACURRICULAR: BUDDHIST UNIVERSITIES AND THE PUBLIC

What we have seen and discussed up to now are issues faced by the modern Buddhist higher education system, including changes to legal structures and the creation of the modern Japanese education system, and what those issues have meant for the training of priests, the teaching of Buddhism, and the content of that teaching. Buddhist universities have evolved from institutions designed to train priests to comprehensive institutions for which the education of priests is but one of their many functions. Following we will examine efforts to reach out beyond the borders of the university to educate and engage the public at large.

Unlike their modern Christian counterparts in Japan, which were initially designed with the express purpose of spreading the Christian teachings and increasing the number of converts, Buddhist institutions in the modern period rarely, if ever, saw their primary role as propagation of the teachings beyond the priesthood. As they expanded from institutions for the teaching and training of priests to comprehensive universities, their role in the propagation of Buddhism came into question.

Temple Buddhism in the postwar period has come under increasing scrutiny. Many within Temple Buddhism see the need to respond to critics, at the very least, by engaging the public through community service, social activism, or spiritual care. John Nelson, Mark Rowe, Nathan Michon, and others have written on the activities of members of Temple Buddhism that have been shaped in mutual interaction with the ways Temple Buddhism is viewed—from the creation of new practices and institutions to the reimagining of familial bonds and the personal relationship one has with Buddhist teachings, practices, and institutions.[127] Like other institutions of Temple Buddhism, today Buddhist universities in Japan are no less involved in activities to raise public awareness of Temple Buddhist teachings and practices and to make manifest a vision of Temple Buddhism as an engine of public service. This public outreach at the universities is not only the product of sincere engaged priests or university administrators looking to increase enrollment through public advocacy programs; it is also connected to their standing as legally recognized institutions of higher education. Every university is asked to respond to questions about how it implements the founding ideals and vision of the institution and how the institution engages the public beyond the classroom in their accreditation reports.

The publication of research results is listed in all university self-examination reports as a common means for disseminating knowledge of Buddhism to the wider community. Anyone involved in university administration in the United States, and likely anywhere else in the world, knows that the dissemination of research results is widely seen as one of the most important ways that universities contribute to the general good, so it should come as no surprise to see it listed by Japanese Buddhist universities. Along the same lines, academic conferences are seen to encourage further study of Buddhism and the exchange of ideas about Buddhism. Publication and conferences tend to have a very limited audience of academics. A third means of communicating Buddhism to the public is lecture series. Komazawa University notes that the public lecture series offered by its Faculty of Buddhist Studies is one of the most popular at Komazawa and that it is the series most closely tied to the university's founding ideals. According to their data, 94 percent of the attendees are over fifty years old, a fact the report's authors see as evidence of "meeting the learning needs of seniors seeking to deepen their understanding of Buddhism."[128] Hanazono University also offers a lecture series on Buddhism that is attended by roughly thirty people on Monday mornings. The lecture takes the format of zazen (in this case sitting in chairs) followed by chanting of sutra and a sermon or lecture.[129]

In addition to its fall and spring open lecture series, which regularly draws audiences of one hundred or more, Kōyasan University offers a unique and popular summer lecture program called "Kōyasan University Lifelong Learning Lecture Series in Koyasan" (previously called "Kōyasan University Open Lecture Series"). The program began in 1986 and was initially designed as a refresher course for temple priests and others associated with local temples. Beginning in 1995 the curriculum was changed to allow participation by the general public. Since 1996, the three-day course has regularly had over two hundred attendees. Topics for this special series range from mandala to "the history and culture of the Silk Road" to "the form of Mahayana precepts in esoteric Buddhism."[130]

Hanazono University and Komazawa University also highlight the role of their museums in opening the teachings of Buddhism to the public. The Hanazono University Museum of History has four areas of focus, one of which directly touches on Buddhism: Art and Zen Culture.[131] This area seeks to draw attention to the ways that Zen influenced aspects of Japanese culture, from art to literature. Komazawa University founded its Museum of Zen Culture and History in 2002. Attendance at the museum rose steadily from 6,800 in 2005 to 11,780 in 2011.[132] Beginning in 2012 a lecture series based at the museum was also created, and attendance there appears to be robust. The museum also hosts "Buddhism in Practice" seminars that offer opportunities to practice sutra copying and zazen.

Taishō University offers a wide array of examples of outreach that go beyond the traditional lecture series. One example is the Center for the Promotion of Buddhist Social Responsibility (previously the Office for the Promotion of Buddhist Social Responsibility, BSR Suishinshitsu) housed in Taishō University's Institute for Regional Development (地域構想研究所, Chiikikōsō kenkyūjo). The center combines research and outreach.

Japanese Temple Buddhism has been undergoing a period of self-reflection following critiques in the modern period about its role in society. This self-reflection reached critical mass following the 2011 Tōhoku earthquake and tsunami, which led to multiple efforts by virtually every denomination to examine priestly training and how Buddhist teachings are disseminated.[133] From as far back as the late seventeenth century, Temple Buddhism had become increasingly identified with death care. As that role came under intense criticism in the postwar period, and as individuals within Buddhism as well as the public came to demand a more socially engaged Temple Buddhism, many Buddhist professionals turned inward to reflect on what it meant to be Buddhist within Japanese Temple Buddhism. What should Buddhist practice in today's world look like? What does Buddhist action in the face of tragedy or social ills look like? Should Buddhists seek to move beyond the temple and its traditional lay member base? Could they do so even if they wanted to? Taishō's BSR Center is an effort to understand just what Buddhist social responsibility is, can be, or should be, and to disseminate those findings so that priests at temples across the country can act on them.

Hoshino Eiki, one of the early BSR Office advisers, writes in the first BSR newsletter (published in 2014) that until recently Taishō was seen as having two pillars—education and research—but that going forward it had to develop a third pillar: service to society and the region.[134] The BSR Center has as its mission the analysis of surveys and practical examples to begin to understand how to define Buddhist social responsibility, with the understanding that there are potentially many varieties including at the level of local temples, denominations, and the university. At least in the beginning, the BSR efforts did not foreground or focus on the wide body of literature on Engaged Buddhism or Humanistic Buddhism, two movements within modern Buddhism outside Japan that seek to understand the roles Buddhism should play in society. In the first newsletter, the explanation of social responsibility provided drew not on the literature or terminology of Engaged Buddhism but on the definition of social responsibility outlined in the International Organization of Standardization (ISO) 26000 guidance, which focused (as the newsletter details) on corporate responsibility. Hoshino raises seven specific points: (1) the need for organizations to clearly explain the impact of their activities on others, (2) transparency, (3) ethical action, (4) respect for the interests of stakeholders, (5) respect for the rule of law, (6) respect for international rules of action, and (7) respect for human rights.[135] Hoshino gives examples of these as applied to temple life, such as explaining the meaning of funerals and making temple finances transparent. He also points out that the research planned and coordinated by BSR will have an impact beyond the university, which itself must be understood as a Buddhist actor in terms of Buddhist social responsibility. Research conducted through the BSR includes the nature of religion as a public good and of temples as public welfare corporations (公益法人, *kōeki hōjin*).

At the end of the first year of the BSR initiative, these seven points were revisited. What becomes clear is that the focus of research is the priesthood. Although the "Buddhist" in Buddhist Social Responsibility was tentatively left open, from Hoshino's opening remarks it was obvious that the priesthood would become the central focus. Given Taishō's historical mission as a place for the training of priests and its continued focus on the education of the next generation of Buddhist priests, the direction BSR took is unsurprising. In the year-end issue of the first year of the BSR newsletter, the seven points listed above are revisited in light of the focus on the priesthood. The revised version of the seven points adds the following explanation to each, respectively: (1) communicate the meaning of various activities including Buddhist ceremonies (such as memorial services and funerals), (2) aspire to make the priesthood and temple finances open, (3) act based on the Five Precepts and the Ten Good Precepts, (4) always consider the temple's lay members and local citizens, (5) obey and respect the laws of Japan, (6) study the teachings and activities of Buddhists in other countries, and (7) never forget to act with thoughtfulness and compassion toward everyone.[136]

The BSR newsletter is designed to underscore the key areas of BSR work. Each issue introduces a book on Buddhism that highlights current critiques of Buddhism, such as funeral Buddhism (in which Temple Buddhism is portrayed as overly focused on income-generating funeral rituals); the proper role of priests in society; the current issues facing Buddhism, such as the depopulation of rural temples; or the history of Buddhist higher education. The bulk of each issue is dedicated to "Research Notes." This section introduces the results of ongoing BSR research and, examined longitudinally, shows the increasing efforts to delineate the outlines of what Buddhist social responsibility might look like in practice. The three areas that are given the most space across multiple issues are an introduction to the new field of Clinical Religious Care Professionals (臨床宗教師, *rinsho shūkyōshi*), suicide, and the trans-sectarian activities of young

Buddhist priests (in which the topic of Engaged Buddhism is examined in some depth). The research notes also provide an opportunity to publicize the various conferences and workshops that BSR members are attending, which in turn exposes the reader to the variety of projects going on in this field.

In addition to highlighting research into Buddhist social responsibility, the newsletter also serves to advertise upcoming talks and events at Taishō or organized by Taishō in the local area. One example is the "Mobile Buddhism" course (出張仏教講座, Shu'chō bukkyō kōza), which takes place at the Toshima District People's Plaza (豊島区区民広場, Toshima-ku Kumin hiroba). The newsletter highlights the first four courses: "Buddhism Basics," "The ABCs of Buddhism" (which served as an introduction to funerals, memorial services, graves, Ōbon, and Higan), "Super Simple Meditation Methods" (introducing breath counting and the Moon Meditation), and "Sutra Copying Practice." The courses were taught by BSR-affiliated faculty.[137] The Mobile Buddhism Course is an example of transdenominational propagation and is one way the university sees itself as fulfilling its mission of outreach and community service.

Debates within Buddhism, and in particular within Taishō, regarding the direction that Buddhism and the study of Buddhism should take in the future are also discussed in the newsletter. For example, the cover story of issue number 14 is by a professor in the Buddhist Studies Department, Noguchi Keiya, who writes that Buddhist graduate education needs to change in light of societal demands. He writes that traditional graduate studies in Buddhism consist of in-depth textual studies on doctrine and the presentation of research results. However, he calls for a shift to Applied Buddhist Studies (応用仏教学, Ōyō bukkyōgaku), in which graduate students approach Buddhist studies or sectarian studies from a variety of angles so that they can apply the results of their studies in the field.[138] This view of the need for an Applied Buddhist Studies is in line with the "Research Notes" of the newsletter's last issue covering the first year of the BSR office. Looking back over the research and other activities of the year, the authors conclude that future research should concentrate on the topic "BSR in a society of many deaths" and write that they have been awarded a three-year grant from the Japan Society for the Promotion of Science (日本学術振興会, Gakujitsushinkōkai). Given the prediction that the number of people dying each year will increase by 30 percent in the coming years due to the increasing number of senior and super-senior citizens, and Buddhism's traditional association with death care, the authors proposed to study priestly interaction with the death process before, during, and after the moment of death. This research, centered in Taishō University and its BSR initiative, was designed specifically to have a practical effect well beyond the walls of the university.[139]

The BSR initiative is closely tied to a new temple that was erected on Taishō's campus in 2013. The new temple is called Ōdai Sazaedō (鴨台さざえ堂, or Sugamo Ōdai Kannondō, 巣鴨鴨台観音堂) and is located behind the university library facing the street. There were already two places for prayer on campus, the prayer hall and a statue of Shakyamuni as a child in front of one of the main classroom buildings where the annual celebration of the Buddha's birth is held. The erection of a pagoda on campus was designed specifically to highlight Taishō's Buddhist character and to serve to link Buddhism at Taishō to the world outside Taishō. BSR staff surveyed the number of visitors in its first six months and found that over ten thousand people had visited. Over half the visitors were over fifty.[140] Fieldwork conducted by students in Taishō's clinical psychology program found that area residents were aware of the new temple but did not know whether it was open to visitors and suggested better signage.[141] In 2018, signs in the area subway stations that once pointed only to Taishō now also point to Sazaedō. Monthly ceremonies are conducted by priests from Taishō University's four denominations of Buddhism as well as the Ji denomination to help to draw visitors and to bridge the gap between the town, Taishō, and Buddhism. The site has become a stop for walking groups, likely coming through on their way to or from the nearby famous Obāsan no Harajuku (Sugamo shopping district famed for its elderly clientele), and it has seen increasing numbers of visitors from temple lay member groups from the denominations associated with Taishō.[142]

Each year the temple is open for *hatsumōde* (first visit of the new year), when Japanese visit temples and shrines to renew their talismans and seek blessings for the new year. By 2016 those visiting Sazaedō to ring in the new year numbered over six hundred. While this is nothing compared to the tens of thousands that visit Sensōji in Asakusa (浅草寺, a famous pilgrimage site in Tokyo), it is certainly a sign that the temple is making headway in becoming a regular part of the local community. The temple is staffed by student and local volunteers who serve to guide visitors or answer questions. With the addition of Sazaedō, Taishō became one of four local sites to host the annual Sugamo Nakasendō Chrysanthemum Festival, held in November.[143] Along with two area temples and one area shrine, Taishō has become one of the four hosting sites for a stamp rally conducted as part of the festival in which visitors walk to each site and collect a stamp in their stamp book. This practice goes back to the practice of pilgrimage in Japan and the collecting of stamps at each temple visited. Again, this serves to strengthen community ties while also identifying Taishō as a Buddhist site.

A pilgrimage temple without an *omamori* (talisman) for visitors to take away could hardly be called a temple in Japan, so common is the practice. *Omamori* are sought after for a variety of reasons, including the religious (for healing, success in business or school, protection, etc.) and the secular (as a keepsake from a trip, to give to friends and family as a special gift). Sazaedō is no exception. A special *omamori* was created for the temple. On the outside is the name of the temple, and on the inside is a thread made up of the five colors of Buddhism.

The educational vision of Taishō (Compassion, Self-Reliance, the Middle Path, Coexistence)[144] is written on the wrapping of the *omamori*. The thread is made by a local bakery, an NGO that employs the homeless and disabled. The thread is then blessed by a staff member who is a Buddhist priest. This *omamori* is an example of the move at Taishō University to re-emphasize its Buddhist origins, connect with the local community, and engage in socially responsible actions.

Sazaedō and the BSR project are two examples of the ways Taishō University is seeking to express its Buddhist nature by making use of new and traditional methods of spreading the Buddhist teachings, and by reinterpreting Buddhism for the modern period. The BSR effort leverages the traditional research activities of a university for the spreading of Buddhism and for the reimagining of Buddhist practice in the modern period. Unlike the efforts of some research institutes affiliated with specific denominations, Taishō's BSR is a transdenominational effort to study contemporary Temple Buddhism and to explore whether and, if so, how Temple Buddhism needs to change to remain relevant in contemporary Japan. The creation of a temple, Sazaedō, to draw people toward Buddhism—the use of a spectacular physical site to encourage people to visit and learn more—is nothing new. Linking that site to a new style of pilgrimage (*stamp-puri*) is also taking advantage of traditional methods to draw people to the site. Working to make the university a center for community life is also nothing new—universities in Japan and elsewhere have often seen community outreach as an important mission—and it is not an unfamiliar role for temples. Temples in Japan have long been the center of communities, serving as a gathering place throughout the year. And temple priests often take a leading role in community life. What is new is using a temple to tie a university to the local community and, in so doing, emphasize the Buddhist nature of the university.

This brings us to our third example of Taishō University's public outreach geared toward enlightening the public about Buddhism or at least about the university's Buddhist nature. In 2011 Taishō held its first Bon Odori (Bon Dance) since student unrest in the 1960s forced the closure of its postwar Bon Odori linked to its children studies program. Bon Odori are a regular feature at local temples throughout Japan and range in size from very small groups representing the lay members of a particular temple to larger affairs connected with town or city offices. They have long been understood as both a religious rite for the dead and a community-building effort that serves to bring together members from across the community in the event's planning and execution.

The impetus for reinstituting the Bon Odori at Taishō was the 2011 earthquake and tsunami disaster in eastern Japan. The new iteration of the Bon Odori, called the Mitama Festival (*mitama matsuri,* or Festival of the Souls), was planned and executed completely by students with faculty oversight. The 2011 festival was hurriedly put together and was done on a shoestring budget in connection with Taishō's NCC Local Region Seminar. Students in the seminar had been tasked with finding something that would bring members of the community onto campus. Student leaders felt the Bon Odori would highlight Taishō's status as a Buddhist university, serve to transmit traditional culture, and be a fitting way to recognize the tragedy that had befallen Japan that year.[145] The Mitama Festival was held to pray for those lost in the disaster and served to express Taishō's Buddhist nature and the link between Buddhism and folk traditions. It also served as a form of community outreach and service. Shiori Hōdō, one of the first faculty advisers for the festival, expressed his hopes that students would learn about and continue traditional arts through the festival.[146] The festival was well attended and became a regular feature at Taishō. Fifty yen was donated for disaster relief for each person that attended wearing a *yukata,* the traditional Japanese summer robes worn at festivals. The emphasis on *yukata* was a way for Taishō to encourage participants to maintain traditional aspects of the festival. In its seventh year it attracted approximately 4,500 people from the Sugamo area, over 1,000 of whom came in *yukata.*

During its first three iterations it was called the Mitama Festival, but it came to be felt that the name was "too religious" and might be limiting attendance. Planners wanted to reach local children to introduce them to the tradition, and some of those planners thought the name did not communicate that goal well. The fourth festival was renamed the Ōdai Kodomo Bondori (Ōdai Children's Bon Dance). Ōdai refers to the local region. That name was later shortened to simply Ōdai Bondori (Ōdai Bon Dance).[147] Despite changes to the festival's name, its religious nature is still highlighted. A Buddhist rite for the dead (施餓鬼, *segaki*) is held to open the festival, and Buddhist priests are among those performing during the breaks between dances. The president of Taishō, a Buddhist priest, begins the festival with a speech that serves to tie together Buddhism, Taishō, the region, and the Bon dance tradition. An article in the local online news captured the religious nature of the event with a large picture of priests performing the *segaki* rite as the lead for the article.[148]

As far as the spreading of the Buddhist teachings go, Taishō's Bon Dance is perhaps best understood as a form of religious sentiment education. Although there is a speech and a religious rite to open the festival, otherwise the program has very little that, at a glance, would appear to be Buddhist or religious in nature. After scanning Twitter and Facebook pages, newsletters, and news reports on the event, it is clear that the overt religious character of the event gets little attention beyond an occasional photo of priests performing. This may be partly because the religious nature of the Bon Dance is believed to be understood by Japanese, since it is such a regular part of Japanese festival life and therefore needs little introduction. Nevertheless, most of the material produced by Taishō regarding the event focuses on its success as a form of community outreach that serves local needs while embedding Taishō within the community. It also stresses that the event is a form of service learning for the students. Interviews in Taishō newsletters with students all focus on this aspect, although a few students and staff use the line "As a Buddhist university this is something we can excel at," implying an understanding that the event is Buddhist in nature.[149]

IS THERE A FUTURE FOR BUDDHIST HIGHER EDUCATION?

Changes in the content and delivery of Buddhist studies, attention to the founding ideals, and attempts to infuse the general education curriculum with a Buddhist spirit may all be for naught if Buddhist universities fail to survive the higher education winter that Japan is suffering. Japan has seen a steady decline in the number of children being born, which has meant a steady decline in the number of people entering university. This comes after years of buildup in Japanese education facilities to accommodate the baby boomers, which created a surplus of institutions. Competition among universities for survival is fierce, and most experts foresee the closing of numerous two- and four-year institutions. The pressure to enroll students is without a doubt behind many of the initiatives, including curricular changes, that we have seen.

For some schools, such as Taishō, the return to the founding ideals of the university is seen as a way of creating and emphasizing a unique identity that might make them stand out in a crowded field. Returning to their religious identity can help with recruiting in other ways, too. At Risshō University during the early postwar period, when students were plentiful, there was a move to tone down the religious aspects of the university. But once the population bubble popped, ties to the denomination and its thousands of temples came to be seen as useful for student recruitment.[150] Reaffirming their Buddhist nature also serves as a way to assure the denominations, which contribute considerable financial support each year, that the universities they support remain a force for the propagation of Buddhism and a place where priests can get the education they will need to assure the viability of the denomination and Temple Buddhism for the future.[151]

Student enrollment numbers also have an impact on the role of the Buddhist university as the site of educating the next generation of priests. Many Buddhist Universities saw their enrollment increase significantly in the postwar period. Komazawa University, Bukkyō University, Ryūkoku University, and Taishō University saw an increase in students, which meant they could be more and more selective in admission decisions. Enrollment caps in individual programs are determined through application to MEXT. Unlike in the United States, for example, where department chairs or deans often can increase enrollment or restrict enrollment depending on the needs and capacities of the department, in Japan those capacities are predetermined when programs are created and then approved by MEXT. This means that a particularly successful program may be at capacity and therefore very selective and would be unable to change those capacities without a major curricular redesign submitted by the university to MEXT.

One way around this problem is to set aside slots and to create a separate entrance examination for the children of temple priests (or for those people who plan on becoming priests). Not every university does this officially, but most develop some mechanism to assure that priests in training can enroll in their Buddhist Studies or Sectarian Studies Departments. Ryūkoku University, for example, found that the increase in students made it harder for temple family members to enroll. This situation was considered dire enough that it became the center of discussion at the Diet meeting of the Jōdo Shin denomination, Nishi-Hongaji branch. In 1991 the Recommendation-Based Entrance System for Missionaries (伝道者推薦入試制度, Dendōsha suisen nyūshi seido) was introduced. This gave preference for entry into the Shinshū Department (Sectarian Studies) in the Faculty of Letters to those who had ordained or promised to ordain.[152] That opened a window of opportunity for temple children to enter the main university associated with their denomination.

In order to attract more students as enrollment numbers dropped, in 2002 Ryūkoku University opened the special bracket to priests in training from any denomination. Ryūkoku widened the number of departments and programs available to them to also include the Buddhism Department, the major in Buddhist History offered through the Buddhist Historical Studies Department, and the Community Management Department in the Faculty of Social Studies.[153] Nevertheless, the head of the Entrance Exam Group noted that those who could not get in could always study Shinshū Studies at either the junior college associated with Ryūkoku or at Chūōbukkyō gakuin (中央仏教学院), which serves as the Shinshū seminary. He states, "While we obviously feel a sense of mission as a denomination school toward temple children, it does not mean that we have to take just anyone without any qualifications."[154] Terakawa Shunshō, president of Ōtani University, similarly stated that watering down requirements for the children of temple families would only be detrimental to the denomination and that those who could not get into the flagship school could still study to become priests at Ōtani University's junior college or at Ōtani Senshūgakuin (大谷専修学院, the Ōtani branch's seminary).[155]

Other schools, however, felt it best to make special accommodations for at least some of these potential students. Bukkyō University, for example, opened a bracket for recommendations from the denomination in 1995, and in 1997 it opened a bracket for children from temples.[156] Much as with Ryūkoku University, Komazawa University leadership felt the need to address the enrollment issues faced by temple children who might not otherwise do well enough on the standard entrance exam to get into the school. According to a 1995 Sōtō denomination survey cited in *Jimon Kōryū,* roughly 60 percent of all temple head priests and assistant head priests were graduates of Komazawa. This led denomination leaders to worry about temple children going elsewhere for their education, since they could not guarantee the standards of that education as it applies to becoming a priest.[157] The head of public relations, cited in the same article, states that while there is no special bracket for temple children, there is a common belief among temples that if they submit their proof of priesthood from the denomination along with their application, they will receive special dispensation. To meet these expectations, those who submit proof of priesthood are accepted with scores a little under the required level in the Faculty of Buddhism.[158] Aichi Gakuin University, also associated with the Sōtō denomination, handles applications in a similar fashion.[159]

Taishō University created a special exam for temple children in 1994. The Missionary Entrance Exam (伝道者入試, dendōsha nyūshi) bracket had a set of requirements not unlike those at other schools with special entrance exams for temple children or those wishing to become priests. Requirements include that the applicant must either currently be a priest or promise to become a priest, be willing take over a temple, and show promise of studying further in the future. The exam questions developed in 2000 give us a better sense of what is being sought from the applicant: "(1) Why did you apply? (2) When did you first become interested in Buddhism and what was the reason? (3) What role do you think it has and what role should it play in society today? (4) What field in Buddhism or what approach to Buddhism would you like to study? (5) What type of work do you want to do in the future? Please explain and give concrete examples."[160] This system changed over time, and in the 2013 self-evaluation report the Faculty of Buddhist Studies had two special entrance exam brackets. The first, the Special Entrance Exam for Denomination Children (宗門師弟特別入学試験, shūmon shitei tokubetsu nyūgaku shiken), remains essentially the same for those in or going into the priesthood. The second, the Adult Special Entrance Exam for the Buddhist Studies Department (仏教学科社会人特別試験, Bukkyōgakka shakaijin tokubetsu shiken), is a nod toward the changing demographics of Japan and is aimed at nontraditional students, especially those over sixty.[161]

AN EVER-CHANGING BUDDHISM

This examination of Buddhist higher education shows us a Buddhism that is constantly adjusting to its social, cultural, and political environment. Changes in education that occurred in the prewar period due to changes in legal codes, the influx of Western educational models, societal pressures, and the needs of the various factions within Temple Buddhism have had a lasting impact on Japanese Buddhism. Education at a Buddhist university has come to dominate priestly training, to the point where ranking within the priesthood is often defined by educational achievement. Course content has shifted from the early modern sectarian studies model to the modern academic Buddhist studies model, even within contemporary sectarian studies. Changing realities of temple economics and local demands have pushed Buddhist educators to reexamine the purpose of Buddhist education. This has led to gradual changes in the content and aim of the course offerings at Buddhist universities, from textual and historical studies to Applied Buddhist Studies. These changes are attempts to find ways to increase Buddhist engagement with society. At the same time, university enrollment pressures have forced Buddhist educators to look at Buddhist education not primarily as a means to educate the priesthood but instead as a form of Buddhist outreach that will influence secular students and shape the way Buddhism is understood by the public at large.

4

MORAL EDUCATION AND BUDDHISM

Morals change with the times, but Buddhism is the Truth and it applies all the time.

—Sumida Keikō

In the late 1980s, I had the pleasure of teaching English in rural Japan on the JET program.[1] I can remember my Japanese colleagues telling me that our school had been designated as a moral education experiment. At the time, I was too busy learning about and enjoying my rural town and environs to pay much attention to what that meant in the grander scheme of things. Nevertheless, I did have a sense of what living in a moral education experiment meant in my everyday life and for the quotidian reality of my junior high school students. Apparently, not long before my arrival, the school had had issues with student behavior. By the time I got there, all boys were required to sport the *marubozu*-style haircut (a close-cropped crew cut), and the girls had limits on their hairstyles as well. And, of course, uniforms were de rigueur. Teachers were expected to correct the behavior of students no matter where they encountered them—on campus or off, during school hours or afterward. It did not take students long to realize I held little coercive power. If they were riding their bicycles without helmets on a weekend and they saw me, they would first cry out, "Yabai!" (Oh no!), but when they realized it was only me they would say, "No worries, it's just Steve Sensei" and wave happily at me.

What sort of moral depravity had befallen Japan that teachers would drive around town after school to scold students for riding their bicycles without a helmet or for buying juice from vending machines? Did these bareheaded, juice-swilling twelve-year-old easy riders represent the doom of Japan's future? To the wide-eyed recent college grad from California, there did not appear to be any moral collapse worthy of the level of handwringing that seemed to be going on around me. Nevertheless, to many in Japan, especially among the conservative leadership, Japan was heading down a moral slippery slope. This perceived moral collapse was thought to be pushed from behind by fears that contemporary moral education was too lax—a reaction to the lasting memory of state enforced moral education during wartime Japan—and pulled from in front by what was perceived to be Western decadence and individualism.

When we fast-forward to today (2023), school bullying and violence are still hot topics in popular media, government circles, and religious institutions. The worries of the 1980s did not fade away. Instead, they gained even more traction. The firebrand governor of Tokyo from 1999 to 2012, Ishihara Shintarō (石原慎太郎), was quoted in the *Yomiuri Shinbun* in 1999 as saying, "Japan is the only nation among the Group of Seven industrialized nations in which middle and high school girls date for money to buy luxury goods. . . . We have to teach them morals."[2] What is to blame for this perceived moral decline? From all directions one can hear complaints that Japan has lost its way and its moral center has been hollowed out. There are three interconnected commonly made explanations for Japan's perceived moral decline: (1) the Japanese have cut themselves off from their history in the aftermath of World War II and have thus lost their identity; (2) in cutting themselves off from their history, Japanese people have lost the "unique" values of their past; and (3) a "religion allergy" has taken hold, resulting in weak morals. The "allergy" is said to be the direct product of blaming religion for Japan's wartime aggression. Many Buddhist and political leaders further argue that the Allied Occupation is to blame for these three factors, citing the imposition of Western values on postwar Japan.

In the *Japan Echo,* Nakanishi Teramasu writes in 2000 that Japanese society is out of balance, that its material and spiritual well-being are out of sync, and that tradition and progress are off-kilter.[3] These feelings are echoed by Onishi Kenmei. Writing in a volume about Buddhist kindergarten education, he states, "On the face of it, the modern period gives one the feeling of being a rich and fulfilling moment but, in reality, it suffers from impoverishment of heart/mind."[4] Nakanishi continues, "History and culture are the social values that were most neglected by postwar Japan. This neglect was the source of the decline of Japanese civilization."[5] Writing in 2001, the social commentator Hosokawa Ryūichirō pins the blame for Japan's "poorness of heart/mind" squarely on the Allied Occupation following World War II:

> Immediately after the war, Gen. Douglas MacArthur ordered that the Imperial Rescript on Education be abolished along with ethics as a subject of study. The Imperial Rescript, which was given to the people of Japan by the then Emperor on Oct. 30, 1890, lists basic virtues such as respect for parents, fraternal love, friendship and conjugal harmony, while ethics was meant to teach children concrete ways of living these virtues.
>
> MacArthur denied the Japanese the opportunity to be taught about such important matters. This is the root of the deluge of murders in present-day Japan, even between husbands and wives or brothers and sisters.

> Some portions of the Imperial Rescript may not be suited to contemporary Japan. But the rest of it contains eternal truths.[6]

Prime Minister Hosokawa Morihiro (細川護熙, in office August 1993–April 1994), also writing in 2001, blames the abandonment of "traditional" values and the wholesale adoption of Western (particularly US) consumerism for Japan's moral decline. He laments the gain of material wealth at the expense of spiritual wealth.

> Since World War II ended, we have blindly accepted the U.S. system of mass production and consumption, abandoning the old Japanese tradition. We bought new-model cars, brand-name bags and condominiums in resort areas. This resulted in the economic bubble, which eventually collapsed. . . . Japanese then [in prewar Japan] did not throw out old goods. Many people had only one set of nice clothes. They used to wear the same kimono for their whole lives. While they did not have material wealth, they were not poor, spiritually speaking.[7]

Many point to the postwar Constitution and the Fundamental Law on Education, the law that guides education policy and administration in Japan, as the culprits behind Japan's spiritual and moral decline because of the way they treat religion in education. A local temple priest, writing in his temple blog about conversations his temple study group had following the 1995 Aum Shinrikyō sarin gas incident, points out what he sees as the double-edged nature of these new laws. He blames them for the elimination of religion in public education. And he sees their guarantee of freedom of religion as allowing people to be drawn to whatever belief system they fancy no matter how harmful those beliefs might be.

> One conclusion was that the Japanese, upon reflection following the end of World War II, removed religion from education and at the same time guaranteed freedom of belief. As a result, people began to step away from being rich in heart/mind. In the realm of education this is seen in the emphasis on ranking, and in incidents of bullying and truancy. On the other hand, freedom of religion led to religious groups devoid of truth that simply use religion for their own purposes.[8]

He is joined in this view by Nakajima Yūjun, then the head of the Tendai Denomination Division of Doctrine (教学部, Kyōgakubu). In an interview in *Gekkan Jūshoku* in 2014 for an article on the realities of moral education efforts within Temple Buddhism, Nakajima states, "Religion is unnaturally absent from moral education. You cannot discuss right and wrong or beauty only by talking about 'morals.' There is so much more. It is necessary, for example, to discuss religion. If you are going to teach morals, you must allow students to come into contact with religion more often."[9]

The view that religion has been cut from postwar Japanese education and that there must be a return to a past when religion was ostensibly the basis for moral education highlights an interesting point. As we saw in chapter 3, religion was specifically banned from education throughout prewar and wartime Japan. Instead, beginning in the 1930s, what was offered in prewar and wartime Japan was religious sentiment education. This included visiting Shinto shrines and participating in Shinto ceremonies. Shinto was defined not as a religion but as an integral part of Japanese culture and identity. For many in Buddhist education and elsewhere, when arguing for a return to religion in public education, the term "religion" is referring to Japanese values, which tend to be those spelled out in the Imperial Rescript on Education and in Shinto and Buddhist teachings about nature and the ancestors, and to religious sentiment. The definition of religion in Japan has been in flux since at least the nineteenth century. Josephson-Storm unpacks the history of the term "religion" (宗教, *shūkyō*) in his book *The Invention of Religion in Japan.* He describes how contemporary understandings of religion came to be constructed through negotiation between Western and Japanese diplomats, religious leaders, and politicians who were seeking ways of understanding each other to complete diplomatic agreements that would have far-reaching effects.

Religion was a realm in which Western and Japanese ideas competed and indeed came to shape and inform each other. In our discussion of Buddhist colleges, we saw the government's desire throughout the prewar period to control Western ideals, such as liberalism, that were making their way into the mainstream through the education system, especially through Christian schools. Nolte writes that since as early as the Meiji period, many in Japan have struggled with how best to understand individualism within the Japanese sociocultural context and have come to believe that the straight adoption of Western individualism was not possible.[10] Today some in Japan see Western individualism as having usurped Japanese values within contemporary education. Katō Junichi of Japan's Young People Association stated in an interview with the BBC, "I think our moral decline has been shameful. It all started when we turned our back on Asian values 130 years ago and Westernized our education."[11]

In this chapter we will explore the history of moral education in modern Japan and look at Buddhist views on moral education to contextualize Buddhist thought on the topic. Examples of contemporary moral education at Buddhist junior and senior high schools will be examined along with secular efforts to invigorate moral education, including *kokoro no kyōiku* (heart/mind education) and the Buddhist response to it.

THE IMPERIAL RESCRIPT AND PREWAR MORALS

In our discussion of the Doctrinal Instructor system, we saw that the Japanese state understood that it was necessary to inculcate a common set of values both to help create a sense of shared participation in the nation and to ensure a peaceful and compliant populace as Japan underwent radical change in the Meiji period. The Doctrinal Instructor system was one aspect of this effort. Tours of the country by the emperor so he could see and be seen by his subjects and thereby create a sense of belonging to a unified nation were another part of the project.[12] This project to mold the minds of the citizens of the emerging nation came to be seen as increasingly important as Western ideals began to spread throughout Japan.[13] Klaus Luhmer writes, "The year 1878 marked a turning point for the educational system as such and moral education (*shūshin*) in particular. Emperor Meiji visited different parts of the country and was concerned about the effects of indiscriminate absorption of Western learning on the morality of his people. . . . The emperor lamented the general decay of public morals, for which he blamed the influx of Western learning."[14]

Ban and Cummings write that modern nation-states came to rely on schools for moral education.[15] In prewar Japan, the Imperial Rescript on Education and the *shūshin* class are evidence of the state's desire to use the new compulsory education system to inculcate morals. The Imperial Rescript on Education was promulgated in 1890 and set the tone for the government's view on moral education. As the scholar Inoue Kyoko writes, "During the late 1870s and throughout the 1880s, as new political, economic, and social institutions began to take root in Japan, strong reactions against Western ideas and practices, and particularly Anglo-American individualism and utilitarianism, began to emerge."[16] In 1882 the Principles for Early Education (幼学綱要, *Yōgaku kōyō*) were created. These included twenty virtues, such as filial piety, benevolence, sincerity, and perseverance.[17] The Rescript furthered these goals and reads as follows:

> Know ye, Our subjects:
>
> Our Imperial Ancestors have founded Our Empire on a basis broad and everlasting and have deeply and firmly implanted virtue; Our subjects ever united in loyalty and filial piety have from generation to generation illustrated the beauty thereof. This is the glory of the fundamental character of Our Empire, and herein lies the source of Our education. Ye, Our subjects, be filial to your parents, affectionate to your brothers and sisters; as husbands and wives be harmonious; as friends true; bear yourselves in modesty and moderation; extend your benevolence to all; pursue learning and cultivate arts, and thereby develop intellectual faculties and perfect moral powers; furthermore advance public good and promote common interests; always respect the Constitution and observe the laws; should emergency arise, offer yourselves courageously to the State; and thus guard and maintain the prosperity of Our Imperial Throne coeval with heaven and earth. So shall ye not only be Our good and faithful subjects, but render illustrious the best traditions of your forefathers. The Way here set forth is indeed the teaching bequeathed by Our Imperial Ancestors, to be observed alike by

> Their Descendants and the subjects, infallible for all ages and true in all places. It is Our wish to lay it to heart in all reverence, in common with you, Our subjects, that we may thus attain to the same virtue.[18]

The Rescript is a combination of Confucian and Shinto values and places emphasis on filial piety, harmony, benevolence, and modesty. Nolte writes that the Imperial Rescript "was defined as a moral rather than as a legal or political document."[19] The morals outlined in the Rescript in many ways remain definitive in the conception of so-called traditional Japanese values today. We have seen a number of these values expressed, for example, in the teachings of Buddhist kindergartens. These are the very teachings that many in contemporary Japan who call for a return to "religious sentiment" education in public schools are seeking to return to.

The philosopher and educator Inoue Tetsujirō (井上哲次郎, 1856–1944) was influential in advancing these values as an integral part of Japanese life. According to Onishi Hajime and Sharon Nolte, "Inoue Tetsujiro saw the Rescript as constituting a state religion."[20] They also note that for Inoue the Rescript was a defense against Christian teachings of universalism and individualism. Inoue's arguments regarding the Rescript were fundamental to how it was understood in Japan, though he had his critics on all sides of the political spectrum. Davis writes that Inoue believed the following: "The movement of evolution was from religion to morality (or real religion). Without real religion one is a 'spiritual cripple (*seishinjō no fugusha*).' Real religion, he thought, is 'a kind of emotion in one's heart toward the universe' and is the one and only source of the varieties of religion that appear in history. National education can be associated only with real religion."[21] As we shall see, today's emphasis on religious sentiment education owed much to this notion.[22]

The moral behavior outlined in the Rescript was eventually incorporated into textbooks for the *shūshin* class in schools. Inoue Kyoko writes, "After the Imperial Rescript on Education was established in 1890, however, the government decided that middle school boys should all be given lessons on the Rescript in the first year *shūshin* course."[23] Especially prior to the Rescript's appearance, *shūshin* textbooks often featured a collection of moral lessons that frequently drew on Western examples.[24]

The Rescript was also made an integral part of the learning experience outside the classroom. The regular reading of the rescript was carried out in a ritual performance at schools across the country and its contents committed to memory by schoolchildren. Yoshimitsu Khan describes the ritual in detail:

> At the front of the hall was a portrait of the Emperor and Empress covered by a purple curtain. The celebration assembly opens with the singing of the national anthem and all made profound obeisance before the Imperial portrait. . . . The most senior teacher, wearing a pair of white gloves,

> held up to his eye level the wooden box [that] contained the Rescript, and walked with a bowed head. The school principal respectively received the Rescript handed over by the senior teacher. After bowing once the principal untied the string and opened the box. With both hands, he lifted the rolled Rescript from the box and bowed once again.[25]

The highly ritualized manner in which the Rescript was treated is identical to the way contemporary Shinto and Buddhist ceremonies in Japan often treat sacred objects. It is also similar to methods of religious sentiment education we have seen at Buddhist kindergartens, where religious sentiment is nurtured not necessarily through study and reflection but instead through ritual and repeated exposure to a unique atmosphere. The Rescript was treated as a sacred object whose influence "pervaded the entire school atmosphere."[26] All of this was designed to model proper behavior and create an atmosphere of reverence toward the emperor and for the contents of the Rescript. The Rescript was used in this manner until the end of World War II, when it was eliminated from education after having been identified as playing a central role in shaping Japanese national identity as intrinsically linked to the discredited emperor system and militarism.

In addition to the *shūshin* hour at school, at which the Rescript came to play a prominent role, the government stressed manners. According to Khan, imparting of proper manners throughout the school day was often considered more important than the moral education hour.[27] As we saw in the chapter on kindergartens, the emphasis on manners and proper behavior remains today.

In 1975, decades after the Rescript was taken out of the Japanese education system, Prime Minister Tanaka Kakuei (田中角栄, 1918–1993) let it be known that he believed the Rescript was still of value.[28] In 2000, Hosokawa Ryūichirō (細川隆一郎, 1919–2009, political reporter and managing editor for *Mainichi Shinbun*) wrote, "Education during the Occupation was intended to turn the Japanese into weak, lazy people. Education regarding history and morals was neglected."[29] The rancor over the moral collapse of postwar Japan came to the attention of overseas news outlets as well. A *Detroit News* article titled "Japanese Young Forget Their Manners" cites a Ministry of Education official: "'Parents must be told things that once were considered common sense,' says Hiromasa Goto, an official with the Education Ministry. 'No one is telling children what to do anymore. . . . The government is so concerned that it has set up a committee to add more emphasis on morals to Japanese education standards and launched a campaign to teach young parents how to raise well-behaved, socially responsible kids.'"[30]

EDUCATING HEARTS AND MINDS (心の教育, *KOKORO NO KYŌIKU*)

Following Japan's defeat in World War II and the removal of the Imperial Rescript on Education from schools, a debate arose about what values should be taught in schools, and especially about the connection between values and religion. Inoue writes,

> The Japanese government officials were particularly bothered by the idea of prohibiting religious education in public schools because they did not distinguish religious education from education about religions. They viewed education about religions, in particular, the moral values to which different religions subscribed, as an important means of teaching morality. As a consequence of the nation's defeat in the war, the Japanese social fabric had been severely damaged and everyone in Japan seems to be out for themselves. The leaders were gravely concerned about rebuilding morality, which they hoped to do by teaching about religions and cultivating religious sentiments, the core of which was the reverence toward the supernatural. They could not understand why the Americans were prohibiting religious teachings.[31]

As early as 1946, the Ministry of Education sponsored a gathering of representatives from Buddhism, Shinto, and Christian groups, together with the principals of sixteen sectarian schools, to discuss religious education. The result of the Zenkoku shūkyōhakyōdan shukansha kyōgikai (全国宗教派教団主幹者協議会) was the following statement: "We seek to serve for world peace and social welfare through the rebuilding of Japan following its defeat by thoroughly promoting the spread of religious sentiment education."[32] The next year, 1947, a Ministry of Education document titled "An Explanation of the Fundamental Law on Education" (教育基本法の解説, *Kyōiku kihonhō no kaisetsu*) defined religious education as "that which perfects human character, requires delivery of knowledge of religions in broad terms, nurtures religious sentiment and thereby develops the human religious heart."[33]

As in the prewar period, debate centered on how to define religion. Klaus Luhmer draws our attention to this problem as it was debated in the early Meiji period when considering the Imperial Rescript on Education and how to understand its contents. The issues he identifies from the Meiji debate resonate within the postwar debate.

> One difficulty in the struggle to define the role of religion in moral education resulted from the confusion that it was not at all clear what was meant by religion. Apparently in the mind of all concerned there was no doubt that Confucianism did not constitute a religion. With Shinto the case was more complex. Terms such as kami, which we translate as "God(s)" (there is no distinction between singular and plural in Japanese), do not necessarily raise the same associations in the mind of the Japanese as in the West. The same applies to terms as, inoru, to pray; reihai, worship; ogamu, adore, and the like.[34]

As if the very question of how to define religion were not enough, the question of how to treat religion in public education was further clouded by the Fundamental Law on Education, which was promulgated in 1947. Article 9 of the law concerned religious education and advocated valuing religious tolerance in education but forbade religious education or activities for a specified religion. While it might appear that this clearly forbids sectarian education while allowing for teaching about religion, when read together with the Constitution's Article 20, it led most educators to err on the safe side and avoid anything but the most cursory mention of religion. Article 20 of the Constitution states: "No person shall be compelled to take part in any religious act, celebration, rite or practice. The State and its organs shall refrain from religious education or any other religious activity."[35] Given that many believed religious education was important to the cultivation of morals, the question became, "How do we teach morals while drawing on religion without creating a constitutional crisis?"

Concerned with the moral character of the Japanese, in 1963 the government charged the Chūō Kyōiku Shingikai (中央教育審議会, Central Council on Education), led by Kōsaka Masaaki (高坂正顕, 1900–1969), with developing a document that described the ideal citizen. In 1966 the Shingikai made public its "Image of the Desired Human" (期待される人間像, *kitai sareru ningenzō*).[36] One desirable trait to be cultivated was that of a heart of reverential awe.[37] The explanation of this heart of reverential awe explicitly links it to religious sentiment, *shūkyō jōsō* (宗教情操):

> Regarding everything discussed above [regarding the image of the ideal human], its foundation lies in one critical aspect of humanity. That is having a mind of reverential awe toward the source of life. Love of humanity and human love are based on this. The source of all religious sentiment lies in this mind of reverential awe for the source of life. We did not give birth to our own life. The source of our life is in our parents, our ethnic group, and humanity. "Life" as it is used here does not refer to the flesh-and-blood body alone. We have a spiritual life. True religious sentiment is a mind of reverential awe toward the sacred that is the source of this life. Human dignity and love are based on this. A deep sense of gratitude wells forth from this. And true happiness is based upon this.[38]

This idea remained important throughout debates on morals and religious education. Päivi Poukka cites a MEXT commentary on moral education that states that such education develops respect for human life on the basis of reverential awe.[39] This phrase is also found in the 1989 *Guide for Instruction* for fifth- and sixth-year elementary education and for middle schools published by MEXT.[40]

In 1986, the Ministry of Education revisited moral education through its Supporting Committee on Survey Research concerning Moral Education (道徳教育に関する調査研究協力会議, Dōtokukyōiku nikansuru chōsakenkyūkyōryokukaigi).

This group found that one cornerstone of moral education should be instruction in one's relationship with nature or the sublime (崇高, *sūkō*). Buddhist education scholar Katō Saigō cites a 1987 Ministry of Education newsletter that delineates how studying changes in nature not only leads to a deeper understanding of the relationship between humans and nature and of human potential but also "serves to create a heart/mind filled with reverential awe for something beyond human power."[41]

Possibly the biggest educational movement to come out of this lasting debate over the necessity to teach religion or religious sentiment as a part of moral education centers around *kokoro no kyōiku,* or the education of heart and mind. The concept can be traced back to the mid-1980s and the *kokoro no jidai* (心の時代), or "age of the heart." The term *kokoro no jidai* is said to come from the then-head of the Agency for Cultural Affairs (文化庁, Bunkachō), Kawai Hayao (河合隼雄, 1928–2007), who was trained as a clinical psychologist and published works on the Japanese psyche as revealed in fairy tales and on the Buddhist monk Myōe's (明恵, 1173–1232) works on dreams. Kawai sought to infuse clinical psychology into education in part as an antidote to what was believed by many to be an overemphasis, bred of economic success, on *mono no yutakasa* (物の豊かさ), or "material richness." What was called for was *kokoro no yutakasa* (心の豊かさ), or "to be rich in heart and mind." Anyone studying religion or education in Japan in the 1990s or 2000s would undoubtedly have heard these terms pitting material richness against a rich heart/mind or spirit ad nauseam. Certainly, while conducting fieldwork in Buddhist temples throughout the 1990s and early 2000s, I heard these terms repeatedly.

According to the psychologist Itō Tetsuji, this call to shift away from materialism and toward a life of the heart was further brought to the fore following the devastating 1996 Kobe earthquake, after which we see widespread use of the term *kokoro no kea* (心のケア), or "care for the heart and mind."[42] This call for a "return" to an emphasis on a rich heart over material riches is seen in a Central Council on Education report published in 1998 that called for "cultivation of *kokoro* [heart/mind] to meet future challenges."[43] The call for a return to cultivate a rich heart and mind was made manifest within the education system with the 2002 publication of the supplementary moral education textbook *Kokoro no No-to* (心のノート, *The Heart and Mind Notebook*), which was distributed to schools all around the country.[44]

The *Kokoro no No-to* were a series of supplementary texts for moral education. As these were designed as supplements and not technically as textbooks, they skirted the usual requirement for vetting by a MEXT committee, which became a source of controversy. Nevertheless, they made their way into nearly every moral education classroom in the Japanese public school system, where, according to a MEXT survey, 97 percent of schools made use of them (though the same survey noted that only 57 percent of schools managed to meet the desired target of thirty-five hours per school year in moral education).[45] The focus of these books, which are designed for use in elementary and junior high schools, is the development of an awareness of self and of one's relationship to others and to the nation. Notably, the books also aim to develop an understanding of one's relationship with nature and the sublime, which is described as "furthering one's self-awareness through one's relationship with the beautiful and that which is beyond human power."[46] In short, these texts seek to cultivate religious sentiment in students as a critical part of moral education.

The textbooks describe practices and ideals that should sound familiar from our discussion of Buddhist kindergartens, and they will be discussed at length in chapter 5. Here I will condense the rich research of Päivi Poukka on these textbooks and the practices contained within them.[47] The textbooks include teachings on self-control, perseverance, duty, sincerity, being bright and spirited, thoughtfulness, and gratitude. Poukka writes regarding thoughtfulness (思いやり, *omoiyari*) that "good manners and *omoiyari* are both presented as a means to convey kindness and caring, but while etiquette is promoted through formalities, or sophisticated social conventions, *omoiyari* assumes the cultivation of affective qualities. *Omoiyari* stresses the importance of reading another person's feelings and thoughts as well as showing sympathy for the person concerned."[48] Poukka further notes, "Gratitude can be regarded as the fundamental power for the promotion of social responsibility. According to the textbooks, there is no self-evident thing in human life: everything is made possible by the enormous efforts of individuals, but not without somebody's help."[49] As students progress through their schooling, the textbooks build out from the personal to the interpersonal and eventually connect to nature and something beyond human power. Poukka writes, "Moral education speaks about forces that exceed human power and abilities, associating these forces with nature and the cosmos. This includes some reference to supranatural powers."[50] Sugawara Nobuo concurs with this assessment.[51] In an article in *Jimon Kōryū* he writes that the *Kokoro no No-to* series uses discussions about the environment to guide the students from thinking about environmental issues, to thinking about nature, to stirring feelings, to thinking about life, to generating a sense of reverential awe and from there to developing an awareness of something beyond human power.[52]

The teachings outlined and the way they begin with a focus on the individual, expanding out to society, nature, the sublime, and finally "that which is beyond human power," sound uncannily like the "common worldview" that Kisala outlines for new religious movements in Japan. "The world is seen as an interconnected whole, and activity on one level will affect other levels. Therefore, a transformation on the most immediate level of the inner self will have repercussions within one's family, the surrounding society, and eventually on the universe as a whole. Consequently, emphasis is placed on individual self-cultivation, centering on the virtues of thankfulness, sincerity, and harmony."[53] This teaching, which Kisala links to the New Religions (including Buddhist lay movements) but which I would argue is typical of the teachings of Temple Buddhism in Japan today as well, draws on a long history of moral teachings in Japan.[54] In particular, Kisala draws our attention to the philosophy of the heart (心の哲学, *kokoro no tetsugaku*) proposed by the historian Yasumaru Yoshio (安丸良夫, 1934–2016): "It posits an essentially unlimited potential for the human heart, and offers a means to the realization of the power of the human spirit through the practice of a 'conventional morality' (*tsuzoku dōtoku*). The cultivation of the virtues of filial piety, loyalty, thrift, frugality, diligence and so on was offered as the answer to the social problems caused by the economic upheavals of the time, in essence reducing these problems to a matter of personal ethics."[55]

The *Kokoro no No-to* series lasted from 2002 until 2015, when it was replaced with a new series, *Watashitachi no dōtoku* (私たちの道徳, *Our Morals*).[56] The new textbook coincided with a shift in the standing of moral education from a supplementary course to a standard course. The shift represents a more forceful attempt on the part of the government to instill values within Japanese youth, who, decades after the "Age of the Heart/Mind" and heart/mind education, are still believed to be living without a firm moral grounding.

BUDDHISM AND BUDDHIST EDUCATORS AND HEART/MIND EDUCATION

Buddhist educators and members of the leadership of the various denominations of Temple Buddhism for the most part appear to share government leaders' concern regarding the state of morals in contemporary Japan. Echoing the common "material abundance and spiritual poverty" argument, Buddhist scholar Hasebe Yūkei argues that following World War II the Japanese pursued economic growth and a convenient lifestyle at the expense of manners and a spirit of compromise.[57] Okaya Akio states much the same argument, extending it further into the past by noting that the widespread adoption of Western rationalism and scientific thinking set the stage for the postwar period, in which "the outstanding values of Japan were just thrown away."[58] In turn, he argues, this led to the pursuit of material wealth at the expense of damaging Japan's spiritual culture (精神文化, *seishin bunka*). And that, in turn, led to the bullying, suicide, crime, and disruption of sexual morals that are plaguing Japan's youth (in his view). Leaders of the Tendai denomination's lay engagement movement (一隅を照らす運動, Ichigu wo terasu undō), use the same language of material prosperity. They wrote in 2000 that the country's focus on economic growth overlooked "true prosperity," which is prosperity of heart/mind and peace for all.[59]

The scholar Suzuki Toshiro states that children today "do not know thankfulness."[60] And, echoing the government's call for heart/mind education that instills a sense of awe in something beyond human power, another scholar, Komatsu Makiko writes, "What is important for the youth of Japan today is to know the limited nature of human life and to return to a point where they experience a sense of reverential awe at something that is beyond human knowledge. Not [just] teaching that life is important and about the importance of living on one's own power, but teaching in a way that balances that with [teaching about] the limited nature of human life."[61] Suzuki Kiyū states definitively that "religious sentiment education is *kokoro no kyōiku*."[62] And in discussing religious education from the point of view of proselytizing (教化, *kyōka*), the scholar Narita Hiroshi explains that religious sentiment education is "that which creates awareness of the individual life and the universal life, that which makes one aware of the unseen world, that which awakens one to connectivity."[63] Just as the government's textbook calls for understanding self as part of a larger whole and thereby perfecting moral practice, Narita writes that those conducting Buddhist proselytizing must understand that "it is not the perfected self that leads the other to salvation but the realization that the perfection of self comes through interaction (connectivity) with others."[64]

The call to understand the role of Buddhism in heart/mind education, or for interpreting Buddhist teachings in light of heart/mind education, can be found not only in the writings of Buddhist academics but also on the websites of temples, in sectarian newsletters, and in the publications of various denominations. An online newsletter for a Jōdo Shinshū temple declares *kokoro* a keyword in contemporary society and attempts to explicate heart/mind education and Buddhism's potential role in it.[65] The author writes that it was the gruesome 1997 murder of a child in Kobe by another child that led to the widespread call for heart/mind education. The author then goes on to describe what such education should look like based on the writings Morotomi Yoshihiko, a professor of psychology at Meiji Gakuin University. He writes that one must nurture, first, a heart/mind that cares for the self; second, a heart/mind that cares for others; third, a heart/mind of service toward society and groups; and fourth, a heart/mind that is able to see the self from the point of view of something greater than the human level. The author then relates how these ideas overlap with the teachings of Pure Land Buddhism. The first point relates to the Buddhist ideal of relying on yourself. The second is similar to Buddhist teachings about the importance of having good companions in practice. The third relates to the community of priests, which forms one of the three pillars of Buddhism: the Buddha, the Dharma (the teachings), and the Sangha (the community of monks). And the fourth can be likened to the wisdom of the Buddha.

In 1996, the Tendai denomination held a symposium on bullying. The introduction to the symposium proceedings, written by a leading Tendai priest, Sugitani Gijun (杉谷義純, 1942–) points to what Tendai leadership believes is the source of the problem: "Parents and educators are often identified as the source of the bullying problem, more so even than the children themselves. But really, we must question the failure or absence of a moral and ethical worldview in society as a whole. Morals and ethics that are not backed up by religion are like grass without roots, their colors will soon fade."[66] In short, religious education is seen as providing the bedrock of moral education.

In 2005 the Tendai denomination held a symposium titled "Thinking about Heart/Mind Education." The symposium proceedings include two parts.[67] Part 1 is a transcript of the symposium, and part 2 is a how-to guide for priests to use at their temples and educational facilities. The how-to guide includes a bibliography on works that can be used in the classroom. It also contains a series of mini-dharma talks that can be readily utilized by priests in their sermons, at their educational facilities, or in public talks.

As might be expected, the introduction to the symposium begins with a statement about the modern turn toward materialism and away from an abundance of heart. The introduction also discusses what the author (Kumoi Shōzen) sees as a growing lack of trust and a decline in morals and civility in modern Japan. As in other writings on heart/mind education, the author envisions expanding rings of responsibility. First, he urges the teaching of manners and morals in the home as the first line of defense. Second, he writes that schools have an important role to play but that contemporary education allows little room for kids to be kids and to bring out their own individuality. (Schools, Kumoi claims, are about ranking and sorting; he implies that they sacrifice moral education for academic achievement.) The third influence after family and school is the social environment, which Kumoi also blames for the current problem. Although these three influences are important, Kumoi notes that the biggest influence has been the lack of religious education and or heart/mind education in the postwar period.

The symposium proceedings draw our attention to the Fundamental Law on Education because it places restrictions on religious education in public schools and is often pointed to as a barrier to successful moral education. But this, some Buddhist educators argue, can be overcome through reframing religious education as human sentiment (人間情操心, *ningen jōsōshin*). Reflecting the common terminology of the times, Kumoi writes that Japanese culture has been grounded in a heart of reverential awe. This sense of reverential awe comes from respect for the *kami* and belief in the Buddha. Reverence begins with the notion that we live not as isolated individuals but within a web of relationships with nature and the people around us, and that we are given life through those people and relationships. This argument is similar to the argument Katō Saigō makes regarding the government's understanding of the term *ikei* (reverential awe). Katō states that instilling reverential awe is religious sentiment education and that it is clearly brought up and intended as such in moral education guidance from the government.[68]

The introduction to the symposium proceedings sets up a clear stance for the Tendai denomination: society is breaking down, morals are in decline, and religious sentiment education that instills a heart of reverential awe is the means by which the decline can be reversed and social bonds strengthened. The proceedings, however, follow the introduction with the speech of the first guest speaker (Yamaguchi Kazutaka), who quickly sets about upsetting that vision by asking how one distinguishes "good" religion from "bad" and posing the question "Is it okay to teach traditional values?" Teaching "traditional values" may seem a rational choice, but in a modern society that is rapidly becoming multicultural, such a move could infringe on the rights of some.[69] The guest speaker is cautioning his audience to think carefully about urging increased religious or religious sentiment education in the public schools and is pointing to the difficulty of defining religion.

While some may express caution about religious sentiment in public education, there is less debate about the role it should play in sectarian schools. Uryūzu Ryūshin, president of Kyoto Women's University, a Buddhist university, writes that education "is, in a word, the nurturing of human beings. The goal of this education can only begin to be realized through an awareness of [our] humanity, which is the essence of religion."[70] He further states, "It is necessary to recognize that it is extremely important to cultivate a religious heart within heart/mind education."[71] It has been argued by many in Buddhist education that heart/mind education through the cultivation of religious sentiment underlies the founding spirit of sectarian schools. A book produced by Hōsen Junior and Senior High Schools notes:

> The type of education most lacking in postwar Japan is heart/mind education. . . . Ever since the Chūo Kyōiku Shingikai released as its midterm report to the minister of education "How Heart/Mind Education Should Take Place from Infancy" in April of 1998, [heart/mind education] suddenly became the center of attention. But at Hōsen Gakuen it has been a pillar of the education [offered] ever since the school's founding [1928]. The founding spirit of Hōsen Gakuen has become the needs of the times.[72]

Indeed, some Buddhist schools, especially in primary and secondary education, have viewed the link they believe exists between their founding spirit and heart/mind education as a unique selling point in the competition for scarce students. It is clear from interviews and reading the home pages of many schools, as well as literature produced by them, that they perceive a fear among parents that public schools may fail to inculcate proper values in their children. Sectarian schools are put forward as safe learning environments in which good behavior and proper moral grounding is provided. In the following sections, we will examine moral and heart/mind education at several Buddhist secondary schools. First, though, we will look at the writings of two Buddhist educators to ascertain their views on contemporary Japan, morals and heart/mind education, and Buddhism's role today and thereby provide more insight into the approaches taken by Buddhist educators.

HIRAOKA TATSUTO (平岡龍人, 1940–)

Hiraoka Tatsuto is the younger brother of Hiraoka Hidenobu (平岡英信, 1929–), another well-known Buddhist educator.[73] He joined the family business, Seifū Gakuen (清風学園, a Buddhist educational association), and worked there as an educator, vice principal, and board member before moving on to become the head of the board of directors for Seifū Meiikusha (清風明育社), which runs the vocational school Seifū Jōhōkōka Gakuin (清風情報工科学院), where he serves as principal. He also enrolled in and completed the PhD program in Buddhist studies at Koyasan University.

He shares a common vision of the problems facing Japan today. Following World War II, "Japan built the world's most prosperous economy and achieved the longest lifespans. Nevertheless, today most people around the world do not place their faith or seek comfort in the Japanese."[74] This, he insists, is evidence that in gaining material prosperity Japan lost something as well. The crux of the problem as he sees it is the elimination of religious education. He argues that even though State Shinto was the target of measures to curb state and religion interactions after World War II, it was religion as a whole that came under attack. He blames this broadside against religion on left-wing political groups and the Allied occupation authorities (118). Another target of his ire is multiculturalism. Multiculturalism, he argues, does not provide for a firm grounding in a tradition. "Where do all the problems in education come from?," he asks. It is when the values of the students, the parents, and society do not coincide. They have no common ground rules on which to rely (71). One answer to this problem is religious education. As a result of no religious education, he says, "smart kids do horrible things" (20). If you do not have a religious heart, he explains, then you will not have within you the rules needed to provide order in your life and in society. Someone lacking such a heart cannot be respected or relied upon. He writes that foreigners will not trust someone like that and claims that in the households of the intellectual elite of the West, and at the best private schools in the West, faith and religion are strictly taught and everyone goes to church on Sundays (119).[75]

Hiraoka defines religion thus: "What is religion? To make people happy (salvation) is the number one point of religion. 'People' refers to yourself but also to others. Why? Because one cannot live on one's own. We are given life thanks to many people. Therefore, we must give thanks and return the favor to society" (18). He adds, "People are free to believe what they want to. But that must come with the precondition that it is based on happiness for all people" (21). Religion, he continues, is something shared by all humans and is innate to human nature: "I believe that in the bottom of their hearts all humans have a religious heart. . . . Humans from the beginning have a religious heart, a heart of faith" (19).

Furthermore, Hiraoka sees religion as the source of values. He writes that religions have for millennia taught unchanging values. Religions ask, "What is just?" and "What does it mean to be human?" He argues that something all great world religions have in common is to do good for others or society. He states that in Japanese the term used for this is *ritagyō* (利他行), or practice done to benefit others. He adds that in Buddhism the extreme example of this is sacrificing yourself to save another (74). Buddhism, he notes, is about finding the appropriate medicine to relieve the suffering of self and others (86). In particular, Buddhism is about compassion, which he defines as "just as you treat yourself, so should you treat others" (89).

According to Hiraoka, the shared essence of all religions is faith (121). Indeed, he claims that faith is what differentiates humans from animals (119). "What is faith? It is that which gives one the strength to live and that which gives purpose in life. . . . If you have faith then no matter how unstable of a situation [you find yourself in], there will always be a Buddha or a god for you to consult" (122). Faith, he continues, means not relying on things that change with the times but on something that never changes. In this way his definition of faith and religion strikes a familiar chord with government calls for reverential awe toward something greater than human power as a foundation for moral education. And, as such, faith is the foundation for knowing what is right from what is wrong (123). This is why he argues that religion is not just about praying and hoping to get some benefit, which he fears is the way most Japanese approach religion (70). It is about putting in effort based on faith. This is the source of miracles (191). He defines religion, as we have seen, as that which brings happiness (he uses the term "salvation" interchangeably with "happiness"), as something that is innate to human beings, and as the basis for values such as compassion and the acts pertaining to those values (self-sacrifice, hard work).

Because he believes religion, and in particular faith, which he is sees as a foundation of religion, is fundamental to being human, he believes that it is critical to teach the proper way to approach religion (19). He worries that the Japanese have lost their way and will no longer be taken seriously should they abandon religion (121). After the war, he writes, the Japanese stopped thinking about religion. They must receive an education that reconnects them to their religious self.

In addition to his worries about how religion is viewed in Japan, Hiraoka declares that Japan has created an educational system that makes people hate studying and is in dire need of change (15). "What is education? It is the drawing out of the limitless power that humans possess" (26). Hiraoka sees the Japanese education system as overly influenced by Western ideals for which Japan is not prepared. In particular, he believes the emphasis on individuality found in the Japanese education system today is flawed. Japan has no experience with individualism, so while it might work in the West, where it comes out of a long tradition, there are no guardrails built into the Japanese system (67). When this focus on individuality is added to the postwar efforts to rebuild Japan's economy, it leads to material affluence that is no longer morally grounded.

Education in postwar Japan was geared toward creating affluence. Once that goal was reached, Hiraoka tells us, there had to be a new education system with new goals in place lest the Japanese lose their way. Nevertheless, there was no change to the system, so Japan floundered (80).

Hiraoka sees education for affluence based on individualism as coming from Western, Christian culture, which he views as based in competition. Within that system there are winners and losers, and it becomes the duty of the winner to look after the loser. Japan did not prepare for affluence after the war and did not teach the rights and duties that come with winning (75–76). Quite the opposite: traditional Japanese values stem from a period of difficult times. Hiraoka tells us that there was a beauty found in suffering. With today's focus on affluence those "traditional" values are disappearing and there is no underlying system in place to balance the emphasis on affluence and individualism (75).

Hiraoka draws our attention to Kūkai, the founder of Japanese Shingon Buddhism, who warned that when practicing to benefit oneself, one can easily fall into self-righteousness. This, Hiraoka warns, is what Japan has done. It is the path of the hungry ghosts (*gakki*), creatures that through their cravings are reborn to a fate of insatiable desires (78). That path was opened for Japan when it began following Western models. Japan, he argues, needs its own model and not what he sees as the noblesse oblige of the West, in which the winners in a competitive system of individuals are required to help those less fortunate (his understanding of Christian compassion). He recommends the Buddhist model, which he sees as fundamentally different from the Western ideal of "forced generosity" (83). The Buddhist model of caring for others comes from the tradition of *fuse* (布施, donation), service based out of gratitude for being allowed to serve, since service is a practice toward one's own perfection/salvation (82).

Hiraoka gives the example of the Three Poisons—greed, ignorance, and hatred—as a way in which Buddhism provides a path for Japan that does not end up with Western individualism. Buddhist practice typically focuses on realizing that greed, ignorance, and hatred are empty through coming to understand the interdependent nature of being, which in turn leads to liberation. Hiraoka views the Three Poisons from the point of view of Shingon Buddhism: they are seen not as something to be avoided but as something that, when approached with the right mindset, can fuel one's practice toward liberation. He writes that the Three Poisons are what drives humans. Learning to harness that energy is a powerful way to move toward enlightenment (30). It takes limitless effort to live without desire, and Buddhism, he writes, teaches the way to limitless effort (36). In Shingon, he continues, it is understood that anyone will work hard to benefit themselves. The key is learning how to take that energy and control it so as to not harm others as you benefit yourself (37).

Hiraoka lays out another threefold concept: *toku* (徳, morality), *ken* (健, health), and *sai* (財, economic stability). Living a moral life is fundamental to Buddhism. Moral practice is seen by Hiraoka as living a life centered in an ever-expanding set of concentric rings of caring, beginning with the care of a mother for her child and the child for its parents, and expanding out to incorporate a broader sense of caring for all (33–34). He writes this is what forgetting self and benefiting others is all about. In Christianity, he claims, there is a duty of care for others, but that is a second-tier understanding of moral practice. Hiraoka claims that in Buddhism care for others is first-order—it is something innate within all that needs to be drawn out and polished through practice. When practicing "forget self and benefit others," the goal cannot be about seeking praise for one's efforts. Forgetting self and benefiting others is a practice for overcoming false perceptions of self and is grounded in the idea of emptiness. Hiraoka ties this to the practice of *hōon kansha* (報恩感謝, returning a debt of gratitude). To highlight this, he presents the four debts as described by Kūkai: (1) the debt of gratitude we owe to our parents and ancestors, (2) the debt of gratitude we owe the Three Treasures, (3) the debt of gratitude we owe our country, and (4) the debt of gratitude we owe those around us and society. By realizing that we are indebted to others, we overcome attachment to self and live a life of service (146–147). The very act of doing good for the world becomes the greatest joy (43).

The second aspect is health. Hiraoka spends considerably less time explicating the importance of this. Essentially, he believes it is important to the practice of morality because ill health impedes progress. This view is common in Buddhist practice. Practice regimes at temples across Japan today continue to emphasize diet and exercise.[76] This includes cleaning and other forms of manual labor that help to keep priests in shape so they can endure long bouts of meditation.

Hiraoka ties the third concept, economic stability, to the earlier discussion of the Three Poisons. Everyone, he writes, craves economic stability. This energy can be harnessed to bring about prosperity for all (45). Just as great effort is required to channel the energy of the Three Poisons into the realization of liberation from suffering, so too does harnessing the desire for economic gain require great discipline. Careful attention must be paid to income and expenditures, to monitoring careful and steady progress. Education, he writes, is similar to this. Education requires great patience. It is about the accumulation of knowledge and wisdom. It is about steady progress—setting goals and patiently working toward them while avoiding the trap of wallowing in success along the way (45–53).

MIYASAKA YŪKŌ (宮坂宥洪, 1950–)

Miyasaka Yūkō holds a PhD in philosophy from Nagoya University and serves as the head priest of Shōkōji (照光寺), a temple of the Shingon denomination, Chizan branch, in Okaya City, Nagano Prefecture. In addition, he serves as the *inchō* (director or dean) of Denpōin (伝法院), the organization within the denomination that is tasked with maintaining doctrinal orthodoxy. Much like Hiraoka, he believes that the education system in Japan today is flawed. He believes Buddhism could salvage Japan's education system. Indeed, one of his first books was called *Buddhism Can Save Japanese Education* (*Bukkyō ga skū nihon no kyōiku*, 仏教が救う日本の木教育).[77] That work will form the basis of our examination here. Much like Hiraoka, Miyasaka points toward the postwar pivot in education away from the premodern and prewar forms of Japanese education as a key problem. He writes, "That denial continues even now, but isn't it mistaken?" Education, he continues, must both teach and communicate. "The [lessons] of our ancestors is what must be communicated. If we deny everything about our ancestors, what is there left to teach?" (5). He pulls no punches in his analysis of this abandonment of tradition: "Our ability to have history and tradition is what separates us from the animals" (6).

The postwar restrictions on religion within public education is something that Miyasaka, like so many others, believes undermined education in Japan. He writes, "For much of history, everywhere around the world, public education was primarily shouldered by religion" (6). He then goes on to engage in a type of wordplay that is not uncommon in Japanese religion. He examines the characters for the word "religion" (宗教, *shūkyō*). *Shū,* he claims, can be read to mean "primary," "fundamental," or "most important," whereas *kyō* can be read as in *kyōiku* (education). Therefore, he summarizes, *shūkyō* means the most fundamental teachings, the most fundamental education. Given that, he continues, how can education without religion be accomplished?

The denial of religion as a fundamental aspect of education has serious consequences, according to Miyasaka. "If religion is denied, morals cannot exist." He sees Japanese schools as having fallen back to a primitive religious state that existed before Buddhism or Christianity, one in which sacrifices (bullying, suicide) are offered (13). "The corruption, use of bad language, lack of manners, and absence of common sense among today's children is the worst it has ever been in Japanese history" (45). Moreover, the denial of religion in education, he believes, leads to the rise of cults (7) because children are unable to distinguish suspicious religion from good religion (27). It has also led to other countries not taking the Japanese seriously.[78] Others, he fears, think, "Is this guy a monkey? A dog?" Why? Because it his understanding that what separates humans from animals is religion. Therefore, no religion in education means animal education: "Public education has completely become monkey education" (25–26).

Miyasaka extolls "traditional" education in Japan. "Even considered on the global stage, Japanese education has an outstanding history. The background for this outstanding history is traditional education. Put another way, humanistic education with morals as its pillar, the way of personhood, the most important things for one to learn as a human, were all thoroughly taught. . . . I am not denying all postwar education. I am sure there are good aspects to democratic education but the time has come to reflect" (7). He believes to return to traditional education the Japanese should seek out the good parts of religion in education and find ways to bring them back, but he notes that there should be some restrictions: the "limitless religious freedom" guaranteed under the Constitution is problematic; limits that existed in the prewar era, such as "not disrupting order" or not interfering with a citizen's duty to the state, are acceptable remedies for Miyasaka (9).

His cry to return to religion in education is rooted in his belief that Japanese traditions are being destroyed by outside (Western/Christian) influence. He argues for a return to the past, to a time before this external pressure. The turn away from the past, from the ancestors, undermines the development of moral values. "No matter what, showing respect for those who have gone before is basic manners in human society. Learning thankfulness like 'Because of your effort and sacrifice, I am the person I am now' is the proper way to learn history." He writes, "If I was a student today, I would scream 'teach me the values of the country I was born in, not these borrowed values!'" (224).

Christianity, he declares, is to blame for at least part of the moral quandary Japan finds itself in today. He argues Christianity teaches absolute equality (41–44). This idea of equality strikes him as going against Japanese tradition in many ways. He views women's rights, for example, as one way that Western ideals of equality disrupt time-honored traditions. He spends considerable time arguing about Article 24 of the Constitution, in which marriage is based on the acceptance of equality of the sexes. He rages that this denies other traditional practices. It is the denial of such traditions that leads people away from knowing right from wrong (28–29). Differences between men and women, he exclaims, are a part of nature, not discrimination. The postwar Constitution, which he sees as having been foisted upon Japan by the victorious Allied powers, is to blame for the destruction of tradition.

Miyasaka sees this imported sense of equality as most insidious with regard to the practice of democracy. He gives the example of someone who is rich versus someone who is poor: their understanding of politics is going to be different, yet for some reason they get an equally weighted vote (41): "Why do fermented bean paste [*miso*] and shit [*kusō*] get the same vote?" Regarding education, he continues, equality leads to teaching to the lowest level (44).

Religion is crucial to moral education, but it needs to be the right religion, not imported Western traditions. He gives the example of the most basic of Buddhist teachings on proper behavior: "It is said that the most fundamental teaching of Buddhism is: Do no evil, practice good acts, purify your heart" (14). This type of basic teaching, he argues, is found only in religion, therefore religion must be taught in schools. "Whether it is gods or ancestors, people direct their prayers to something that is transcendent. Therefore, where there is no prayer, there can be no morals. That being the case, in today's schools where religion is denied, it is not possible to discuss good and evil" (15).

Miyasaka argues that incidents of violent crime in Japan would decrease if people had a religious grounding. Murder, he states, is forbidden because of religious feeling. It cannot simply be a social rule "like rules to a game." He writes that criminals must have an awareness of sin, which is a religious feeling. Without religious feeling it is impossible to judge murder as right or wrong (14). For Miyasaka lack of morals grounded in religion results in the many problems Japan now faces, whether on the international stage or at home. Educational reform based on Buddhist values, he believes, will solve these problems.

MORAL EDUCATION IN BUDDHIST SCHOOLS

We can see from the above discussion that Buddhist educators believe moral education grounded in religion is important and that Buddhist schools have a role to play in the moral education of Japanese citizens. We have already seen the important role instilling manners and basic morals plays in Buddhist kindergarten education. Below are brief examples of moral education in practice at four Buddhist secondary schools.

Our first example is Seifū Gakuen. At Seifū Gakuen, religious sentiment education is seen as crucial. One of the most common forms of integrating religious sentiment education into school life at many sectarian schools is to hold morning services at which either the whole school gathers in the gymnasium or students gather by grade. The general pattern is to briefly chant scripture and follow that with a short talk. At Seifū Gakuen, for example, a school related to Shingon-shū Koyasan-ha, all students chant the Heart Sūtra during the morning service.[79] The webpage for Seifū Gakuen notes that chanting sutra not only cleanses sins but also helps to focus one's mind. It is said to accomplish this by stopping the actions of the bad or impure side of one's soul and allowing only the good side to flourish. Doing this "improves the blood, enhances the working of the brain, and leads to a healthy spirit and body."[80] Following the morning service the principal gives a short speech to the students in which he seeks to communicate a fundamental teaching based on Buddhist principles. On the day I arrived in Osaka to speak with the principal of Seifū Gakuen, he talked about the concept of "forget self and benefit others."[81] As he explained to me, however, he teaches the material in very simple terms. He emphasized that he doesn't even teach religion, meaning, as best as I could tell, that he doesn't see himself as explicating doctrine. Rather, he sees himself as introducing life lessons to the students. Is this method effective? His answer was to compare the daily speeches to a cup of sake. After filling and emptying it many times, the sake may be gone, but the smell of sake lingers on. In other words, it was his hope that students who were exposed to religious values daily would eventually absorb, if not understand, basic values.

Religious sentiment education can also be accomplished through annual and semiannual ceremonies at which priests preside and speeches are given. Additionally, many schools also have field trips designed as religious sentiment education, such as Seifū Gakuen's trip to Mt. Fuji or to major temples and shrines.[82] Probably the single most frequently discussed method for accomplishing heart/mind education is *aisatsu* (挨拶, greetings) campaigns. Except for the elite Shiba Gakuen (芝学園), most schools I visited or researched online mentioned that teaching students to greet one another and the staff as a routine matter of daily life, was an important part their morals or *kokoro* education.[83] The principal of Seifū Gakuen spent a great deal of time discussing *aisatsu* during my interview with him.

> What sort of society is it that we live in today? People on the trains ignore each other. This is no different than not living at all. The world has become terribly lonely. If I say hello and you do not respond, or vice versa, our heart-to-heart communication is cut off. If [we] respond [to each other], then there is some connection there between our hearts. In this lonely society we have to begin [to overcome our situation] through heart-to-heart exchanges. It is from this that a society in which we can communicate with one another is built.[84]

Although it can be argued that this is a purely secular concern (after all, many public schools put considerable effort into *aisatsu* campaigns too), within Buddhist institutions *aisatsu* are often viewed as the first step toward learning such concepts as interdependence and compassion. Daily greetings are seen as a basic method for overcoming attachment to self through engaging others. Greetings are, in part, about overcoming ego. The principal continued, "In the past, you had to rely on others to get things done. Now there is no need for people to help each other. There is no chance for heart-to-heart conversations anymore. Before you had to always think about the standing of others. You don't have to do that anymore. People have become more egoistic."[85] The practice of daily greetings helps to create and maintain relationships and build an understanding of self as part of a larger social group, which aids in overcoming ego.

The emphasis on *aisatsu* found in some schools is linked to MEXT calls for increased moral education. When asked about the MEXT push for more such education, the principal of Seifū Gakuen responded:

> Some is necessary. Currently nothing is being done. Not even teaching about George Washington and the cherry tree, which I learned about in school. Japan lost the war and so moral education and the like was linked to militarism. The kids don't know anything. The parents don't know anything. When we were young, we learned things like giving up our seats to the elderly. Parents now, born after the war, don't teach their kids to give up their seats. They don't see what could be wrong with that. That's also why they don't do *aisatsu*.[86]

Just as greetings are a way of gauging how someone else is feeling, as well as demonstrating an awareness of social hierarchies and relationships, the manner in which one acts and carries oneself is also an important way of gauging one's inner state of mind. At our next example, Hōsen Gakuen, a link between outward form and inner purity is stressed. From this point of view, if one dresses or acts poorly, it not only reflects an unsettled outer state but also leads to the degradation of one's inner state, or *kokoro*.[87] A person of character must be one who not only has their heart under control but whose outward form is also controlled (23). This teaching follows the school's emphasis on education as the project of building people and not merely imparting knowledge.[88] This emphasis on character building is part of a larger project of education of the heart/mind, which the school stresses is foundational to nurturing people of character.[89] This stress on form before understanding—the idea that when form is perfected, the inner state is also perfected—is basic to most forms of so-called traditional practice in Japan.[90]

Like Seifū Gakuen, Hōsen also emphasizes greetings. They are how one shows respect and gauges how the other person is feeling: "The face is a window to the heart/mind" (12–13). Looking deeper, *aisatsu* are a way of demonstrating a heart of thankfulness. They seek through their school to nurture "someone who can say 'Thank you' earnestly" (14). In addition to *aisatsu,* we can also see a link made at some schools between Buddhist teachings and a call by the Chūo Kyōiku Shingikai for integrating into school education volunteer activities in the welfare field. At Hōsen Gakuen there has been a strong effort to involve students in volunteer activities. Such activities are tied to the Buddhist act of *fuse,* or donation. In Buddhism, it is explained, volunteering is done neither for someone else nor at the command of someone else, but as part of one's own practice for liberation (16). One cannot seek recognition for one's giving. At Hōsen a primary form of volunteering is cleaning around the school. The idea is that students clean their mind as they clean the school: "In Buddhism it is said that first you clean, then you practice, then you study" (32–33).

According to a book produced by Hōsen Gakuen, Buddhist voluntarism is necessary because of weaknesses in government voluntarism campaigns. As an example, the authors of the Hōsen book point out that the government has called for extracurricular activities such as volunteering to be considered in college applications. Such plans, Hōsen leaders fear, will only inspire students to volunteer to pad their applications.

The government call for instilling a sense of reverence for life, or for something beyond human power, is echoed in the belief among some Buddhist educators that practices such a voluntarism should well forth from the heart of anyone who recognizes that life is given by the greater life force of the cosmos. Hōsen educators state, "If we can gain awareness of the fact that we humans are given life by the life[force] of the cosmos, then we will be equipped with a heart of compassion and thankfulness, have a heart of gratitude, and will do whatever we can to return [the favor of this gift of life]" (17). The founder of Hōsen sought "universal character." By this he meant one who is moved by all of creation and can sense a life force beyond human knowledge (14). According to the Hōsen book, we tend to think we live on our own power; we forget that we are given life from the universe, in short from the sun and the air, as well as the rice, vegetables, meat, and fish we consume. If we awaken to this, then we naturally give rise to a heart of compassion and thankfulness and become "someone who is filled with a spirit of service" (15).

Proper behavior is grounded at Hōsen in the Ten Good Precepts (十善戒, *jūzenkai*), which are themselves grounded in the *shichibutsu tsūkaige* (七仏通誡偈): "Do not give rise to evil, practice all good acts, purify your heart, these are the teachings of the many Buddhas" (19). Students at Hōsen learn these precepts at the morning assembly or in homeroom, where they are chanted daily (20). This, in turn, creates "someone filled with a heart of compassion" (21). The Japanese word for compassion is *jihi.* Hōsen defines *ji* as "to treat others with friendship and thoughtfulness," and *hi* as "to feel/appreciate the suffering of others" (22). Compassion is linked to thankfulness: "The Buddha always has a heart of compassion for all living things. . . . We must be thankful for that. . . . In that way, a heart of compassion is connected to a heart of thankfulness" (23).

While schools such as Seifū Gakuen and Hōsen Gakuen generally emphasize the religiously grounded morals their student will learn to embody if not fully understand, many other schools find themselves forced to move away from their origins as religious schools. In a critique of sectarian schools, Sunada Yoshihiro writes: "In the postwar, religious education took place at private schools. Yet, believing that student enrollment would drop if religion was put forward as the educational goal, the founding spirit of such schools, which was based on religious thought, was given but lip service. The emphasis instead has come to be placed on education that meets the needs of the times, parents, and students."[91] Today the demand for academic success leading to admission to top universities, which in turn guarantees access to the best jobs, can force schools to focus less on character building and more on studying to pass college entrance exams. The pull to focus on academics rather than religion is strong at elite junior and senior high schools, such as Shiba Gakuen in Tokyo, which is related to the Jōdo denomination of Buddhism. These schools are faced with considerable pressure to concentrate their educational program on the college entrance examinations.

Religion is taught at Shiba Gakuen. Students study the life of the Buddha, basic Buddhist history, and the life and teachings of Hōnen, the founder of the Jōdo denomination. But in my conversation with the principal, it became clear that religious sentiment education and moral education were not high priorities—placing students in elite universities was *the* priority.[92] At Shiba Gakuen in the first three years (junior high school), students receive one hour per week of class time in moral education, and in their three years of high school they receive no moral or religious education in years 1 and 2, and four hours in year 3.[93] The desire for elite schools such as Shiba Gakuen to focus on getting their students into elite colleges is confirmed by the scholar Fukase Shunji, who notes that parents, not students, put their hopes in the religion class as a source of moral training, but the number one reason parents choose a high school is that it will assure their children's entrance into a good university.[94] Difficulties in implementing the founding principles and placing religious sentiment education at the heart of the educational experience are not limited to sectarian secondary education. For example, in chapter 3 we saw Ishii Seijun of Komazawa University, a major Buddhist institution, speak of resistance within the university to efforts to enforce a mandatory university-wide two-year religious studies course.

Most of the schools I visited or researched online offered very little in the way of classes on religion or morals. Such classes were usually either dedicated to a basic introduction to Buddhism, often ending with the founder of whatever branch of Buddhism that school represented, or to moral education. In general, religion classes doubled as moral education classes, or there was no religion class offered. Sugawara Nobuo confirms that many religious schools may offer a moral education class and not a religion class, and that what is taught varies from school to school. He highlights Shiba Gakuen as a religious school that does not offer a religion class.[95] In my interview with the principal it was clear that students did get a brief introduction to the history of Buddhism leading up to and including the history of the Jōdo denomination. They use three short textbooks along with a booklet on the subject published by Jōdo denomination headquarters.[96] The short booklet is based on the idea that readers should be able to respond to three typical critiques: "There is no way Amida exists," "There is no such thing as a Pure Land," and "There is no real value in chanting the *nenbutsu*." It is unclear how well students respond to or absorb this material, but the goal is to provide a basic introduction to the teachings of Pure Land Buddhism and to help the students refute critiques of the faith in a nod to the school's founding principles.

The last school we will look at is Tsurumi Joshi Chūgakkō/Kōtōgakkō (鶴見女子中学校・高等学校). This is (or was until 2008) a women's junior and senior high school connected with the Sōtō denomination of Zen Buddhism. Our discussion here primarily concerns the school before it became a coed school in 2008, a step it most likely took to combat dwindling enrollment. The school's webpage sums up its educational goals in a brief statement by the principal: "This school, following Buddhist teachings, seeks to educate empathetic women as people, as women, as mothers, and as women sure in right belief who can contribute to the building of a peaceful 21st century society in which culture flourishes."[97] Following up on this, the home page also states the school's guiding principles: "(1) expand your nature—let's work hard on our studies, (2) love your work—let's nurture our physical strength, (3) don't forget your debt to others—let's give our all for society, (4) strengthen your belief—let's take joy in our existence." In stark contrast to the elite Shiba Gakuen, there is a strong emphasis from the start on the Buddhist character of the school. The thirty-page color brochure produced by the school likewise highlights the Buddhist nature of the school and the type of moral education the children will undergo before going on to detail courses, classrooms, and extracurricular opportunities. Here the principal, who is also the head priest of a leading Sōtō temple, points to the enlightenment of the Buddha. He writes that following the example of the Buddha's enlightenment, "it is important to refine wisdom and sensibility and to possess self-reliant powers of discernment."[98] The same brochure notes that school is not just about studying at your desk; it's vital to learn about one's heart/mind as well. For this reason, it goes on to say, the school offers morning services, volunteer activities, and annual rituals.[99] Volunteer activities are couched in terms of repaying the gift of life and giving rise to a heart of thankfulness.[100]

The daily, monthly, and annual cycle of ceremonies and rituals is highlighted in the school handbook and elsewhere. The repetition of ritual is understood to create a rhythm in the life of the students that serves to help them embody the moral and religious teachings that are seen to underlie the academic program and thereby create well-mannered, wise, and compassionate young women. Morning rituals start with greetings at the gate to the school and bowing toward the main Buddha/Lecture Hall. Daily morning practices include quiet meditation, sutra chanting,[101] the singing of Buddhist hymns, a brief prayer for the success of the students' endeavors and for the happiness of all living beings, the recitation of the four bodhisattva vows, and a second round of quiet meditation. This may sound like a full day's work, but it is accomplished in ten to fifteen minutes. At lunch students recite a prayer before eating. At the end of the day, in their homeroom, they practice a short round of quiet meditation once again. Once a month there is a prayer service led by the principal, and there are multiple annual rites for the Buddha's birthday, the founder of Sōtō, and others. Much as in the kindergartens we learned about earlier, these regular rites serve to create a Buddhist atmosphere. They are a form of religious sentiment education. They also are a form of moral education in that they are designed to communicate Buddhist teachings about how to live one's life—if not always through the ceremonies themselves, then through the dharma talks given at them.

The foreword to the school booklet, handed out to all students, serves to stress the importance of learning proper behavior and manners by pointing to Dōgen's equating of etiquette with the Dharma and manners with practice. The rest of the booklet outlines the various ceremonies, rituals, and other practices the students will engage in throughout the year. This includes photos of how to sit properly for meditation or the chanting of sutra.[102]

Unlike the schools we observed earlier, the teachings and practices at Tsurumi were aimed at creating well-mannered young women who could fulfill their role in society. The principal related to me that most entered the workforce after graduating, with roughly 40 percent going on to community college and only 1 or 2 percent going on to four-year colleges. It was clear that the goal was to train young women and prepare them to become mothers and to fit into the traditional roles expected of women (graduate, work briefly, marry, have children).

Buddhist schools, each in their own way, implement some form of moral education. Elite college-bound escalator schools may do little, while others see such education as something critical to their mission and infuse it throughout their curriculum and daily activities. Practicing greetings, daily chanting of Buddhist teachings, and some study—often very limited—of fundamental Buddhist concepts and history is common. Learning to repay a debt of gratitude to family while nurturing a belief in something beyond human power are also common practices—ones that are mirrored in government moral education campaigns. Manners and etiquette as well as some introduction to prayer or meditation are also found at most schools. Schools tend to echo the government call for teaching reverential awe toward a higher power as necessary for moral education. And all of this is frequently couched in terms of responding to a moral crisis that is gripping the nation's youth, leading to those helmetless soda-swilling easy riders who would wave at me from across the rice fields over thirty years ago.

5

LEARNING TO PERSEVERE

The Popular Teachings of Tendai Ascetics

Today that "come-what-may" fighting spirit is all but gone. And there is no longer the disposition to patiently persevere. Without this, how can an international superpower be built?

—Hagami, *Kaihōgyō no kokoro*

Up to now we have looked at the teachings and teaching of Buddhism in modern and contemporary Japan primarily through the lens of Buddhist education. In this chapter we step away from Buddhist education to study the teachings of an elite group of Buddhist ascetics. What we will find is that the core of their teachings is in harmony with the public-facing teachings of Buddhist kindergartens, schools, and colleges.

The following sections introduce the teachings of three contemporary practitioners of Tendai Buddhism. All three successfully completed the grueling thousand-day circumambulation (千日回峰行, *sennichi kaihōgyō*), in which practitioners walk distances equal to the circumference of the globe over a period of seven years. The teachings of Temple Buddhism denominations are usually understood as those of the founders or other prominent priests from the distant past. For example, at Taishō University young Tendai priests are required to study the Tendai classics known as the Three Great Texts,[1] as well as the teachings of the founder of Japanese Tendai. At Gyōin (行院), the main training temple on Mt. Hiei, all priests must complete an intensive and exhausting two-month program in which they master esoteric ritual and ceremonial protocol, review the teachings of Tendai founders Saichō (最澄, 767–822) and Zhiyi (智顗, 538–597), and read the Lotus Sūtra, the central text of Tendai. What is taught at both places as "Tendai teachings" is drawn from the texts of the founders of Tendai and the writings of later famous priests such as Ennin (円仁, 794–864). For example, Zhiyi's "three thousand thoughts in a single moment" (一念三千, *ichinen sanzen*) and the categorization of Buddhist teachings attributed to him, "the five periods and eight teachings" (五時八教, *gojihakkyō*), are required learning for all prospective Tendai priests.[2]

This same material is drawn on by Western and Japanese scholars in any discussion of Tendai teachings. While these teachings play an important and formative role in the study and practice of Tendai today, they nevertheless represent only a fraction of the material that needs to be examined to understand the teachings of Tendai as a living tradition. The teachings of contemporary Tendai must be sought not only in the classical texts but also in the collected stories, sermons, and articles found, for example, on the Light Up a Corner of the World Activities webpage.[3] This campaign, directed primarily at lay members, is now over fifty years old and is representative of Tendai activities today. The movement seeks to increase Tendai lay members' awareness of basic Tendai teachings and to engage priests and laity in public welfare, international aid, and environmental activities. Every year across Japan meetings are held at which priests and laity involved in the movement gather to celebrate that year's successes and to participate in the chanting of sutra and other activities.[4]

In many ways the Tendai denomination is little different from other denominations of Temple Buddhism. Each has a standard training curriculum, a required period of practice to master basic rituals and ceremonial protocols, and a set of classic texts taught within a sectarian history. They also have programs similar to Tendai's Light Up a Corner of the World Activities and noted practitioners who teach to a variety of audiences in different venues.

A theme throughout this book has been that contemporary Buddhist teachings must be sought not only in classic writings but also in the curricula of Buddhist educational institutions, the writings of Buddhist educators, and the practices of Buddhist primary and secondary schools. This is especially true if we think of outward, public-facing teachings—those that are taught not only to priests but also to the laity and that, by far and away, are the best-known teachings. This chapter looks at the writings of three practitioners of one of modern Japanese Temple Buddhism's most extreme ascetic practices. Together they have produced or been the subject of dozens of books, articles, videos, and documentaries, and arguably they have a greater direct impact on society than the cerebral ruminations of scholar-priests and academics.

For many Buddhists, practice serves as the wellspring of Buddhist teachings. The *kaihōgyō* practitioners examined here, for example, draw on the physical act of walking and persevering. There are few open references to classical texts in their writings. The main emphasis is on what they learned through practice. One states plainly that he does not seek outside material as a source for his teaching: "What I have to say does not come from having read scholarly works or books, nor does it come from something I heard from a schoolteacher. The heart of what I talk about comes from things I realized as I was walking and which I never forgot."[5]

Many years ago I asked two priests who had completed the first one-hundred-day segment of the *kaihōgyō* as part of their three-year retreat on Mt. Hiei if they believed that *kaihōgyō* practitioners derived their teachings from classical Buddhist texts. The response was a resounding no. While they felt there was influence, they believed the source of their teachings was the physical practice of walking and persevering.[6] Despite such statements, we cannot entirely discount classical sources for some of their teachings, since each priest was indoctrinated into classical Tendai teachings during his training.

Hagami Shōchō (葉上照澄, 1903–1989), Mitsunaga Kakudō (光永覚道, 1954–), and Sakai Yūsai (酒井雄哉, 1926–2013) have all completed the *kaihōgyō* (Sakai twice) and have all written for popular consumption.[7] In addition, they have been in demand as guest speakers at temples and other venues around the country. They are part of a small cadre of the Buddhist priesthood in Japan today that commands a broad audience of readers and faithful. In Hagami, Mitsunaga, and Sakai's cases, they have been able to reach a wide audience primarily through renown at having completed the *kaihōgyō.* The *kaihōgyō,* in which the practitioners engage in walking meditation by traversing a mountainous route of over thirty kilometers daily for one thousand days, is perhaps the best-known traditional Tendai practice today. The mystique of "living Buddhas," as successful practitioners are known, making their way over ancient mountain trails in flowing white robes before the first light of dawn draws popular and, to a lesser extent, scholarly attention.[8] Pictures of these practitioners can be found on the Tendai denomination webpage, in magazine and newspaper articles, on travel brochures, and on the covers of books about Tendai or Mt. Hiei. NHK (the Japanese national public television station), the BBC, and most recently a French documentary filmmaker have all produced documentaries about the practice.[9] A quick search online for references in English finds numerous articles in magazines aimed at marathon runners and triathletes.

To better understand the source of their charisma and their teachings, and by way of providing background into the foundation of their teachings, a brief introduction to the *kaihōgyō* follows. The practice developed over time and is said to have its roots in the practices of Sōō Kashō (相応和尚, 831–918).[10] The outlines of its current form can be traced to the Muromachi period (1392–1573). Records of the practice as it existed before the Muromachi period appear to have been lost when Oda Nobunaga (織田信長, 1534–1582) razed the temples of Mt. Hiei. Einami Sogen (叡南祖賢, 1903–1971), a powerful reformer of postwar Tendai, and himself a successful practitioner of the *kaihōgyō,* shaped the practice as it is known today.[11]

Just fourteen people have completed the practice in the postwar period, and only fifty since 1585. The practice today is made up of ten one-hundred-day segments spread over a seven-year period. During each segment, the practitioner is required to walk from one site to the next, over the entirety of Mt. Hiei's three main peaks, covering a total of over thirty kilometers and as many as three hundred sites per day. The following summarizes progression through the *kaihōgyō:* The practitioner awakens at midnight to begin his practice, is back in time to perform morning services, and then begins his regular daytime priestly duties. He must proceed with his practice regardless of the weather or his own physical condition. At each stop along the way he must chant the proper mantra and/or sutra and perform the proper mudra. After the seventh segment the practitioner undertakes *dōiri* (堂入り), literally "entering the temple," prior to which a living funeral is performed for him. He remains in the temple without sleeping, eating, drinking, or lying down for nine days. There are assistants present to make sure he fulfills the requirements as well as to support him should he need help. During this period he is expected to perform daily services, recite Fudō-Myōō's mantra 100,000 times, and chant the complete Lotus Sūtra once.

During the eighth one-hundred-day segment, a trip to Sekizanzenin (赤山禅院), a temple in Kyoto, is added to the journey, increasing the route by approximately twenty kilometers. This is called *Sekizan kugyō* (赤山苦行, Sekizan austerity or, literally, the suffering practice of Sekizan). The ninth segment is called the *Kyoto omawari* (京都お巡り). During this period the practitioner makes a long circuitous trip through Kyoto, and along the way he blesses the faithful who line the streets.[12] After the fiftieth day he is expected to stop occasionally to pray at the homes of those who request his presence. This brings the length of the route to nearly ninety kilometers.

He begins his last one-hundred-day segment not long after completion of the *Kyoto omawari.* He is then invited to perform a prayer ceremony at the Imperial Palace in Kyoto, where he is allowed the rare honor to enter the palace with his sandals on (though they are a special set used for the occasion). Sometime after completing the *kaihōgyō* (generally two to three years later), he is expected to perform the 100,000-stick fire ceremony. This ritual requires one hundred days on a special diet in which the five grains and salt are forbidden. The fire ceremony lasts seven days, and the practitioner is not permitted any food or water during that time. The nickname for the practice is "the hell of being bathed in flames."

The practice up to *dōiri* is referred to as *jōgubodai* (上求菩提), or "practice done looking up toward achieving enlightenment." Practice following *dōiri* is called *gekeshujō* (下化衆生), or "practice looking back toward those still in need of aid." The first half is thus preparatory practice in which the practitioner readies mind and body for the task of saving others. Once he has mastered himself, he is ready to turn around, in bodhisattva tradition, and aid those farther back on the path. This is why in the second half of the practice (post *dōiri*) the practitioner spends considerable time walking off the mountain, as far away as Kyoto.

There is also evidence that Tendai practitioners from as early as the medieval period saw the mountain as a map of their practice. Jacqueline Stone cites an early source that describes priests climbing up Mt. Hiei as progressing from a state of unenlightenment to that of Buddha and those going down the mountain as manifesting enlightenment in the phenomenal world much as the practitioners of the *kaihōgyō* are understood to bring the benefit of their practice off the mountain to help others.[13]

The practice and the successful completion of *kaihōgyō* transforms the practitioner into a charismatic figure. Shimazono Susumu, writing on charisma in the New Religions of Japan, states that there are two types of "supernatural" charisma: (1) primary, which is possessed divinely or innately; and (2) secondary, which is endowed to certain classes of individuals such as monks.[14] *Kaihōgyō* practitioners can be understood as possessing both secondary charisma, through the office of "*kaihōgyō* practitioner," and primary charisma, through the completion of a practice that turns them into living Buddhas. The practice itself is a source of charisma not simply due to the "office" but due to the long association in Japan of mountain austerities with the acquisition of exceptional powers. In his research on Shugendō, Miyake Hitoshi makes clear the special nature of mountains in Japanese religious practice and the manner in which those who undergo austerities in the mountains can be transformed in the eyes of the faithful into exceptional beings.[15]

Shimazono further remarks that charisma depends on a specific kind of relationship between individuals in which the charismatic figure serves as a vessel for the aspirations of the followers. This, in turn, is closely linked to Shimazono's definition of charisma as resting "on the keen awareness of differences in individual ability."[16] Many regard the *kaihōgyō* practitioners as having completed a task far beyond the abilities of average people. Their followers, in turn, invest great emotional and at times financial capital in them to see their own hopes fulfilled through them. This image is particularly strong in videos of the practice, in which one can see people lining the streets or waiting by mountain roadsides in the predawn hours to be blessed by the practitioner. There are also those who work in support groups to assure the practitioner's needs are met. Their hopes for salvation are linked to his success. One of Catherine Ludvik's informants told her that lay support group members are there solely for the benefit of the monk and that any personal spiritual interests are simply out of place.[17] Be that as it may, members seek a visit to their home by the monk to pray for their ancestors, seek rank within the support group in part for social capital, and even seek after articles of the monk's attire, particularly the sandals he wears (and replaces regularly) throughout his practice. Ludvik mentions the desire for *zuiki* (随喜), "a Buddhist term meaning the rejoicement in another person's practice of good actions."[18] Such rejoicing should be found without consciously seeking it. Perhaps this is what her informant meant: the true blessings of helping the monk are those found in giving oneself completely over to another in service. This is line with what we learned in chapter 4 about service as a practice.

The above discussion regarding charisma helps to explain the popularity of the *kaihōgyō* practitioners among the laity closely associated with and in close proximity to the practice. It also may explain their popularity within the Tendai denomination more generally. This popularity is seen in the regular demand for their appearance at Tendai events across the country, but it does not as readily explain their more general appeal as authors. For example, one of Mitsunaga's books, *Sennichi kaihōgyō,* originally published in 1996, is already in its eighth printing. He has also written three additional books since then, and Sakai Yusai had at least nine books to his credit by the time of his death, some of which have gone through as many as nineteen printings. He has also had five books written about him. This appeal may be more directly linked to what Shimazono calls "prophetic" charisma, which is defined as "the ability to address the existential core of the life of the believer." *Kaihōgyō* practitioners direct their teachings to the *kokoro,* or heart/mind: "What they intend to overcome is not the crisis posed by particular or immediate problems, but the crisis of the heart, the existential crisis that permeates one's whole life."[19] The writings of the *kaihōgyō* practitioners, while often addressing specific issues, seek to explain what is wrong with the world in a broad sense and how one can solve one's existential crisis—transform one's *kokoro*—by placing one's own problems within the greater context.

HAGAMI SHŌCHŌ

Background

Hagami Shōchō was born in 1903 in Okayama Prefecture. He did not begin training on Mt. Hiei until the age of forty-four in 1947. Before entering the priesthood, Hagami studied German philosophy at Tokyo Imperial University (now the University of Tokyo, Japan's most elite university), married, and worked for a newspaper. His wife passed away when he was thirty-three. A self-described "semi-intellectual," he chose to enter the priesthood because he felt he "must change his life." He could no longer go on "just being someone who uses only his head."[20] The famous Buddhist studies scholar Unno Tetsuo relates the following story regarding Hagami's decision to join the priesthood: "Immediately after World War II, Hagami happened to be on a platform at the San-no-miya Station. Just then a train pulled up and American soldiers tossed packs of cigarettes out of the window. As he watched, men, women, and even children scrambled frantically on their hands and knees for the cigarettes. For Hagami, this scene symbolized the physical as well as the spiritual devastation of his beloved country."[21] Motivated by a desire to be more than just an intellectual and to work to restore his country, Hagami joined the priesthood.

Hagami completed the *kaihōgyō* on September 18, 1954, at the age of fifty-one. He began his practice at a time of great change for Japan. World War II had just ended and the country was still under occupation. By the time his book, *Dōshin—kaihōgyō no taiken* (道心—回峰行の体験, *Will to Enlightenment: The* Kaihōgyō *Experience*), was published in 1971, Japan had experienced what many felt was a miraculous recovery and was just through a period of high growth.[22] While the economy boomed, many in educational, political, and religious circles began to agitate for a return to the so-called traditional Japanese values believed abandoned in the aftermath of World War II. It was hoped that such values would counteract the perceived greed, unfettered consumption, and excess that accompanied economic success. Hagami, too, as will be shown, emphasized a return to traditional values. He clearly believed that the youth of Japan are in dire need of moral guidance and thus recommended a worldview steeped in traditional values and character building.

Hagami on Contemporary Society: In Defense of Tradition

Hagami longed for the past, for a simpler time when people admired and aspired to traditional values. In addition to looking back on the prewar period emperor system with nostalgia and lamenting the attitude of contemporary youth, he also spent considerable time defending Buddhism from critiques that it was not fit for the modern world.

Born in 1903, in the Meiji era, in which the imperial household was central to state ideology, Hagami expresses great joy at being able to pray for the imperial family in the final rite of the *kaihōgyō*.[23] Throughout his writings he self-consciously remarks on the importance of this rite, at one point stating, "We think the Imperial Palace is the greatest place, maybe because we were born in the Meiji period."[24]

Related to his nostalgia for the emperor, he also discusses the critical nature of nation-defending rites in the Tendai denomination. Hagami notes that each day practitioners turn to face the direction of the palace gates and offer prayers. "Despite all that has been said about the emperor system after the war, I think that performing empowerment rites [facing the Imperial Palace] every day for eight hundred days over six long years is meaningful."[25] Cutting across sectarian boundaries, the practice of performing rites to defend the nation has a long history in Japan. Tendai, in particular, has been so closely associated with nation-defending theories that a leading postwar member of the Tendai denomination felt it necessary to include a reference to such teachings in a short essay he wrote apologizing for Tendai's contribution to Japan's modern wars.[26]

Hagami's reflections on the past are related to his uncertainty about Japan's present and his fear for Japan's future. He imagines Japan as moving away from traditions too easily dismissed following defeat in World War II and worries that Japan, shorn from the past—which he sees as the anchor of morals—has been set adrift. Throughout his writings Hagami seeks to convey the view that past traditions can be of great contemporary value, especially as a means to establish common moral groundings.

Contemporary Japanese youth, for example, appear to be far different from those Hagami remembers growing up with as a child in the Meiji (1868–1912) and Taishō (1912–1926) eras. He repeatedly notes with trepidation that contemporary youth are overly materialistic, divorced from a religious moral base, and disrespectful of the traditions that once provided the foundation for Japanese moral character. According to Hagami, this contempt for their country's past has led to a loss of self-esteem. He believes that because traditional values were removed from the curriculum at public schools, those charged with educating Japanese youth are faced with the difficult task of instilling pride in their charges while avoiding discussion of traditional values. And he notes, "Without pride you can only fall."[27]

Critiques of traditional values center on the failed wartime state and on the view that they are premodern. In a line of argument that calls to mind Meiji-period defenses of Buddhism, in which Buddhism was framed as a philosophy as opposed to a primitive "religious" or "magical" system, Hagami argues that tradition is "not a foolish thing; it continues to exist for logical reasons."[28] The *kaihōgyō,* he maintains by way of example, is precision tuned. It survived one thousand years for a reason. Each act, the order of the acts, and the times at which they are carried out are designed to push the practitioner to his limits without killing him. Echoing Meiji arguments that Buddhism was fit for the modern world, he frequently portrays Buddhism as scientific and logical in nature. He relates the story of how when he first decided to undertake the *kaihōgyō,* he had reservations about the attire:[29] "To be honest, [this practice] can only be understood as complete 'nonsense' if seen simply as running around and around the same place day in and day out praying to trees and rocks wearing an anachronistic costume."[30] Hagami says he soon realized that each article of clothing as well as each action had a purpose. The attire was very "logical": the lotus hat was streamlined, making it just the right fit for narrow tree-lined mountain trails; the straw sandals were light and flexible, yet their construction forced one to tread softly and carefully. He concluded, "There are few things that are as scientific and as deeply religious as this" (9). The jacket cover for his book makes clear his aim, with the selling point written in bold: "As a science it has surpassed science: the inner teachings of the *kaihōgyō.*"

In fact, Hagami continues, the whole of the *kaihōgyō* practice is based on logic and thus can be understood as scientific. Like science, it combines experience with repeated testing (14). Thus, the *kaihōgyō* demonstrates that Temple Buddhism is not something that should be forsaken as a useless vestige of the past but is instead very "logical" and "scientific" in nature and therefore relevant to the modern world. Traditional practices, he argues, survive because they retain their relevance by proving themselves time and again. Moreover, the pride derived from participation in time-honored traditions leads to self-esteem. Here he is clearly addressing the aforementioned lack of confidence among Japanese youth.

Hagami goes on to emphasize, however, that, in addition to being scientific and logical, Buddhism is super-rational: that is, it goes beyond the limits imposed by purely rational thought. Returning again to the *kaihōgyō* as an example, he states that though based on scientific logic, it is also a "deeply religious" practice and, therefore, something that surpasses science (14). What allows this is faith (14, 32). This is what Hagami believes gives Buddhism its power and why he recommends it over other alternatives: it is rational and yet super-rational, scientific and yet capable of penetrating beyond the limits of science, locally based and yet international in scope (120). Hagami is not alone in his use of the term "international"; the Tendai denomination and many other religious groups also seek to demonstrate the quality of their practices by showing that their effectiveness is not limited to Japan.

As James Edward Ketelaar has shown, the move to describe Buddhism as a global or world religion, stretching beyond the limitations of regional sectarianism, was a major part of the resignification of Buddhism that began in the Meiji period. Hagami never informs the reader directly that he is conscious of his own mimicking of Meiji arguments. Yet it is evident that he feels continuing critiques of Buddhism as premodern must be answered. Hagami seeks to demonstrate Buddhism's relevance to the modern world, just as his Meiji predecessors did. The critiques Hagami faces often are more oblique than Meiji-period critiques, which were regularly leveled directly by government authorities, Shinto nationalists, and National Learning (国学, *kokugaku*) scholars. Contemporary critiques are perhaps more popular in nature, appearing in the mass media or by word of mouth among disgruntled laity. The success of new religious movements (NRMs) and lay Buddhist movements is often interpreted as a critique of Temple Buddhism.

Hagami expends considerable effort defending Temple Buddhism against the New Religions. He states, "That which is old but new is the real thing, that which is old and dated is not, and that which is simply new disappears" (173). By this he means that traditions that survive and retain their relevance are to be trusted, unlike trendy fads. Hagami is addressing the dramatic increase in the strength of NRMs during his time, especially that of Sōka Gakkai, a lay Buddhist movement that he sees as an NRM.[31]

Hagami attacks Sōka Gakkai for its radical exclusivism. He also attacks Nichiren, on whose teachings Sōka Gakkai is based. "If I had to put it in to words I would say, Nichiren is from what, about six hundred years ago? For us modern people he's like Sōka Gakkai today, which goes around calling everyone else false religion. That's not Buddhism" (63). By attacking the relative newness of Nichiren or Sōka Gakkai, Hagami attacks their legitimacy. Sōka Gakkai today, he asserts, is the same as Nichiren in the Kamakura period (1185–1333). It is an upstart newcomer that feels it must define itself by attacking all that came before. Its success, Hagami appears to believe, only speaks to the worrisome condition of contemporary Japanese character.

Hagami attacks Nichiren, and by association Sōka Gakkai, by continuing a centuries-old debate regarding exclusivist single practices: "In Japanese Buddhism during the Kamakura period there was a strong tendency to stress simply one [practice]. From the point of view of faith that, too, may be a real option, but I think there is something odd about an anti-others, self-righteous attitude" (24). Hagami writes that whereas the focus and effort of these schools should be applauded, their exclusivism is potentially dangerous because it denies other viewpoints. This opinion mirrors the standard Tendai rhetoric of inclusivism as taught to all Tendai priests during their training. Indeed, Tendai, in a move that places it at the historical, religious, and cultural center of Japanese Buddhism, is commonly depicted as the mother of Japanese Buddhism from which sprang later exclusivist offspring. One section on Tendai's home page is dedicated to this metaphor, replete with a picture of Mt. Hiei and Saichō in the center and, flowing out from there, the founders of the new Buddhist movements of the Kamakura period: Nichiren, Shinran, Hōnen, Eisai, and Dōgen. The picture is titled *The Mother: The Mountain as Mother.*[32]

Against the alleged exclusivism of the New Religions and other Buddhist denominations, Hagami argues that the openness of Saichō and the inclusive nature of the (Tendai) Lotus teachings are what is needed to bring unity and a solid religious foundation back to Japan. Tendai's inclusivity, Hagami teaches, is what made it great and what allowed these other schools to form.

Hagami's reservations concerning exclusivity also reflect anxiety about Tendai's contemporary situation. In the postwar period, changes in the laws governing the incorporation of religious organizations made breaking away from the parent denomination easier than before. In particular, the head priests and lay leaders of large temples, which could easily financially afford independence, began considering severing their ties with the denomination.[33] Hagami appears to have worried about this trend: "Now, once again, in this small Tendai denomination the wave of schisms is flowing. Yet, especially given this situation, I believe now is the time to build a new and true unifying principle and base" (24–25). Faced with exclusivist New Religions and schisms within the Temple Buddhism denominations, Hagami argues that Japan needs to "return" to a unified Buddhism. This echoes Meiji- and Taishō-period reform efforts that focused on promoting trans-sectarian Buddhism. We saw an example of this in our discussion of the founding of Taishō University. He is not specific about how to go about creating a unified Buddhism, though he does offer trans-sectarian pilgrimages as one example where such a unified Buddhist practice is in evidence. Regardless, he stresses that a firm, unified religious (Buddhist) base is necessary if Japan is to rebuild itself.

Hagami on Practice: Character Building

Based on his experience of the *kaihōgyō,* Hagami's teachings include perseverance, sincerity, interdependence, and the importance of role models. Hagami frequently laments the woeful state of education in Japan and the lack of resolve among the nation's youth. He writes that it is to Japan's loss that schools no longer instill strength of character in students. They fail to teach the young to patiently persevere: "Today that 'come-what-may' fighting spirit is all but gone. And there is no longer the disposition to patiently persevere. Without this, how can an international superpower be built?" (85).

To nurture the ability to persevere and realize the strength of character found therein, Hagami teaches that people must learn that the fruit of practice is the process itself. Focusing on the result would make practices such as the *kaihōgyō* nearly impossible and would obscure their true lesson. Hagami reminds the reader that what is needed in life, and what the *kaihōgyō* teaches, is an attitude of *nanikuso,* or "come-what-may determination" (84). One must always show resolve and see things through to the end. This is true not just for the *kaihōgyō* but also for daily life; one cannot allow oneself to be overwhelmed by difficulties (121–123). Here he is directly appealing to the members of Japan's workforce, the fabled salarymen, whose life has been lionized in numerous manga, television dramas, and business schools around the world as an example of unwavering dedication and stubborn determination. Hagami's practice of completing seemingly impossible austerities appears to both strike a familiar chord with the salarymen and serve as a role model for them.

In addition to perseverance, Hagami teaches the need for sincerity. He draws on the founder of Japanese Tendai, Saichō, as an example. He writes that Saichō was different from other great teachers, such as his contemporary rival Kūkai. Hagami claims that an examination of their calligraphy shows that, although Kūkai may have been a genius, he lacked Saichō's sincerity, a quality that Hagami claims all true religions must possess, though he fails to explain just how a lack of sincerity is determined through examining someone's handwriting. "The spirit of Hieizan is sincerity. Put another way it is purity. It's *pi-yu-ri-ti* [emphasis in original]. Religion and art are meaningless without this. Even Mt. Hiei is valueless without this."[34] Hagami points to Saichō's teaching that one must forget oneself and work to benefit others (忘己利他, *mōkorita*) as an example of how to live in a state of sincerity.[35] Only by overcoming attachment to the self can one be understood as living in sincerity.

Tied to the teaching of sincerity is that of interdependence. People must realize that they are part of a larger group and are therefore dependent on those around them. To explain, Hagami draws on his experience in the *kaihōgyō* and describes the annual summer retreat for practitioners.[36] A *kaihōgyō* practitioner has not officially completed his practice until he attends this retreat. There he is recognized by his peers and reports his success to Sōō, the legendary founder of the *kaihōgyō.* This ritual is meant to remind practitioners that the individual practice of *kaihōgyō* is still dependent on a larger group that includes those who have been through it before and those who will attempt it in the future. This creates a sense of interdependence and humility vis-à-vis other practitioners, and with the lay support groups for the *kaihōgyō,* without whose help little would be possible.[37] The implication is that even "living Buddhas" must accept that they are a part of and dependent on society and be thankful.

Linked to the teaching of interdependence we find that Hagami stresses the positive function of role models. The Bodhisattva Never Disparaging (Jōfukyōbosatsu, the central figure in chapter 20 of the Lotus Sūtra) serves as a role model for practice. Bodhisattva Never Disparaging is said to have seen Buddha nature within everyone he encountered. Therefore, he venerated all people as Buddhas. Hagami remarks that it is imperative to follow Bodhisattva Never Disparaging's example and not just respect all people but venerate them.[38] Hagami relates the story of a man who came to see him on occasion. The man bowed properly, which moved Hagami. The man's mother, Hagami tells us, took him daily to a shrine to make offerings and taught him through her words and actions how to behave respectfully.[39] In Hagami's view, the job of those further along the path, whether parents, teachers, or priests, is to instill in others proper behavior through exemplary practice.[40]

Believing that anything that has survived the test of time is a proven good, Hagami teaches his readers a way of life that takes pride in tradition. He defends Temple Buddhism against those who would see it as backward or moribund. He emphasizes "traditional" Japanese character, including "come-what-may determination," as especially pertinent in today's world. He also encourages readers to avoid exclusivitic practices, such as those offered by the New Religions. People must instead seek out inclusivitic practices and recognize their dependence on those around them and live a life of sincerity. Finally, Hagami warns that Japan needs to re-educate its youth to give them a firm, unified (Buddhist) faith, one that will provide the grounding from which to secure their (Japan's) future.

SAKAI

Background

Sakai Yūsai was born in Osaka in 1926, the eldest son among eleven siblings. His father ran a rice and vegetable shop, which failed, leading his family to move. At age five Sakai traveled with his family to Tokyo. While attending night school, he worked cleaning in a lab at the Army Medical School. He did not know much about what went on in the lab, only that working at a military lab was likely to keep him from getting sent off to war. He later came to know that the lab was the home of the infamous Unit 731, which conducted human experiments in China. Because of the amount of work he was doing, his grades at school dropped, and he was given the option of failing out or graduating early and joining the military. So at eighteen years old, in 1944, he enlisted in the Yokaren (予科練, Japanese Navy Preparatory Flight Training Program) in Kumamoto Prefecture. He trained there for six months and then trained with the Miyazaki air force. From there he was sent to Kagoshima Prefecture's Kanoya airfield, a Tokkotai (特攻隊 Special Forces—Kamikaze) base where, in Sakai's words, the suicide pilots were the best-educated and most talented students. He was not in that group and spent his time filling in holes on the runway left from Allied bombing runs. As his comrades were killed, he asked why someone like him lived while others died. He says he came to believe not that he survived but that he was left to live on and that there was meaning to his remaining alive.[41]

After World War II, he held a variety of jobs, including working at a university library. He also ran two businesses with his father: a noodle shop, which burned down, and a stockbroker shop that went bankrupt. He married at age thirty-two, but his wife left him after one month and, after they reunited for a short period, she took her own life. His wife's mother took him to Mt. Hiei to seek relief from his suffering. Though he claims not to have thought much of it at the time, later he walked there himself from Osaka, and stayed. He was ordained in 1965 at the age of thirty-nine. He completed his first *kaihōgyō* in 1980, and his second in 1987 at the age of sixty-one. After completing his second *kaihōgyō,* he began a series of pilgrimages around Japan. He also made pilgrimages in China, Italy, Spain, and Cambodia.

Sakai on Contemporary Society

According to Sakai, Japan is facing a crisis of the heart and mind. Until the Japanese learn resolve, reestablish community ties, and completely renew their educational system, the country, he believes, will continue its downward spiral. The healing process for Japan, Sakai remarks, will take over a century, and if it does not begin soon, Japan will decline so far as to be beyond any hope of revival. People "must have this sense of danger," he declares.[42]

Connecting the healing of Japan to his own experiences during the *kaihōgyō,* he goes on to say that in practice it is said that it takes three times as long for an injury to heal as it does for it to occur: "In the same way, if we consider that it has been over fifty years since the end of the war and that during that time the country has fallen into disrepair, then in order to restore things to how they were in the past, it will take three times as long as that, or one hundred and fifty years."[43] Echoing Hagami, Sakai believes the healing process will require a complete overhaul of the education system, a return to strong family and community ties, and the invigoration of a spiritless salaryman class.

In Sakai's view, Japan's extended recession drained Japan's workers of their will to continue and made them apathetic. Round after round of layoffs in a society where layoffs were not supposed to happen left Japan's salarymen timid. Responding to a dramatic increase in the number of suicides among middle-aged men, Sakai states, "Life isn't something you throw aside just because things aren't going well now."[44] Elsewhere he writes, "There is no one who lacks talent, there is no life that is without meaning."[45] He urges them not to dwell on the present, and to look instead to the promise of tomorrow. While this might be construed as emphasizing goal over process (in contradistinction to Hagami's views), Sakai is not asking salarymen to focus on a distant goal when he urges them to look to tomorrow. He is instead asking them to see their present situation as part of a longer ongoing process. Those who have been laid off "are too wrapped up in what is directly in front of them. They think only about what their rank and salary should be, when they should just go out and take any work that is available."[46] Their pride and narrow understanding of what working is about (material gain in their view, something to be grateful for and learn from in Sakai's) is a stumbling block to moving forward. "I have this to say to salarymen: just let it be. Don't dilly dally about in your current situation, grasp the real situation and keep moving forward."[47] Today's salarymen, Sakai fears, overemphasize past accomplishments, school records, and qualifications. "Don't get wrapped up in what you have been up to now," he advises. "Suck in your gut and live your life to the best of your abilities."[48]

The picture of dejected salarymen that Sakai paints is powerful, but in his view they are more symptom than cause. Echoing what we saw in chapter 4, he sees the cause of Japan's decline as directly related to a collapse in morals. Sakai views this collapse as having started in the aftermath of World War II. He states, "After the war people have come to think only of money."[49] While Sakai clearly sees selfishness as a problem, he does not, like Hagami and many conservative commentators, place the blame squarely on the introduction of Western values, such as individualism, or the elimination of religious education from the school system. Instead Sakai links the postwar collapse in values to the hardships people underwent in the immediate postwar period. Income was hard to come by, food was scarce, and life in the cities was a day-to-day struggle for many. Sakai states that because of the difficult times they experienced, many parents sought to give their children whatever they asked for. This was gradually made possible by the economic boom that extended through the 1950s and 1960s. Sakai worries, however, that "when those children grow up, they lose the sense of gratitude toward things. Kids raised like that are now becoming adults."[50]

Sakai also points to the weakening of community ties as a reason for the decline in morals in postwar Japan: "If you were to mention duty and human feeling [義理人情, *girininjō*] in today's society, you would probably be laughed at."[51] *Girininjō,* Sakai suggests, develops and is maintained through neighborly interaction. As urban life shifted away from the long houses he remembers from his youth—in which neighbors would pop in to borrow salt, look after each other's children, and generally have a high degree of contact—to large-scale apartment complexes, interaction between neighbors ceased. "In the box-like apartments today that kind of interaction does not exist. If horizontal bonds disappear, the world is bound to grow crazy."[52] As part of this large-scale architectural assault on community bonds, Sakai also sees the advent of individual rooms for children as an attack on family bonds. Furthermore, he notes that the competitive school entrance examination system has created a society in which individuals are encouraged to look out for themselves, placing the bonds of friendship behind the individual's desire for personal (material) success.[53] Taken together, the emphasis on personal gain and the weakening of horizontal community and family ties have led to a decline in morals in Japan, according to Sakai. Referring to a series of political and business scandals, he states, "There has been an explosion [in the number] of incidents that make you think morals have been lost."[54] Sakai argues that moving beyond this competitive way of life is important. Success comes from realizing equality. "From the point of view of the Buddha, everyone is equal. Make the most of the life that you have been given and just keep moving on a bit at a time."[55]

Like Hagami, Sakai places his hopes for the regeneration of Japan on the education of the youth. He also places much of the blame for what has gone wrong up to now on the educational system:

> It is not good enough to simply look at what is right in front of oneself and judge whether or not something went well. I believe that the various problems that have arisen from the end of the war until now are because we have not learned to look at things comprehensively. . . . [Postwar] education has not served to comprehensively broaden individuality to give people something that they can hold up and say, "In this, I will lose to no one." . . . Because they have not had a complete education people feel uneasy, thinking "I can't do anything."[56]

Sakai believes there is a pressing need for restructuring the education system so that it can produce forward-looking, community-oriented, well-trained individuals: "If Japan cannot engage in a human resources education that leads to Japanese being needed around the world, then it will not survive."[57] Unlike with Hagami, restoring religious education to the classroom is not on Sakai's agenda. Sakai seeks a complete overhaul of the education system to foster individual talent and thereby rebuild Japan's economy.

Rather than supporting the current educational system, with its emphasis on producing pliable workers ready to fit into corporate life, Sakai takes a line of argument similar to many who are seeking to reform Japan's ailing educational system, including the Ministry of Education, Culture, Sports, Science, and Technology.[58] He argues for emphasizing and nurturing individual capabilities over uniform training. In his view, this type of education must begin from very earlier on:

> Regarding education from here on, we must put into place an education system that seeks to foster the uniqueness of children from a young age. . . . Particularly in the case of Japan, which is becoming an aging society in which there are fewer and fewer young people. To be on par with the rest of the world, it is important to implement an education that gives life to the special talents of each individual. . . . When you look at a country like China with its massive population, for Japan to be a big player in the world, each and every Japanese must become someone with a special talent.[59]

Sakai seeks to create workers who will drive Japan's economic engine and assure Japan's survival. Sakai's views on specific education reforms differ from those of Hagami, but their goals remain the same, and those goals tend to underscore those of the state. Indeed, Sakai writes in his book *You Have the Strength to Find Happiness* (あなたには幸せになる力がある, *Anata ni wa shiawase ni naru chikara ga aru*) that *yutori no kyōiku* (ゆとりの教育) is what is needed. *Yutori no kyōiku* refers to the type of education that was promoted in the 2002 education reforms in Japan but has roots as far back as the 1970s. It includes a reduced school schedule and more emphasis on allowing students to learn at their own pace. Sakai says this kind of education must begin "with understanding the 'flavor' of each person" and require that students study what they like or what they are good at.[60]

For this type of education to work, Sakai feels that there must be close cooperation between the family and the school. He draws on his experience as a Tendai priest to describe what is necessary: "Within our practice is something called *jōgyō sanmai* [常業三昧], and within that is body, speech and mind. Success occurs when these are in harmony. When I think about education I see it in the same way as this. Namely, the child, parent and school or teacher must become one."[61]

Sakai describes an educational plan in which parents watch their child closely, note any specific talents he or she might have, and relate those to the kindergarten or elementary school teachers, who then design a curriculum suited to inspire the child to develop his or her talents to the fullest. To waste these talents is to deprive the nation of their potential and the individual of fulfilling his or her promise. Believing that children are the nation's treasure,[62] Sakai writes, "People are born because the Buddha has given them each a special talent. Most people go through life without ever discovering that talent. Life's practice is finding one's life path through the leaves and branches. Finding the root, entering from there, and persistently heading down that path."[63]

For Sakai, education plays a crucial role not just in saving the country from economic ruin but also, at a more primary level, in allowing individuals to realize their true nature. Once they grasp their Buddha-given talent, they will be able to proceed down their unique path in life and fulfill their purpose.

In sum, Sakai believes contemporary Japan is mired in a swamp of materialism in which individual desires are seen as more important than national or community needs. Nevertheless, he remains hopeful that if the Japanese return to an emphasis on horizontal community and family bonds and that if they pursue educational reform with the intent of allowing everyone to give full play to their Buddha-given talent, then Japan will recover from its postwar moral decline and regain its position as an important world power. Here we see a tension in Sakai's teachings between his belief in the powerful emotional and moral support roles of community and his desire to educate unique individuals. This tension may be resolved if we turn our attention to Sakai's hopes for creating a Japan capable of surviving in the twenty-first century. Sakai can be understood as advocating the importance of individuality, but not at the expense of the larger community. Individuals are not encouraged to seek after their own gain; rather, they are expected to apply their unique gifts and school-honed talents to the restoration of Japan.

Sakai on Practice: Live Each Day as If It Were Your Whole Life

Sakai recommends practices that directly address problems in contemporary society such as the emotional and moral weakness he believes plagues salarymen. Foremost among his teachings is an emphasis on living each day as if it were one's whole life. This, and his emphasis on persistence, are clearly derived from his *kaihōgyō* experience as well as his life struggles before entering the priesthood. He also teaches the importance of empathy and gratitude and emphasizes the significance of role models.

Like Hagami, Sakai addresses the salarymen of Japan: "I really want to tell the lethargic managers and mid-ranked administrators that 'each day is your whole life.' Even if you failed today, you can still try hard tomorrow. At any rate, instead of doing nothing and just sitting about lifeless, try everything that you can. It won't hurt to have some samurai spirit."[64] His teaching to "live each day as if it was your whole life" is not a call to live each day as if there was no tomorrow but, rather, a call to try one's best each day. "If there is something you don't like, [remember that] today's self ends today and try again tomorrow."[65] Drawing from his own experience of the *kaihōgyō,* Sakai reminds his readers that the focus of each day must be on getting through that day's practice. Any practitioner who dwells on what lies ahead or on the pain they are suffering on any given day will never be able to complete the long journey.[66] Practitioners must see themselves as being reborn each day. Each morning as they leave their temples to circumambulate the mountain, they don white clothing, representing their death to the world.

Sakai also draws on his other life experiences. Evoking the human touch that helps readers identify with him, he relates that he used to feel the first forty years of his life were wasted, a life spent bouncing from job to job. As he says, "My life has been a series of things not going well."[67] But when he looks back now, he sees those experiences as preparing the way for his practice on Mt. Hiei.[68] In a similar manner, salarymen who have lost their jobs should not view their life as a waste but should instead learn from their past and move forward. Sakai encourages his readers to take time at the end of each day to reflect on what happened and identify any problems that may have occurred and how they might make things work better the next time.[69]

Sakai's views, born of practice, can be seen as somewhat anti-intellectual, but they are not necessarily anticanonical. "In Buddhist studies they do a variety of difficult things. But for someone like me, who comes from an awareness developed through practice, practice is living each day as though it were your whole life."[70] Though he bases his ideas on his personal experience, he also implies that his teachings are grounded in classical doctrines.

> There is a teaching of Dengyō Daishi's [Saichō] called *isshin sankan*.[71] There are a lot of difficult ways of understanding this, but it means things like obtaining simultaneous understanding of the three truths. The more I think about it, though, the more confused I get. So, if people ask "What is *isshin sankan*?" I tell them it is understanding nature just as it is. When you hurt, hurt. When you are sad, be sad. Death is waiting for all who are born. It's about being able to accept such a reality just as it is. Sincerely know yourself just as you are.[72]

Here, to further explain his teaching of living each day as if it were one's whole life, Sakai draws briefly on Saichō and the concept of *isshin sankan* (一心三観), only to state how difficult explicating such a teaching is, and then to switch to his own practical knowledge of it. Sakai thus draws on classical Tendai thought to give depth and legitimacy to the idea of living each day as if it were one's whole life. By claiming intellectual ignorance but physical understanding gained from his practice, he validates his teaching and suggests that those with intellectual knowledge alone cannot truly understand.[73]

Sakai believes that the teaching of living each day as if it was one's whole life is connected to an understanding of the "true" nature of things. Only through sincerity, by being open to accepting things as they are in each situation, can one truly live each day as if it was one's whole life. Accepting this leads to gratitude. Recounting his feelings at looking at the sunrise over Lake Biwa, he states, "I don't know how to describe it, but it is like life is a stage, and when this happens, feelings of gratitude just pour forth of their own accord."[74] In an interview given near his death, Sakai admits that he is upset with himself for failing to take his own advice. Friends and doctors were telling him he had serious health issues, but he ignored them and thought that someone in such good physical health could never be that ill. When he finally chose to see a doctor, it was too late: he had terminal cancer. He writes that if he had practiced self-reflection and sincerity from the beginning and remembered that life is a gift from all those around him and been grateful for this, things might have turned out differently.[75]

The concept of living each day as if it was one's whole life forms the framework for the rest of Sakai's teachings. The practice he recommends most often within this framework is persistence. Persistence leads to a sense of accomplishment and to practical benefits such as advancement in the workplace, fresh ideas, mental clarity, and so on. He gives his own teachings, derived from his persistent walking, as an example: "The heart of what I talk about comes from things I realized as I was walking and which I never forgot."[76]

The value of persistence is in realizing that practice, and its benefits, can be found within everyday life: "It doesn't matter what, just find something and stick to it, that is practice."[77] Sakai stresses that practice can be anything, even the simple task of greeting officemates every morning, without fail, with "Good morning." He also recommends persistence to retirees: "If you sit there watching TV, especially period pieces, you'll go senile in a flash."[78] Instead he recommends that they find something they excel at and stick to it.

To persistence Sakai adds empathy, compassion, gratitude, and sincerity. These are drawn from his practice but also are clearly part of the "traditional values" that Sakai and many others wish to see revived: "The world today is one in which there is no empathy, or feeling of gratitude, there are no bonds holding people together. There is no way that politics or the economy can go well in such an environment. . . . I want people today to live with empathy and compassion. The reason Japan today has gone off-kilter is that these have been lost."[79]

Sakai views the goal of practice as making these values a lived reality: "It may be the ideal that people possess empathy and a compassionate heart, together with sincerity, but making this ideal a reality is necessary. In Buddhism, making this ideal a reality is called practice."[80] It is through practice that one comes to see the Buddha as manifest in everything, and it is from the realization that the Buddha is manifest all around one that feelings of thankfulness naturally arise.[81]

Like Hagami, Sakai does not believe that Japan can recover without these values in place. It is through role models that such values are taught: "In Buddhism, because as a practice we constantly repeat the same action, people think 'That's incredible!' or 'He's really doing something I could never do.' My practice has been successful if people who see me practicing think to themselves, 'That priest is doing all that. I'm being too easy on myself. Should I go on like this? Maybe I can change myself?'"[82]

Sakai uses himself as an example, but he also writes that the most basic exemplars are parents. Yet he does not limit his search for exemplars to parents. He states that children, too, can be teachers. Indeed, citing the famous swordsman Miyamoto Musashi (1584–1645), he states, "Even a blade of grass can be your teacher."[83] The point is that the world is full of potential role models; one must simply become aware of this. How is it that the world is so full of role models? Sakai writes, "Everyone is born given life from the Buddha, at the core it is all the same life. If you see all the life around you as the manifestation body of the Buddha you will realize that there is much to learn even from small bugs and animals."[84]

In summary, Sakai purposefully avoids scholarly debate, lending his teachings a down-to-earth feel that probably appeals to his readers. His practice of living each day as if it was one's whole life is legitimized through his personal success. Sakai's teachings are very similar to those of Hagami especially as regards the emphasis on perseverance. Where the two begin to differ is in Sakai's insistence on the importance of developing unique individuals, though, as explained above, Sakai does not abandon awareness of interdependence and the importance of communal and familial bonds. Sakai's use of samurai examples is helpful. The popular image of the samurai is twofold. On the one hand, the samurai is representative of Sakai's unique individual. He is someone, like Musashi, who is dedicated to honing his talents and mastering his art. He is engaged in a very solitary enterprise, much like the *kaihōgyō* practitioner. This image differs from Hagami's portrait of an individual existing in a state of interdependence within a larger community. On the other hand, the samurai is often depicted as someone bound to a community, fiercely loyal to his lord, and willing to sacrifice everything for the greater good of the domain or nation. This image of the samurai is perhaps closer to Hagami's views and reflects Sakai's hopes that individuals will act for the greater good. It is Sakai's desire that his readers will take his teachings to heart and change for the better, thereby increasing the likelihood that Japan will "once again" prosper spiritually, morally, and materially.

MITSUNAGA KAKUDŌ

Background

Born in 1954 in Yamagata Prefecture, Mitsunaga describes his childhood as rather uneventful. A loner throughout junior high school, he later went to a technical school where he studied mechanical engineering. Immediately following graduation, he traveled to Mt. Hiei and was ordained at age twenty in 1975. He says that he was drawn to the priesthood because of the freedom he felt it offered. He claims that in the secular world of his salaryman contemporaries, one's whole life was mapped out once hired by a company, whereas a priest never knew what role he might play.[85]

Mitsunaga on Contemporary Japan: Sad Japanese

Mitsunaga was born and raised in the postwar economic boom. His writings address the salarymen who represent the secular ideal of that period and whom Mitsunaga sees as caught on a dangerous path of self-indulgence. Mitsunaga argues that a "return" to a religious moral foundation is necessary. Like Hagami, he states that with the loss of World War II came a repudiation of religion. State Shinto was associated with the war and dismantled. But the dismantling, he argues, did not stop with State Shinto; it expanded to include a widespread undermining of any faith in religion or "traditional" Japanese values as a moral foundation.[86] He titled a section of one of his books "Sad Japanese" and wrote that this sadness stems from the lack of a religious foundation on which to base their lives. In fact, according to Mitsunaga, Japan has contracted a "religion allergy" (161): "Religion is at the root of each person's value system. However, the Japanese swept all religion from their daily lives when the war was lost. This is because State Shinto, the key element in the value system put forth as a guiding ideology during the war, became equated with war, and because of that religion was equated with something bad" (84–85).

The loss of a unified value system resulted in a moral void into which numerous competing value systems rushed: "In short, various value systems such as 'getting rich is good,' or 'becoming powerful is good,' got all mixed together and deciding the value of each was simply entrusted to individuals" (84). The children of the bubble era, those born during Japan's booming economy when Japan seemed unstoppable, are particularly susceptible (74). They fail to understand that a moral foundation can provide an important emotional support system: "Young people have the image that relying on something like religion is uncool. They believe [only] in themselves and live their own lives; religion is not providing support in their lives" (164). As long as they persist in the belief that religion is an "old thing" for "old people," Mitsunaga fears they will further distance themselves from a proper moral foundation.

Mitsunaga does not blame postwar religious education reform alone for the shallowness of the youth or the youth's turning away from religion. He also places some responsibility on Buddhism. Echoing the call for "applied Buddhism" we examined in chapter 3, Mitsunaga claims Buddhism became too theoretically oriented and too separated from the reality of everyday life to have any meaning for contemporary Japanese. This is a great loss, he argues, because the Japanese, through enculturation, possess the "basic Buddhist way of thinking" (164–165). If only that foundation could be shaped and put into practice, he laments, Japan could recover from its moral collapse. In the vacuum created by the removal of religion as a moral foundation, Mitsunaga writes that the Japanese came to rely completely on manuals:

> There are few people who hold to their own convictions. . . . The number of manual people is rising. A large number of people, because they had an education that judged them on a scale, simply measure their own abilities on a scale. "I've gotten to here," they think. They limit themselves to their academic records and where they fall on the scale. Therefore, since they have predetermined the limits of their abilities, even though they have strengths, they are unable to give them play. (33–34)

Mitsunaga feels that the Japanese educate their young by manuals, run their businesses by manuals, and order their lives as though based on manuals. Parents, he says, raise their children by the book and expect everything to work out and are rarely prepared for the consequences if they do not (54–55). The problem with "manual people," he asserts, is that they never push beyond their school records and licenses (34).

According to Mitsunaga, having been raised in an ordered "manual" world, children have no will or values of their own, thus group values can easily take hold (57). He argues that one dangerous outcome of the above is that many young people find order within the New Religions, and thus join new religious movements, cults, and the like (162–163). According to Mitsunaga, NRMs offer a well-defined, manual-like worldview through which the faithful can identify and solve their everyday problems. But such religions, Mitsunaga critiques, do not allow for the growth of wisdom and faith:

> Recently some New Religions use the term "entering the faith." But since faith is something that you do not swear to anyone other than yourself, I don't really like the term. If there is the freedom to "enter the faith," the opposite must also exist. Faith is not something to be forced; it should be within the realm of an individual's free discretion. . . . In the end, faith is a matter of an individual's own free discretion. Something forced upon one by another is not true faith. Having in the bottom of one's heart the desire to put one's hands together in supplication is faith. (95, 211; see also Mitsunaga, *Sennichi kaihōgyō,* 211)

He argues that faith should well up from within and thus assist one in finding self-confidence. He believes New Religions force their faith on others. Forced faith allows only false confidence (95, 171). Moreover, faith should put one's mind at ease and not cause discord within families.[87] Mitsunaga implies that some New Religions end up creating discord within families. This rhetoric of discord as a critique of new religious movements, especially the Buddhist lay movement Sōka Gakkai, is not uncommon and reflects the opinion of many within Temple Buddhism, in which the traditional family is the primary source of support for temple ritual, social, and financial life. Temple Buddhism priests thus tend to roundly critique any perceived disruption to the family.

Mitsunaga on Practice: From Knowledge to Wisdom

Mitsunaga describes for his readers the practices that he believes will give them the foundation they need in life, without leading to discord. Here I describe the six practices he emphasizes most often: turning knowledge into wisdom; perseverance; controlling desire; developing awareness of the fact that one is given life by all those around oneself; gratitude; and people as mirrors.

Mitsunaga stresses throughout his writings the importance of turning knowledge into wisdom. This is a direct critique of the contemporary education system and the "manual people" it produces. Turning knowledge into wisdom means internalizing and embodying information gathered through reading, studying, or daily life. He gives as an example the case of father and son. The father can teach the son about life, but until the son turns his father's teachings into wisdom by reflecting on his own experiences, his father's words can be no more than simple knowledge (45). Practice, he notes in *Kaihōgyō,* is not simply the acquisition of knowledge, but turning that knowledge into wisdom through experience (182).

The foundation of "turning knowledge into wisdom" is the practice of maintaining a routine. This teaching reflects the nature of Mitsunaga's experience in the *kaihōgyō* and his belief that persistence is the key to success. It is very similar to Sakai's definition of practice as finding something and sticking to it. Mitsunaga states that practice is all about committing to a routine and never wavering from it (5–8): "Every day must be seen as practice. Practice is not about maintaining one's current lifestyle, but about advancing one step at a time" (14). Mitsunaga offers the example of *mikkabozu* (三日坊主), a common expression with the literal meaning "three-day priest" that refers to those who give up just a few days after beginning a new project. Mitsunaga turns this expression around by teaching that if one becomes a *mikkabozu* every three days, then one can make great advances. In short, it is very difficult to relentlessly follow a routine over a long period of time in pursuit of a distant goal, so people should think of routine in three-day segments—just as *kaihōgyō* practitioners are encouraged to focus on their next step and not on the distant goal of enlightenment (111–115).

The ability to properly manage oneself—that is, to know one's limits and thereby be able to push beyond them in a controlled fashion—is an important part of maintaining any routine. Mitsunaga advises readers to know themselves and their limits. For example, the ability to complete the *kaihōgyō* is in a large part a matter of knowing how far one can push oneself without overdoing it and then having to stop practice. People should push themselves a little extra every day. If one makes the extreme a part of everyday life, then when unexpected difficulties arrive, one will be prepared and not overwhelmed.

> It's only natural to be able to be strong when all the conditions are right. It's the same at work. When everything is prepared and ready, producing results is to be expected. However, it's not like there will always be perfect conditions. Since that's the case you should push yourself. Train so that you can produce good results even when the conditions are not very good. If you build up such experience, you will be able to confront even more difficult situations, and when the conditions are good your job will be easy.[88]

Through these practices one builds self-confidence.

Controlling one's desires must be part of any routine. Humans, Mitsunaga remarks, are incapable of completely denying desire, but they can control it: "As long as we exist as humans, we cannot deny the three desires [sleeping, eating and drinking, worldly pleasures]. Since they cannot be denied they must be controlled" (12). He states, for example, that the *dōiri* is a crucial part of *kaihōgyō* practice because it is a total denial of all basic desires. Desires are fundamental. We must all eat and sleep. The object of controlling them, Mitsunaga states, is to move closer to the Buddha, to a state of freedom from desire, and thus to move closer to one's true potential.

Mitsunaga notes that desire, when controlled and properly applied, can also be useful. Desire can be understood as the will to improve oneself, though this should not be equated with material gain, according to Mitsunaga. He quotes Saichō's famous line "Within the will to enlightenment there is food and shelter, but within food and shelter there is not the will to enlightenment." Mitsunaga puts this classical line into contemporary terms:[89] "[We are] given life as humans, each with our own abilities. Therefore, we should do that which we have been allowed to do. Because we have been allowed to work, we obtain compensation, so we shouldn't work grudgingly. [The meaning of] 'within the will to enlightenment there is food and shelter' is to do all that you can to the best of your abilities while giving thanks to those around you" (13–14). He advises replacing "the will to enlightenment" with "work" and "food and shelter" with "paycheck." Thus, "within work there is a paycheck, but within a paycheck there is no work." In other words, work should not be about material gain; rather, it should be taken on gratefully as an opportunity to improve oneself. This is similar to the attitude toward service we saw in chapter 4.

Mitsunaga emphasizes throughout his writings that people are given life by those around them: that is, they live interdependently. Thus, the most basic teaching, he says, is both the simplest and the most difficult: it is living with the awareness that life is a gift born of interdependence. "There are too many people living [as though] on their own. There are few who [live with the awareness that they] are given life. If the number of people who feel that they are given life would increase, things would change."[90] Mitsunaga says that practice is a matter of slowly building up awareness that life is given—in other words, that one lives not independently but interdependently. This is true for the *kaihōgyō* practitioner as well as the layperson. His sentiments resonate with those of Hagami and Sakai.

When one realizes that life is a gift, Mitsunaga says, one should express gratitude to all. In particular, gratitude toward the past and toward one's ancestors is important.[91] "I often tell believers that when they put their hands together to pray, the foundation is the ancestors. Give thanks every day to the ancestors. . . . [This] is giving thanks for your own existence" (167). Giving thanks builds merit. Merit, Mitsunaga explains, is like "a bank account." One's ancestors begin by making frequent deposits. The living can then draw on this account of merit.[92] Thus, the act of respecting one's ancestors, and thereby all that supports one's life, is a lesson in how to live properly through the return of debt, by recognizing and respecting interdependence:

> Even though you wake up today, there is no guarantee that when you go to bed tonight, you will wake up. You could be cold and dead the next morning. That we can go to sleep without a worry is, to me, a mystery. To wake up and think "Ah! I am alive another day!" is how it really should

> be. Give thanks that you are alive and think what you can do to repay the gift. First, face your ancestors and give thanks that you can wake up and be there. Then, the rest of the day should be spent thinking how you can repay that debt of gratitude. To give thanks to your ancestors and build up [merit] little by little each day is truly returning the debt of gratitude.[93]

Interdependence is put forward not in strict doctrinal terms but in terms of ancestor veneration—a practice common to most religions in Japan, including Buddhism, Shinto, many New Religions, and even some forms of Christianity.

Coupled to the idea that one lives among and is given life by all those around is the idea that people are mirrors in which one is reflected:

> I tell everyone that just as they say that children are mirrors to their parents, so too are all those one encounters. Therefore, if you give all your heart and try your best to communicate, you are sure to get a similar response. So please lead a life in which you think of what you can do for others, not what others can do for you. Interact with others by trying to give all your heart and do your best to communicate.[94]

Mitsunaga uses the parents who come to him seeking advice about their children as an example. Most parents seek advice because their child either failed to get into the right school or dropped out partway through. He tells them that the child's problems cannot be the child's fault alone. The child's problems reflect trouble within the family. Often the problem is lack of communication, something he sees as occurring between husband and wife as well (53–55).

In sum, Mitsunaga seeks to teach Japanese today how to live more fulfilling, more productive, and less troubled lives. The "manual people" of Japan must learn to go beyond their manuals and turn knowledge into wisdom. They must learn fortitude and resolve, must come to realize that they exist not alone but interdependently with others, and must be thankful for the gift of life and make their life an expression of that gratitude.

TENDAI AJARI AND THE COMMON RELIGION OF JAPAN

Hagami, Sakai, and Mitsunaga clearly hold much in common. Regarding contemporary society they are unanimous in their opinion that postwar Japan suffers from moral decline. As we have seen, the view that postwar Japan is a ship afloat without a moral rudder is by no means limited to them. It is a belief widely expressed by politicians, religious practitioners, social commentators, educators, and others. For example, Ishihara Shintaro, an outspoken and controversial mayor of Tokyo, begins his book *Ima tamashii no kyōiku* (今魂の教育, *Now Is the Time for Education of the Soul*) with the following quote from Takada Kōin

(1924–1998), the head priest of Yakushiji (薬師寺): "If things go on like they are, this country will be rich in material goods, but at loss for heart."[95] In her work on the Buddhist lay movement Risshō Kōseikai, Ranjana Mukhopadhyaya writes that founder Niwano Nikkyō (庭野日敬, 1906–1999) also refers to Japan as "materially rich" but "spiritually impoverished."[96] The publications of Tendai and other denominations are also rife with warnings about the dire state of moral affairs in Japan, as we saw in chapter 4. Yamada Etai, who in 1986 was head priest of Tendai, stated that year, "In the forty years since the war, young and old have been blessed as our country once again became a major economy. However, I dread the fact that, while people have material abundance, they have lost richness of heart and that this has led to a deepening and widening trend of turning their backs on morality and ignoring humanity."[97]

Much as Ishihara Shintarō calls for an education of the soul, Hagami, Sakai, and Mitsunaga all place great value on education. Without exception, they critique the current education system for failing to incorporate religion or moral values. In particular, Sakai and Mitsunaga are profoundly concerned about a system that relies on judging people on a scale and on earning specific qualifications that limit from an early age what one might accomplish in life.

Although they are critical, their primary desire is the creation of a system that assures Japan's global survival. The Japanese government, too, has come to emphasize (in rhetoric if not in practice) an education that develops individuals' talents. In this sense, Sakai and the others are putting forth a teaching about contemporary society that mirrors that of the government.

Linked to their emphasis on moral decline is a shared interest in what are commonly accepted as "traditional Japanese values." The greatest difference among the three on this point lies in Hagami's openly nostalgic reflection on the prewar past and his fondness for the emperor. His reflections on the past, however, in many ways mirror Mitsunaga's view that it was the postwar removal of religion from education that led to moral collapse, and Sakai's view that it will take over a hundred years to recover from the postwar decline in values.

This call for a "return" to so-called traditional Japanese values places Hagami, Mitsunaga, and Sakai squarely within the broad public debate over Japanese character known as *nihonjinron,* a form of argument that seeks to define the uniqueness of Japanese character.[98] It can be understood in the contemporary period as an attempt to create or understand Japanese identity following the loss of the primary prewar and wartime symbols of that identity: namely, the emperor system and the extended family.[99] Their participation in this debate is evidence that Hagami, Sakai, and Mitsunaga are consciously tapping into a large vein of popular concern. Their teachings are aimed directly at what they perceive to be a postwar moral vacuum—an existential crisis facing all Japanese.

Their defense of tradition and call for a return to traditional values to ward off moral decline frames their worldview. There are differences in their writings, though, particularly the weight Hagami places on defending Temple Buddhism and attacking sectarianism. This difference can be explained by reference to the times at which they were writing. From the 1950s to the 1970s, when Hagami was training and writing his book, Temple Buddhism was undergoing major changes, along with shifts in population patterns and laws governing religious organizations that created internal discord within Temple Buddhism. Also, traditional institutions were under close public scrutiny for the role they played before and during the war. Hagami's writings speak directly to these early difficulties faced by Temple Buddhism and are especially focused on addressing the criticism of Temple Buddhism as a traditional prewar practice and value system.

Hagami and Mitsunaga are more in line with each other regarding their attitude toward new religious movements. During the first three decades following the war, when Hagami was most active, the New Religions and lay Buddhist movements were growing dramatically. These were seen as a direct threat to Temple Buddhism. Mitsunaga, writing in the late 1990s, after the sarin gas attack by the religious movement Aum Shinrikyō and the rise of the Komeito Party (associated with the Sōka Gakkai) to political power, was addressing a public concerned about the activities of New Religions. He carries on Hagami's attack on NRMs by describing them as vessels of false faith. We saw in previous chapters that Buddhist educators saw a lack of religious education as a reason that people turn to new religious movements, which they clearly saw as dangerous. Although it is only speculation at this point, the fact that Sakai appears to refrain from attacks on the New Religions may be because he was active in Tendai in the 1980s. This was a period when Tendai, under the leadership of Yamada Etai (whom Sakai lists as one of his mentors), developed close relationships with Buddhist lay movements like Risshō Kōseikai.

Despite differences in emphasis, the teachings of Hagami, Sakai, and Mitsunaga are very similar. Stemming directly from their own practice and speaking to salarymen, they teach the need for perseverance or persistence. If the practice of perseverance is made routine, people will be able to endure the rigors of daily life and continue to better themselves and society. All three also place great emphasis on understanding and embodying the idea of interdependence. The self, they argue, is inextricably bound together with family, community and all sentient (and nonsentient) beings. Life, therefore, is to be understood as a gift born of and nurtured within the bonds of interdependence. By living a sincere life and accepting one's circumstances while also striving for even deeper understanding of one's situation, one can realize one's Buddha nature or Buddha-given talents.

Gratitude, a teaching we saw in earlier chapters, is said to naturally develop from and further deepen one's understanding of interdependence. It is also taught by all three. The teachings of perseverance and interdependence do little to challenge the status quo, but they do enable people to accept and cope with their current situation. If anything, their teachings are a reactionary response to the rapid changes occurring in modern Japanese social relations.

The above examination of their teachings brings to light one conspicuous point. From the high value placed on tradition to the teaching of interdependence and the emphasis on perseverance and gratitude, their teachings are strikingly similar to what we saw in previous chapters and to the worldview of the New Religions and lay Buddhist movements as described by Shimazono Susumu, Helen Hardacre, Winston Davis, and others. These groups often emphasize ancestor veneration, which is closely tied to the valorization of the traditional family. They also stress what Ian Reader terms "the primacy of action."[100] This emphasis on learning through practice is very similar to the way Hagami, Mitsunaga, and Sakai maintain that people must get out and practice and not spend time overly analyzing or questioning their situation. Regarding practice, Hardacre describes four "patterns of action" found within New Religions: people as mirrors, gratitude and repayment of favor, striving for sincerity, and paths of self-cultivation.[101] Each of these can also be found in the teaching of the *kaihōgyō* practitioners, and we also saw them in our discussion of Buddhist education in the previous chapters. For example, "paths of self-cultivation" emphasizes learning through participation and through the imitation of role models. As we have seen, role models are especially important to the teachings of Hagami, Sakai, and Mitsunaga, just as they are within Buddhist education.

Tsushima Michihito and Shimazono Susumu point to the vitalistic concept of salvation as the essence of the worldview of the New Religions, and we can also find this in the teachings of Hagami, Mitsunaga, and Sakai. Although they use their concept to describe NRMs, Tsushima and Shimazono derive that concept from a study of the Buddhist lay movement Sōka Gakkai. The vitalistic concept of salvation can be described briefly as follows: (1) the idea of a primary being that bears and nurtures all living beings; (2) confidence in the inherent goodness of the world; (3) exhortations to thank the deity for its bestowal of life; and (4) an optimistic view of salvation easily attainable in this world.[102] I believe that we can find within Hagami, Mitsunaga, and Sakai's teachings on interdependence, sincerity, and persistence (through which the benefits of practice can be realized in this life) a similar teaching. Within their teachings the Buddha, who is manifest in all through Buddha nature, can be seen as the "primary" source that is to be thanked and awakened to, or unified with. This teaching is also found in official pronouncements of the Tendai denomination, including on the sect's website under "teachings," where it states that Saichō "proclaimed that all people are the children of the Buddha."[103]

Moreover, Hagami, Mitsunaga, and Sakai are clear in their view that this world is inherently good, it is possible for people to attain salvation in this very world, and people must live a life of gratitude. Shimazono notes that this move away from merely emphasizing common moral values and toward this vitalistic concept of salvation, in which moral action is inextricably linked to a greater power, is what propelled the growth of many of the New Religions.[104] Hardacre and others also have argued that this worldview of the New Religions is one of the main reasons for their popularity, and it is no doubt one reason for the popularity of the teachings of Hagami, Mitsunaga, and Sakai, as well as the public-facing teachings we found in our examination of Buddhist education.

Given the similarities between their teachings and those of the New Religions, the tenacity with which Hagami and Mitsunaga excoriate them is all the more remarkable. Then again, Hagami and Mitsunaga do not attack the New Religions' worldview so much as their organization and history. The New Religions are seen as divisive, whereas Temple Buddhism is understood as open; they are also viewed as home breakers (splitting family-based religious affiliations) and as politically motivated (seeking secular power). Moreover, they are portrayed as enticing false faith and thus false confidence and hope.

Hagami and Mitsunaga's condemnation of the New Religions can be linked not to a disagreement over the need for spiritually inspired traditional values as a moral foundation for contemporary Japanese but to a different view on just who has the legitimacy necessary to teach such a worldview. The *kaihōgyō* practitioners emphasize history and experience as the key legitimizing factors. They believe that history has shown that the teachings of Temple Buddhism, when embodied through practice, are effective. The New Religions lack history and thus the test of time. The teachings of Temple Buddhism, on the other hand, are, to borrow from Hagami, "old but new" and thus "the real thing."[105]

Hagami, Sakai, and Mitsunaga apply a similar experiential test of authority to Temple Buddhism doctrines as well. In a clear swipe at the intellectualism of sectarian studies, they downplay (but do not deny) the importance of textual study. They see physical practice—embodiment of the teachings, to paraphrase Mitsunaga's knowledge into wisdom principle—as the measure of authority. They are not outright anti-intellectual (although given Sakai's admitted aversion to reading, he comes close). Each one has gone through a significant amount of training in sectarian studies. They each maintain, however, that only through practice can the classical teachings be truly understood. It is helpful to view them as representative of one faction within contemporary Tendai (and within contemporary Temple Buddhism more broadly). They are the practitioner-monk faction and stand in tension with the scholar-monk faction. To better understand the development of contemporary Japanese Buddhism, we must begin to explore the various factions interacting within Temple Buddhism today. Other factional dividing lines that share similarities across the various denominations of Temple Buddhism include the on-mountain and off-mountain factions (those representing the denomination headquarters and those representing small local temples), the Honzan (denomination headquarters) and denomination university factions, the lay-family background and temple-family background factions, and the sectarian studies and propagation factions. Each faction is in constant interaction with the others, and overlap often exists.

Exploring the multifaceted nature of the teaching and teachings of Temple Buddhism can help to broaden our understanding of what Temple Buddhism is today and what it will likely become in the future. For now, we have introduced the teaching and teachings of Temple Buddhism through an examination of Buddhist education and the writings of the *ajari*. That examination has shown how a certain set of teachings and practices that are designed to be easily grasped and embodied by lay practitioners are shared across different groups within Temple Buddhism—from Buddhist kindergartens to elite practitioners—and how those same teachings are echoed in the teachings of Buddhist lay movements and many new religious movements.

6

CONCLUDING THOUGHTS

When I wrote my first book on Temple Buddhism in Japan, the priests I worked with told me they were worried I was airing their dirty laundry. At the same time, though, they thanked me for publishing my research: they said they could not dare to write about anything contemporary. That was over twenty years ago. Today, especially in the field of Buddhist education, my colleagues at Buddhist universities in Japan are publishing critical work that often challenges the very institutions they work for. In many ways, I believe, this highlights major changes going on in Temple Buddhism today. Buddhist institutions are working, often in an uncoordinated and experimental fashion, to make themselves relevant to the times they live in. They have created new burial formats and new memorial societies, and they have begun chaplaincy programs. And as we have seen throughout this book, they have developed new curricula at their schools and engaged in ceaseless efforts to make the teachings of Buddhism accessible to a broad audience.

I began this book by pointing out some generally well-known flaws in the study of Buddhism. I am the first to admit that I was not presenting much that is radically new. The field has grown considerably since I first began this project twenty years ago. But I also believe those issues in the field's past remain in our system, even if only as ghosts haunting how we see the field. My goal is to urge us to look at Buddhist institutions in all their raw, messy, and very human nature and not to focus solely on texts and broad assumptions in the field about what is and is not "real" Buddhism.

No one book can capture all the many activities and developments taking place in Temple Buddhism today. In this book I have tried to show the ways Buddhist teachings are taught, what teachings are most often taught (especially to a lay audience), and how what is taught in Buddhist education does not differ significantly from what some of the most popular Buddhist preachers teach through their sermons and writings. These teachings have been called "Buddhism light" by some, but they are the popular, accessible teachings that reach large audiences. They represent Temple Buddhism as it is lived today. We also learned that what is taught tends to be very similar to the teachings of Japan's New Religions and, in particular, Buddhist lay movements, as defined by Hardacre, Shimazono, and others.

Engaging Temple Buddhism as a lived tradition, as I have tried to do here, allows us to examine the various, at times disconnected, ways that institutions of Temple Buddhism seek to maintain and rethink their teachings. It also opens the way to think about who is taught and where instruction takes place. This approach reveals many of the factors taken into consideration by Buddhist institutions as they seek change or have change forced upon them by shifting political structures and legal codes. This includes things as varied as government modifications to the education system, contemporary debates about material versus spiritual wealth, and worries over Japan's global status. This approach also draws our attention to a growing need identified by Buddhist educators over the last one hundred years: the need to expand their teaching. Buddhist institutions moved from teaching only those who were bound for the priesthood to teaching the general public, and in so doing, the goals and contents of teaching shifted. This may be why the teachings observed in Buddhist education (kindergarten through college) are similar to the teachings of the *ajari,* new religious movements, and lay Buddhist movements, all of which direct their teachings at lay audiences.

All of this is not to say that textual study of doctrine has somehow disappeared from Japan. Traditional doctrinal studies is alive and well in Japanese Temple Buddhism today. Buddhist universities still teach textual studies, and training temples still train young priests in ritual and the doctrines that underpin ritual. For a more complete understanding of the teaching and teachings of Temple Buddhism, an examination of denomination research centers, *kangakuin,* and other institutions designed to guard orthodoxy, as well as college courses on doctrine, need to be examined further. What is clear from what we have seen is that at Buddhist higher education institutions, how Buddhism is taught, and what is taught as Buddhism, has changed throughout the modern period in reaction to changes in law and government policy and to those within Temple Buddhism who are seeking to make Buddhism relevant to contemporary Japan.

It is clear from the research presented here that Buddhist institutions have put considerable effort into making their teachings accessible. Much attention has been paid to outward-facing, public teachings. From Buddhist kindergartens to Buddhist universities a similar set of outward-facing teachings is taught. Teachings emphasized by Buddhist educators are also reflected in the public teachings of advanced ascetic practitioners such as the *ajari* discussed in the previous chapter. The teachings of these elite practitioners, much like the teachings in Buddhist educational institutions, hold many similarities to the teachings of Buddhist lay movements and New Religions that developed during the modern period. Teachings such as interdependence (often highlighting the connection between family, ancestors, community), symbiosis, sincerity, gratitude, empathy, compassion, thankfulness, and the need to forget self and benefit others play a major role in Temple Buddhism education from kindergarten to university. Other common teachings include taking pride in tradition, self-reliance, reverential awe, and seeing life as a gift.

These outward-facing teachings are matched throughout Buddhist education to a number of different practices designed to allow the teachings to be learned by people of all ages and capacities. The practices tend to rely on the idea of persistence—that is, if you practice consistently and persevere, you will come to embody the teachings even if you do not fully understand the practices' more complex doctrinal foundations. Practices most frequently seen include greetings, the use of role models, and service. They all tend to emphasize process over goal. The key of all of these practices is to embody the teachings. In many cases, such as at the kindergartens discussed earlier, those practicing are not even aware that they are engaged in practice. They are learning through sentiment education in which the teachings are expressed through the atmosphere created by the institution. In the end, practice is understood as living the teachings, of turning knowledge into wisdom through experience, with the goal of making the ideal a reality.

To truly capture the teaching and teachings of Temple Buddhism would require at least another volume. Left uncovered here is an examination of the various Buddhist propagation societies run by every denomination at the local, regional, and national levels. These societies meet regularly to listen to sermons, study past sermons, and learn how to write new ones and deliver them effectively. There is a small industry of publications and materials designed to support priests in writing sermons. Sermon collections are available for every denomination and generic sermon samples can easily be found in industry resources such as the trade journal for priests, *Jimon Kōryū*.

Gender is another area left mostly untouched in this examination. Temple wives play a significant role in interacting with laity, and although they are not frequently called on to give sermons, they are often the ones lay members turn to for advice. What kind of advice do they give? What kind of training do they receive, if any, to give advice? Jessie Starling's recent book *Guardians of the Buddha's Home: Domestic Religion in Contemporary Jōdo Shinshū* is a great first step in understanding this aspect of contemporary Temple Buddhism. The role of nuns in disseminating Buddhist teachings also needs to be examined. In the future, I hope to write about the famous author and Tendai nun Setouchi Jakuchō (瀬戸内寂聴) and others who have published widely and had an impact on Buddhism today, including on the public-facing teachings that are described in this volume. And, of course, the teachings themselves can be gendered. We saw at least some of this in the chapter on moral education, but there is much more that can be done.

In taking the "Buddhism is what Buddhism does" approach in the study of contemporary Temple Buddhism, actually being on-site to observe practice is important. The work presented here could have been stronger with extensive fieldwork to interview parents and children attending Buddhist K–12 institutions as well as those attending higher education. Unfortunately, I was only able to conduct initial fieldwork before becoming bogged down in administrative roles at my university and family roles at home. I can only hope that someone else takes up the baton and takes the time to do more extensive fieldwork to understand how the teachings and practices outlined here are understood by their target audience and whether or not they play a role in their lives beyond their encounters with them in school.

While I recognize these gaps in what is presented here, it is my hope that the reader comes away with a better understanding of some of the most broadly taught teachings of Temple Buddhism today and how those teachings have come to be taught as they are.

NOTES

Chapter 1: Buddhism Is What Buddhism Does

Epigraph: Hagami, *Kaihōgyō no kokoro,* 60.

1. McMahan, *The Making of Buddhist Modernism,* 179.

Chapter 2: Buddhism for Children?

Epigraph: Nakano Kindergarten, http://kosodate-web.com/nakanoy/naiyou/naiyou.html (accessed August 6, 2008).

1. Holloway, "The Role of Religious Beliefs in Early Childhood Education," 2.

2. Nihon Bukkyō Hoikukyōkai (Japan Buddhist Nursery and Kindergarten Association), "Nihon Bukkyō Hoikukyōkai ni tsuite." The number of Buddhist facilities associated with NBHK dropped to 1,050 on the most recent listing (accessed May 13, 2022). All translations are mine unless otherwise noted.

3. Mochida, *Bukkyō to kyōiku,* 246. Yasui Akio provides a complete list from a 1978 NBHK survey that includes a denominational breakdown. See Yasui, "Yōchien / hoikuen ni okeru bukkyō kyōiku," 393. Morinaga Shōshin writes that most temples engage in social welfare activities. He provides survey data from the Nichiren denomination for 1961 and 1971 showing that *yōchien* and *hoikuen* comprised 79.8 percent of all social welfare activities in 1961 and 26.2 percent ten years later (with facilities for elder care, scouting, and cram schools making large gains in the interim). In a Sōtō denomination survey from 1965, 35.3 percent of social welfare activities were daycare facilities. Morinaga, "Bukkyōsha no shakai fukushi katsudō," 374–375.

4. Wakakusa Yōchien, "Kōchō no kangae."

5. Kathleen Uno discusses the reasoning behind age six becoming the line between early childhood and school age. Uno, "Civil Society, State, and Institutions for Young Children in Modern Japan," 170–171.

6. Ministry of Education, Culture, Sports, Science and Technology (hereafter MEXT) and the Ministry of Health, Labor and Welfare jointly introduced a new category of early childhood education in 2006, the *nintei kodomoen,* which is essentially an amalgamation of *hoikuen* and *yōchien.* According to Hayashi and Tobin, movement in this category has been slow. See Hayashi and Tobin, "Continuity and Change in Japanese Preschool Education," 36.

To avoid confusion with this new category, I will use the Japanese terms *yōchien* and *hoikuen.* However, works cited that use the term "kindergarten" will be left as they are.

7. Hayashi and Tobin, "Continuity and Change in Japanese Preschool Education," 35. Even as the experience is becoming similar there are still several differences, in particular hours of operation, child-to-caregiver ratios, and—perhaps most important—the age of the children accepted, with *hoikuen* accepting children from age zero and *yōchien* accepting children from age three. Ozaki, *Kyōikuhō kōgi,* 273.

8. Tobin, Wu, and Davidson, *Preschool in Three Cultures,* 44–46.

9. Wollons, "The Black Forest in a Bamboo Garden," 7; Hendry, "Kindergartens and the Transition from Home to School Education," 53; Ieda, "Bukkyō hōiku no genjo to mirai," 482.

10. Uno, "Civil Society, State, and Institutions for Young Children in Modern Japan," 176.

11. Ideno, "Yōchien ni okeru jōsō kyōiku," 73.

12. Wollons, "The Black Forest in a Bamboo Garden," 6.

13. Hendry, *Becoming Japanese,* 17.

14. Education scholar Kobayashi Tetsuya also discusses this emphasis of the Gakusei. Kobayashi, "Tokugawa Education as a Foundation of Modern Education in Japan," 297. For general information on the early history of early childhood education and care, see MEXT, "Hakusho," http://mext.go.jp/b_menu/hakusho/html/others/detail/1317591.htm (accessed October 18, 2017).

15. Okano and Tsuchiya, *Education in Contemporary Japan,* 15. The "three Rs" refers to reading, writing, and arithmetic.

16. Uno, "Civil Society, State, and Institutions for Young Children in Modern Japan," 175.

17. Naka, "Hoiku no rekishi," 355, 361, 363.

18. MEXT, "Hakusho," http://www.mext.go.jp/b_menu/hakusho/html/others/details/1317510.htm, and "Ministry of Education, Culture, Sports, Science, and Technology Hakusho," http://www.mext.go.jp/b_menu/hakusho/html/hpab201701/1389013_022.pdf, p. 452 (both accessed October 18, 2017).

19. Ieda, "Bukkyō hōiku no genjo to mirai," 482.

20. Nishida, "A Chrysanthemum in the Garden"; Holloway, *Contested Childhood,* 139.

21. Wollons, "The Black Forest in a Bamboo Garden," 13–27.

22. The Imperial Rescript on Education is discussed in chapter 4.

23. Wollons, "The Black Forest in a Bamboo Garden," 9.

24. Ideno, "Yōchien ni okeru jōsō kyōiku," 72.

25. Isoyama, "Bukkyō hoiku no rekishi," 373. See also Imoto, "The Japanese Preschool System in Transition"; and Nakakida, "Early Childhood Education and Care Curriculum in Japan."

26. Naka, "Hoiku no rekishi," 355–359.

27. Nakano Kindergarten, "Naiyō."

28. Okano and Tsuchiya, *Education in Contemporary Japan,* 14.

29. See Khan, *Japanese Moral Education Past and Present.*

30. Kobayashi, "Tokugawa Education as a Foundation of Modern Education in Japan," 293.

31. Ieda, "Bukkyō hōiku no genjo to mirai," 482. See also Nihon Bukkyō Shakai Fukushi Gakkai, *Bukkyō Shakai Fukushi Jiten,* 22.

32. Isoyama, "Bukkyō hoiku no rekishi," 374.

33. Ibid., 375. For more on *haibutsu kishaku,* see Ketelaar, *Of Heretics and Martyrs in Meiji Japan.*

34. Yoshida, *Nihon kindai bukkyō shakaishi kenkyū.*

35. Nishida, "A Chrysanthemum in the Garden," 284.

36. Isoyama, "Bukkyō hoiku no rekishi," 367.

37. Ibid., 367.

38. Mochida, *Bukkyō to kyōiku,* 119.

39. *Japan Times,* "Ozawa Lashes Out with Scathing Remarks on Christianity."

40. Yoshida, *Nihon kindai bukkyō shakaishi kenkyū,* 320.

41. Ibid.

42. Isoyama, "Bukkyō hoiku no rekishi," 376.

43. Ieda, "Bukkyō hōiku no genjo to mirai," 482–483. See also Isoyama, "Bukkyō hoiku no rekishi," 374; Yasui, "Yōchien / hoikuen ni okeru bukkyō kyōiku," 392; and Saitō, *Kindai Bukkyō kyōikushi,* 67–68.

44. Nihon Bukkyō Shakai Fukushi Gakkai, *Bukkyō Shakai Fukushi Jiten,* 277.

45. Saitō, *Kindai Bukkyō kyōikushi,* 69–70.

46. Ibid., 74.

47. Wollons, "The Black Forest in a Bamboo Garden," 30.

48. Saitō, *Kindai Bukkyō kyōikushi,* 71.

49. Isoyama, "Bukkyō hoiku no rekishi," 377.

50. Ibid., 371.

51. A major set of revisions to the Fundamental Law on Education was passed in 2006. Among these changes was the addition of the clause "general knowledge regarding religion." This clause implies the need for Japanese citizens to have a basic understanding of religion. See McNeill and Lebowitz, "Hammer Down the Educational Nail." It does not appear to have affected the funding issue for Religious Juridical Persons that run early childhood education facilities.

52. Suemitsu, "Kyōiku seisaku to Bukkyō," 493.

53. *Gekkan Jūshoku,* "Shūkyō hōjin ritsu yōchien no genjō to mondai," 21. This article also points out that another strike against Buddhist schools was that Christian schools tended to be part of escalator systems in which entrance into the kindergarten led to entrance into the elementary school and so on up to college.

54. Chūgai Nippō, "Rensai Shinsō."

55. *Gekkan Jūshoku,* "Shūkyō hōjin ritsu yōchien no genjō to mondai."

56. Watanabe, "Jiin keiei to zaisei mondai," 145.

57. Satō, "Chiiki shakai to henka," 131.

58. Mochida, *Bukkyō to kyōiku,* 120.

59. Satō, "Chiiki shakai to henka," 131–132.

60. See Mori, "Gendai ni okeru dendō no imi," 219.

61. These regulations include the 1947 Fundamental Law on Education, under which *yōchien* were formally brought into the education system in line with elementary, junior high, and high schools as well as the 1949 law governing the licensing of educators in which *yōchien* instructors were required to have college-level training for licensure. Ideno, "Yōchien ni okeru jōsō kyōiku," 74.

62. Mochida, *Bukkyō to kyōiku,* 249.

63. Zaidan hōjin zen nihon bukkyōkai, "Tekisetsu naru shūkyō kyōiku jitsugen no tame no kyōiku kihonhō daikyūjō kaisei no kansuru onegai," 4. This view is found throughout contemporary Buddhist literature; it is not limited in any way to this organization.

64. Hoiku Plus, "Hoiku Hōhō."

65. Mochida, *Bukkyō to kyōiku,* 238.

66. The online material regarding curriculum and programming of the following universities and junior colleges was reviewed: Ashikaga Junior College 足利短期大学, Chikushi Jogakuen University 筑紫女学園大学, Hakodate Ohtani Junior College 函館大谷短期大学, Higashi Kyushu Junior College 東九州短期大学, Hosen Gakuen College 宝仙学園短期大学, Jin'ai Women's College 仁愛女子短期大学, Kacho College 華頂短期大学, Komazawa Women's Junior College 駒沢女子短期大学, Kyoto Women's University 駒沢女子大学, Musashino University 武蔵野大学, Osaka Ohtani University 大阪大谷大学, Otani University Junior College 大阪大谷短期大学, Rissho University 立正大学, Ryūkoko University Junior College 龍谷短期大学, Seika Women's Junior College 精華女子短期大学, Seitoku University 聖徳大学, Seiwa Gakuen Junior College 聖和学園短期大学, Shukutoku Junior College 淑徳短期大学, Taishō University 大正大学, Takada Junior College 高田短期大学, Tokoha Gakuen Junior College 常葉学園短期大学, and Tsurumi Junior College 鶴見大学短期大学.

67. Tsurumi Daigaku, "Daigaku gakubu—Tandaibu."

68. Jin-ai University, "Department"; Seiwa Gakuen Tankidaigaku, "Hoiku gakka."

69. Kyoto Joshi Daigaku, "Hōshin."

70. Osaka Ohtani University, "Kengaku no seishin."

71. Nihon Bukkyō Hoikukyōkai, *Kodomo no kokoro wo sodateyō,* 27.

72. Hayashi and Tobin, "Continuity and Change in Japanese Preschool Education," 40.

73. Ideno makes a similar claim about how teachers learn to teach sentiment education on the job and not within their college curriculum. Ideno, "Yōchien ni okeru jōsō kyōiku," 81.

74. Bukkyō hoiku kyōkai, *Heisei 24 nendo jigyo hōkuku.*

75. Yasui, "Yōchien / hoikuen ni okeru bukkyō kyōiku," 389.

76. The Chūō Kyōiku Shingikai is a government advisory group under MEXT. This goal is part of a larger plan to reform the Fundamental Law on Education; see MEXT, "Atarashii jidai ni fusawahi kyōikukihonhō to kyōiku shinkō kihonkeikaku no arikata ni tsuite (Chūkan hōkoku gaiyō)."

77. Ibid.

78. Zaidan hōjin zen nihon bukkyōkai, "Tekisetsu naru shūkyō kyōiku jitsugen no tame no kyōiku kihonhō daikyūjō kaisei no kansuru onegai." See also Fujidō, "Shūkyō to kyōiku," 238.

79. See Ozaki, *Kyōikuhō kōgi,* 63–66.

80. See, for example, Mochida, *Bukkyō to kyōiku,* 20.

81. Miyasaka, *Bukkyō ga skū nihon no kyōiku,* 142; Mochida, *Bukkyō to kyōiku,* 10–31.

82. Nihon Bukkyō Hoikukyōkai, *Kodomo no kokoro wo sodateyō,* 6.

83. Hendry, *Becoming Japanese,* 54; also discussed in Tobin, Wu, and Davidson, *Preschool in Three Cultures.*

84. Murakami, "Jiri rita."

85. Holloway, "The Role of Religious Beliefs in Early Childhood Education," 8–9; Holloway, *Contested Childhood,* 161. This is also confirmed by Ideno. Ideno, "Yōchien ni okeru jōsō kyōiku," 76.

86. Tobin, Wu, and Davidson, *Preschool in Three Cultures,* 31.

87. Yasui, "Yōchien / hoikuen ni okeru bukkyō kyōiku," 390.

88. Romanizations follow NBHK readings, which are designed to be nondenominational. Note that the school year in Japan starts in April.

89. Nihon Bukkyō Hoikukyōkai, "Kyōkai hōshin."

90. See Hardacre, *Kurozumikyō and the New Religions of Japan;* Reader, *Religion in Contemporary Japan.*

91. Holloway, *Contested Childhood,* 161.

92. Nihon Bukkyō Hoikukyōkai, *Kodomo no kokoro wo sodateyō,* 31.

93. Tachibana Hoikuen (たちばな保育園); Myōjōkai, "Nursery." A similar set of vows can be seen at other Buddhist facilities. See, for example, Shiroishi Yōchien, "Seimei sonchō no hoiku." A variation that adds the line "We are children of the Buddha" can be found at Fuki Yōchien's website, under kyōiku rinen (Educational Ideals), http://www.cc9.ne.jp/~fuki-you/sub4.html (accessed September 18, 2008).

94. "Nono-sama" (or "Nono-san") is a term used to refer to the Buddha, the dead, and spirits by children.

95. The webpages of the following Buddhist ECEC were examined for this chapter: Azuma Yōchien (あずま幼稚園), Bukkyō Daigaku Fuzoku Yōchien (佛教大学附属幼稚園), Chōshi Yōchien (銚子幼稚園), Fuki Yōchien (吹上幼稚園), Hakodate Daisan Ōtani Yōchien (函館第三大谷幼稚園), Hannō Yōchien (はんのう幼稚園), Hikari Yōchien (光幼稚園), Kōrin Yōchien (光輪幼稚園), Kōzenji Yōchien (光禅寺幼稚園), Miyama Yōchien (みやま幼稚園), Musahino Yōchien (武蔵野幼稚園), Myōjo Yōchien (明星幼稚園), Nadeshiko Yōchien (なだしこ幼稚園), Nakano Yōchien (なかの幼稚園), Ōkurayama Anka Yōchien (大倉山アンカ幼稚園), Ōmori Minori Yōchien (大森みのり幼稚園), Padoma Yōchien (パドマ幼稚園), Sakuragi Hanazono Yōchien (桜木花園幼稚園), Sapporo Ōtani Yōchien (札幌大谷幼稚園), Tachibana Hoikuen (たちばな保育園), Taishi Yōchien (太子幼稚園), Takada Yōchien (高田幼稚園), Wakakusa Hoikuen (若草幼稚園), Wakyō Yōchien (和敬幼稚園), Yanagigawa Minori Yōchien (柳川みのり幼稚園), Yawata Hanazono Yōchien (八幡花園幼稚園).

96. For more on *omamori,* see Mendes, "Ancient Magic and Modern Accessories."

97. Nihon Bukkyō Hoikukyōkai, *Kodomo no kokoro wo sodateyō,* 53.

98. Ibid., 32.

99. Shibamoto, "Yōchien no kyōikukatei no henkan ni kansuru ichi kosatsu," 7.

100. Wakakusa Yōchien, "Shizen no setsuri wo manabu yōchien toshite."

101. Covell, *Japanese Temple Buddhism.*

102. Ideno, "Yōchien ni okeru jōsō kyōiku," 76.

103. Sapporo Ōtani Yōchien, "Ōtani Yōchien nitsuite."

104. Hendry, *Becoming Japanese,* 74.

105. Holloway, *Contested Childhood,* 162.

106. Kōrin Yōchien, "Q&A."

107. Minori Yōchien, "About."

108. Hayashi and Tobin, "Continuity and Change in Japanese Preschool Education," 33.

109. Holloway, *Contested Childhood,* 159.

110. Mombushō, *Yōchien kyōiku yōryō* (1989), 3, cited in Lewis, *Educating Hearts and Minds,* 30.

111. Borup, *Japanese Rinzai Zen,* 120.

112. Holloway, *Contested Childhood,* 141.

113. Nihon Bukkyō Hoikukyōkai, *Kodomo no kokoro wo sodateyō,* 25.

Chapter 3: Buddhist Colleges and Universities

Epigraph: Okamoto, "Kore kara no daigaku no kyōiku to shūmon deshi yōsei ni tsuite," 3–4.

1. The text they cite is the *Shugeishuchiinshiki narabinijo* (綜芸種智院式并序).
2. Kōyasan Daigaku, *Heisei 22 nendo Kōyasan Daigaku ni okeru genjō to kadai,* 3.
3. Hori, "Gakusō kyōiku no shisetsu," 260–262.
4. Saitō, "Nihon bukkyō kyōiku," 273.
5. Hori Ichirō ("Gakusō kyōiku no shisetsu," 264) lists eight Tendai *danrin* and notes that Kichijōji was the most famous Sōtō *danrin.* And on pp. 264–265 he lists eighteen Kanto area *danrin* belonging to the Jōdo denomination.
6. Taishō Daigaku Gojūnenshi Hensan Iinkai, *Taishō daigaku gojūnen ryakushi,* 81.
7. Ibid., 79.
8. Nakai, "Shumongakko kyōiku seido no kindaika katei," 436.
9. In *The Invention of Religion in Japan,* Josephson-Storm draws our attention to changes within the national education system designed to downplay Buddhist and Confucian teachings in public education and to focus on Western sciences. Buddhist institutions were under pressure to offer curricular changes similar to those taking place in the broader education system of the time.
10. Taishō Daigaku Gojūnenshi Hensan Iinkai, *Taishō daigaku gojūnen ryakushi,* 8–9.
11. Grand Council of State (Daijōkan) Proclamation 322, in Shingonshū Buzanha Kyōikujigyōdan, *Buzan kyōikuzaidan shi,* 33.
12. Ketelaar, *Of Heretics and Martyrs in Meiji Japan,* 99.
13. Ejima, "Kindai nihon kōtō kyōiku ni okeru kyōiku to kyōka," 8. Ejima gives as an example of these changes Jōdo Shinshū Honganji branch's addition of history, National Learning, Confucianism, and anti–false beliefs education to their *gakurin* curriculum.
14. Hardacre, *Shintō and the State,* 43. Other layers of teachings were added as the program progressed. See Ketelaar, *Of Heretics and Martyrs in Meiji Japan,* 106.
15. For example, Miura points to Buddhist efforts to offer up the King's Law / Buddha's Law (Shobō-Buppō) argument against Christianity. Miura, "'Gakushū' sareru Bukkyō," 206.
16. Ketelaar, *Of Heretics and Martyrs in Meiji Japan,* 105.
17. For more on this system see also Tanigawa, "The Age of Teaching."
18. Annaka, "Kindai ni okeru nichiren kyōdan no shitei kyōiku," 135.
19. Nakai, "Shumongakko kyōiku seido no kindaika katei," 438.
20. Shingonshū Buzanha Kyōikujigyōdan, *Buzan kyōikuzaidan shi,* 25.
21. Ejima, "Sōryo wo sodateru daigaku e," 71.
22. For more on Sensōji see Hur, *Prayer and Play in Late Tokugawa Japan.*
23. Taishō Daigaku Gojūnenshi Hensan Iinkai, *Taishō daigaku gojūnen ryakushi,* 100. Tanigawa Yutaka draws our attention to the ways in which local temples, tasked with this mission of propagation for the state, were often at odds with local public schools over funding and that, indeed, some school districts made use of temples for their schools, in some cases drawing on the history of *terakoya* (schools for commoners that were widespread in the preceding Edo period). Tanigawa, "The Age of Teaching," 91–93.
24. Under the 1872 Ministry of Doctrine Notice No. 4 (Kyōbushō tasshigaki daiyongō). The "one school, one leader" system was an attempt by the state to streamline control over religious institutions.

25. Order No. 1 from Ministry of Interior 5 (Naimushō bo daiichigō tasshi). Shingonshū Buzanha Kyōikujigyōdan, *Buzan kyōikuzaidan shi,* 34.
26. Abe, "Meiji ni okeru Shingonshū no kyōiku karikyuramu," 203.
27. Hayashi, "Religious Studies and Religiously Affiliated Universities," 167.
28. Nakai, "Shumongakko kyōiku seido no kindaika katei," 438.
29. Takeda, "School Education and Religion in Japan," 217.
30. Saitō, "Nihon bukkyō kyōiku," 296. See also Minagawa, "Bukkyō ni okeru dendō to kyōiku," 113.
31. Ejima, "Kindai nihon kōtō kyōiku ni okeru kyōiku to kyōka," 17.
32. Hayashi, "Religious Studies and Religiously Affiliated Universities," 168.
33. Saitō, *Kindai Bukkyō kyōikushi,* 218.
34. Cited in Saitō, "Nihon bukkyō kyōiku," 310.
35. Takeda, "School Education and Religion in Japan," 219. Takeda does not give the name of the vice minister cited. There were many laws passed and actions taken by the Japanese government to control or eliminate faith healing, fortune-telling, and other such practices, along with New Religions that were determined to be an ideological threat. See, for example, Josephson-Storm, *The Invention of Religion in Japan,* 164–191. See also Garon, *Molding Japanese Minds.* In the case of Ōmotokyō, which was deemed a severe ideological threat, the government used dynamite to destroy its headquarters. Ooms, *Women and Millenarian Protest in Meiji Japan.*
36. Takeda, "School Education and Religion in Japan," 222.
37. Ejima, "Sōryo wo sodateru daigaku e," 73.
38. Ejima, "Kindai nihon kōtō kyōiku ni okeru kyōiku to kyōka," 24.
39. Ibid., 24.
40. Stone, "A Vast and Grave Task," 220–221.
41. Ejima, "Sōryo wo sodateru daigaku e," 72.
42. Stone, "A Vast and Grave Task," 223.
43. Ejima, "Kindai nihon kōtō kyōiku ni okeru kyōiku to kyōka," 24–25.
44. Ejima, "Sōryo wo sodateru daigaku e," 73.
45. Shingonshū Buzanha Kyōikujigyōdan, *Buzan kyōikuzaidan shi,* 48.
46. Ejima, "Sōryo wo sodateru daigaku c," 73.
47. Hayashi, "Religious Studies and Religiously Affiliated Universities," 184.
48. Saitō, *Kindai Bukkyō kyōikushi,* 31.
49. Covell and Rowe, "Round-Table," 433.
50. Annaka, "Kindai ni okeru nichiren kyōdan no shitei kyōiku," 149.
51. Shingonshū Buzanha Kyōikujigyōdan, *Buzan kyōikuzaidan shi,* 58.
52. The document is titled "Sōtōshū shōkaku no hitsuyō nitsuite." Saitō, *Kindai Bukkyō kyōikushi,* 27.
53. Harada, "Taishō shindaigakurei to shūmondaigaku," 138–139.
54. Ejima, "Sōryo wo sodateru daigaku e," 73–74.
55. Takada, "Bukkyō (Shinshū) to kindai kenkyū sosetsu," 210.
56. Ibid., 210. See also Ward, "Genzai to mirai"; and Ejima, "Sōryo wo sodateru daigaku e," 74.
57. Taishō Daigaku Gojūnenshi Hensan Iinkai, *Taishō daigaku gojūnen ryakushi,* 271.
58. Jaffe, *Neither Monk nor Layman.* See also Miura, "'Gakushū' sareru Bukkyō," 210.
59. Miura, "'Gakushū' sareru Bukkyō," 211.

60. Taishō Daigaku Gojūnenshi Hensan Iinkai, *Taishō daigaku gojūnen ryakushi,* 112.

61. Saitō, *Kindai Bukkyō kyōikushi,* 27.

62. *Todanjūkai* and *nyūdankanjō* are two basic initiation rites.

63. Tendaishūmuchō, *Tendaishū shūkishū,* 502. See also Covell and Rowe, "Round-Table," 462–463.

64. Taishō Daigaku Gojūnenshi Hensan Iinkai, *Taishō daigaku gojūnen ryakushi,* 116. See also Nakai, "Shumongakko kyōiku seido no kindaika katei," 440.

65. Kōyasan Daigaku, "Heisei 23 Rinen."

66. Shingonshū Buzanha Kyōikujigyōdan, *Buzan kyōikuzaidan shi,* 35.

67. Abe, "Meiji ni okeru Shingonshū no kyōiku karikyuramu," 204.

68. Ibid., 205.

69. Saitō, "Nihon bukkyō kyōiku," 291.

70. Nakai, "Shumongakko kyōiku seido no kindaika katei," 435.

71. Taishō Daigaku Gojūnenshi Hensan Iinkai, *Taishō daigaku gojūnen ryakushi,* 137. Hereafter, page numbers for this source are given parenthetically in the text.

72. Taishō remains on land donated for use by the Jōdo denomination, which has allowed Jōdo to maintain a level of power the other denominations do not enjoy.

73. Saitō, "Nihon bukkyō kyōiku," 291. See also Nakai, "Shumongakko kyōiku seido no kindaika katei," 436.

74. Annaka, "Kindai ni okeru nichiren kyōdan no shitei kyōiku," 136.

75. Miura, "'Gakushū' sareru Bukkyō," 203.

76. Shingonshū Buzanha Kyōikujigyōdan, *Buzan kyōikuzaidan shi,* 44.

77. Ibid., 55.

78. Abe, "Meiji ni okeru Shingonshū no kyōiku karikyuramu," 211.

79. Ibid., 215–216.

80. For example, Taishō University began with five academic departments and a research department. See Taishō Daigaku Gojūnenshi Hensan Iinkai, *Taishō daigaku gojūnen ryakushi,* 334–335.

81. Hasegawa, "Shūkyōka karikyuramu ni okeru jissenteki kamoku no kōka," 107.

82. Miura, "'Gakushū' sareru Bukkyō," 243.

83. For example, at Taishō University, the journals *Sangegakuhō* and *Tendaishū Gyōshō* came out and in 1916 the *Sangegakkai* (a scholarly conference) was founded (these represent the Tendai denomination's activities at Taishō). Taishō Daigaku Gojūnenshi Hensan Iinkai, *Taishō daigaku gojūnen ryakushi,* 134–135.

84. Miura, "'Gakushū' sareru Bukkyō," 238.

85. Only in the last ten to fifteen years (ca. 2005) have Buddhist studies programs and Buddhist denominations begun to take seriously the training of women as priests. This shift is directly related to shrinking family sizes, which have left some temples without sons to take over.

86. Covell and Rowe, "Round-Table," 430–431.

87. Taishō Daigaku, *Taishō Daiguku Tenken Hyōka Hōkokusho,* 1.

88. Covell and Rowe, "Round-Table," 438. Translations for terms used have been altered from the original translation to reflect the terminology used throughout this book and by Taishō University.

89. Okamoto, "Kore kara no daigaku no kyōiku to shūmon deshi yōsei ni tsuite," 3.

90. Ibid., 3–4.

91. Tada, "Bukkyōkei daigaku ni okeru shōraizō no kōkei (Taishō daigaku no bawai)," 42–43.

92. Ibid., 44.

93. Okamoto, "Kore kara no daigaku no kyōiku to shūmon deshi yōsei ni tsuite," 4.

94. Komine, "Bukkyōkyōiku no arikata nitsuite," 9.

95. Covell and Rowe, "Round-Table," 444.

96. Ibid., 445.

97. For more on clerical marriage see Covell, *Japanese Temple Buddhism;* Jaffe, *Neither Monk nor Layman;* and Kawahashi, "Jizoku (Priests' Wives) in Soto Zen Buddhism."

98. Covell and Rowe, "Round-Table," 440.

99. Shioiri, "Taisho Daigaku ni okeru bukkyou kyouiku to NCC," 15.

100. Ibid., 15.

101. Ibid.

102. Ibid.

103. Ibid., 16.

104. Taishō Daigaku, "NCC no senmonkamoku no risshū."

105. Taishō Daigaku, *Taishō Daigaku ni taisuru Daigaku Hyōka (Ninshō Hyōka) kekka,* 3.

106. Ibid., 5.

107. Ibid., 12.

108. Taishō Daigaku, "Undergraduate."

109. Covell and Rowe, "Round-Table," 435.

110. Ibid., 431.

111. Rissho University, "About Rissho Univ." See also *Jimon Kōryū,* "Jiin ya shitei ni totte ima, shūmon daigaku to wa nanika wo shiru tokushū 3."

112. Hanazono Daigaku, *Heisei 25 nendo Daiguku Kikan betsu ninshō hyōka,* 1.

113. Taishō Daigaku, *Taishō Daigaku ni taisuru Daigaku Hyōka (Ninshō Hyōka) kekka,* 2.

114. Ibid., 3.

115. Ibid.

116. Ibid., 4.

117. These ideals are explained in depth elsewhere in the report (see pp. 4, 26). These four also are explained in English on the university home page as follows: "Compassion—To show love and kindness for all forms of life, The Middle Path—develop a free mind and live life following the middle path, or the right way, Coexistence—To coexist with others and work towards achieving our goals together, Self-Reliance—To search for the truth and learn to rely on oneself in life." Taishō Daigaku, "School Philosophy."

118. Nara, "Daigaku ni okeru Bukkyōkyōiku," 404.

119. *Jimon Kōryū,* "Jiin ya shitei ni totte ima, shūmon daigaku to wa nanika wo shiru tokushū," 74. This viewpoint is shared by others, as we shall see in chapter 4.

120. Nara, "Daigaku ni okeru Bukkyōkyōiku," 405.

121. Covell and Rowe, "Round-Table," 438.

122. *Jimon Kōryū,* "Jiin ya shitei ni totte ima, shūmon daigaku to wa nanika wo shiru tokushū 2," 60.

123. Kashiwagi, "Daigaku ni okeru sōryo yōsei no kadai," 321.

124. Komatsu, "Nihon no gendai no seinen no seishikan to shūkyō kyōiku no kadai," 92.

125. Kashiwagi, "Daigaku ni okeru sōryo yōsei no kadai," 322.

126. For example, Bukkyō Daigaku also holds ceremonies for religious sentiment education purposes. These ceremonies are run by their Religion Faculty. *Jimon Kōryū,* "Jiin ya shitei ni totte ima, shūmon daigaku to wa nanika wo shiru tokushū 3," 84.

127. See Rowe, *Bonds of the Dead;* and Nelson, *Experimental Buddhism.*

128. Komazawa Daigaku, *Kyakkashōko,* 248.

129. Hanazono Daigaku, *Heisei 25 nendo Daiguku Kikan betsu ninshō hyōka,* 76.

130. Kōyasan Daigaku, "Kōyasan University Lifelong Learning Lecture Series in Koyasan" (summer lecture program booklet), 2003 (in author's possession). See also Kōyasan Daigaku, *Heisei 15 nendo Kōyasan Daigaku ni okeru genjō to kadai,* 123.

131. Other areas are Archaeology, Folklore Studies, and History/Documents. See Hanazono, http://www. Hanazono.ac.jp/about/museum.

132. Komazawa Daigaku, *Kyakkashōko,* 242. These are the last dates for which I have statistics.

133. There is a growing body of literature on this subject. See, for example, Graf, "Buddhist Responses to the 3.11 Disasters in Japan"; and McLaughlin, "In the Wake of the Tsunami."

134. Hoshino, "Kantōgen," 1.

135. *BSR Tsūshin,* "BSR toshoshitsu," 2.

136. *BSR Tsūshin,* "Kenkyū no-to: BSR gainen saikō," 2.

137. *BSR Tsūshin,* "BSR Topikksu," 4.

138. *BSR Tsūshin,* "Ōyō bukkyōgaku no kanōsei."

139. *BSR Tsūshin,* "Kenkyū no-to: BSR gainen saikō," 2–3.

140. *BSR Tsūshin,* "Sazaedō dayori" No. 1, 3.

141. *BSR Tsūshin,* "Sazaedō dayori" No. 2, 2.

142. *BSR Tsūshin,* "Sazaedō dayori" No. 4, 2.

143. *BSR Tsūshin,* "Sazaedō dayori" No. 1, 3.

144. The English translation here follows the one on Taishō's home page.

145. Taishō Daigaku, "Ōdai bondori tokushū [dai 4 kai]."

146. Taishō Daigaku, "Ōdai bondori tokushū [dai 2 kai]."

147. Taishō Daigaku, "Ōdai bondori tokushū [dai 3 kai]."

148. See news.livedoor.com/article/detail/13290337 (accessed January 29, 2018).

149. Taishō Daigaku, "Ōdai bondori tokushū [dai 9 kai]."

150. *Jimon Kōryū,* "Jiin ya shitei ni totte ima, shūmon daigaku to wa nanika wo shiru tokushū 5," 81.

151. Buddhist education scholar Minagawa Hiroyoshi, for example, makes the argument that a Buddhist-based education serves as a form of missionizing, the aim of which is to get nonbelievers interested in Buddhism, on the theory that this will help Buddhist schools attract students. See Minagawa, "Bukkyō ni okeru dendō to kyōiku."

152. *Jimon Kōryū,* "Jiin ya shitei ni totte ima, shūmon daigaku to wa nanika wo shiru tokushū," 38.

153. *Jimon Kōryū,* "Daigaku zennyū jidai wo mokuzen ni waga shūmondaigaku no genjō," 61.

154. *Jimon Kōryū,* "Jiin ya shitei ni totte ima, shūmon daigaku to wa nanika wo shiru tokushū," 39.

155. Ibid., 40.

156. *Jimon Kōryū,* "Jiin ya shitei ni totte ima, shūmon daigaku to wa nanika wo shiru tokushū 5," 84.

157. *Jimon Kōryū,* "Jiin ya shitei ni totte ima, shūmon daigaku to wa nanika wo shiru tokushū 2," 68.

158. Ibid., 70.

159. Ibid., 73.

160. *Jimon Kōryū,* "Jiin ya shitei ni totte ima, shūmon daigaku to wa nanika wo shiru tokushū 4," 100.

161. Taishō Daigaku, *Taishō Daigaku ni taisuru Daigaku Hyōka (Ninshō Hyōka) kekka,* 106.

Chapter 4: Moral Education and Buddhism

Epigraph: Sumida Keikō is a local temple priest cited in *Gekkan Jūshoku* (1977), 17.

1. The JET program is administered by MEXT. At the time it was a program primarily designed to send native English speakers into schools across Japan as assistant English teachers; it has since greatly expanded in scope.

2. *Daily Yomiuri,* "Election '99."

3. Nakanishi, "Goals for Japan in Its 'Second Postwar Period,'" 9.

4. Onishi, "Bukkyōhoiku no kongo no kadai ha nanika," 518.

5. Nakanishi, "Goals for Japan in Its 'Second Postwar Period,'" 12.

6. Hosokawa R., "Regaining the Spirit of Prewar Japan."

7. Hosokawa M., "The True Meaning of Civilization."

8. Tokuseiji, "Eshin No. 6."

9. *Gekkan Jūshoku,* "Dōtoku no kyōkaka de chūmoku sareru kaku shū seishōnen kyōka katsudō no jisai," 55.

10. Nolte, "Individualism in Taisho Japan."

11. Frei, "Japan's New Face of Politics."

12. This is a topic Fujitani covers in detail in *Splendid Monarchy.*

13. See Garon, *Molding Japanese Minds,* for more on this.

14. Luhmer, "Moral Education in Japan," 174.

15. Ban and Cummings, "Moral Orientations of Schoolchildren in the United States and Japan," 64.

16. Inoue, *Individual Dignity in Modern Japanese Thought,* 17. See also Nolte and Onishi, "National Morality and Universal Ethics."

17. Khan, "The History and Influence of the Imperial Rescript on Education on Moral Education in Contemporary Japan," 83.

18. Sekicho, "Imperial Rescript on Education." See also Khan, "The History and Influence of the Imperial Rescript on Education on Moral Education in Contemporary Japan," 93–94.

19. Nolte and Onishi, "National Morality and Universal Ethics," 284.

20. Ibid., 285. Davis notes, "The influence of Inoue Tetsujiro on the cultural life of prewar Japan can hardly be overestimated. At that time his books, unimaginative as they are, sold in the millions. As a commissioner in charge of compiling books for teaching moral education in the public schools and as an educator of educators, his impact on the Japanese school system was deep and long lasting." Davis, "The Civil Theology of Inoue Tetsujirō," 33.

21. Davis, "The Civil Theology of Inoue Tetsujirō," 22.

22. Kurita argues that Inoue's ethical religion project may not have been successful in terms of a specific immediate policy but had lasting influence, especially through debate and dialogue with religious leaders. His influence can be seen in practice at Japanese Buddhist schools and in the postwar government's insistence on cultivation of a student's heart/mind. Kurita, "The Notion of Shūyō and Conceptualizing the Future of Religion at the Turn of the Twentieth Century."

23. Inoue, *Individual Dignity in Modern Japanese Thought,* 32.

24. Wray, "A Study in Contrasts," 72.

25. Khan, "The History and Influence of the Imperial Rescript on Education on Moral Education in Contemporary Japan," 99. Khan is citing Katō T., *Kyōiku chokugo no jidai,* 9–14.

26. Luhmer, "Moral Education in Japan," 176.

27. Khan, "The History and Influence of the Imperial Rescript on Education on Moral Education in Contemporary Japan," 135.

28. Ibid., 191.

29. Hosokawa R., "Only Education Reform Can Save Japan."

30. Yamaguchi, "Japanese Young Forget Their Manners."

31. Inoue, *Individual Dignity in Modern Japanese Thought,* 91.

32. Kaizuka, "Senryōka no shūkyō kyōiku seisaku," 62–63.

33. Ibid., 62.

34. Luhmer, "Moral Education in Japan," 175.

35. Prime Minister of Japan and His Cabinet, "The Constitution of Japan."

36. Inoue, *Individual Dignity in Modern Japanese Thought,* 155. The text of *Image of the Desired Human* can be found at http://www.mext.go.jp/b_menu/shingi/chuuou/toushin/661001.htm#1 (accessed May 10, 2018).

37. Koike, "Kyōka to kyōiku," 102.

38. Part 2, chapter 1, section 5 of the *Image of the Desired Human,* MEXT, http://www.mext.go.jp/b_menu/shingi/chuuou/toushin/661001.htm#1 (accessed May 10, 2018).

39. Poukka, "Moral Education in the Japanese Primary School Curricular Revision at the Turn of the 21st Century," 222.

40. Koike, "Kyōka to kyōiku," 102.

41. Monbujihō, *Monthly Journal of Monbushō,* no. 1327 (1987): 117, cited in Katō S., *Shūkyō to kyōiku,* 119.

42. The above is derived from Itō, *Shinrigakusha ga kangaeta "Kokoro no no-to" gyaku katsuyohō,* 5.

43. Poukka, "Moral Education in the Japanese Primary School Curricular Revision at the Turn of the 21st Century," 173.

44. Poukka writes that MEXT spent 1,100 million yen over two years to produce and send the textbook series to 12 million students across Japan. Poukka, "Moral Education in the Japanese Primary School Curricular Revision at the Turn of the 21st Century," 238.

45. Cited in Poukka, "Moral Education in the Japanese Primary School Curricular Revision at the Turn of the 21st Century," 244–245.

46. Itō, *Shinrigakusha ga kangaeta "Kokoro no no-to" gyaku katsuyohō,* 8.

47. Poukka, "Moral Education in the Japanese Primary School Curricular Revision at the Turn of the 21st Century," 233–349.

48. Ibid., 317.

49. Ibid., 327.

50. Ibid., 332.

51. Born in 1941, Sugawara was a writer for *Asahi Shinbun* and in retirement taught as a lecturer at several universities in Japan. He specializes in issues of religion.

52. Sugawara, "Ima gakkō de shūkyō ha dō oshierareteiru no ka (2)," 105.

53. Kisala, *Prophets of Peace,* 3. This same schema is outlined in Hardacre, *Kurozumikyō and the New Religions of Japan;* and Tsushima et al., "The Vitalistic Conception of Salvation in Japanese New Religions."

54. See, for example, Aoki and Dardess, "The Popularization of Samurai Values."

55. Kisala, *Prophets of Peace,* 21.

56. *Gekkan Jūshoku,* "Dōtoku no kyōkaka de chūmoku sareru kaku shū seishōnen kyōka katsudō no jisai," 54.

57. Hasebe, "Bukkyō kyōiku to seikatsu shidō," 6.

58. Okaya, "'Kokoro no kyōiku' wo kannō ni suru ni ha," 107.

59. Tendai Shūmuchō Sōmubu, "Kuakuka no itto wo tadoru shōnen hanzai," 27.

60. Suzuki, "Shūkyō jōsō to shūkyō kyōiku," 163.

61. Komatsu, "Nihon no gendai no seinen no seishikan to shūkyō kyōiku no kadai," 92.

62. Suzuki, "Shūkyō jōsō to shūkyō kyōiku," 167.

63. Narita, "Shūkyō kyōiku no gendaiteki igi," 83.

64. Ibid., 86.

65. Kōkyōji, "Bukkyō to kokoro."

66. Tendai Shūmuchō Dōwasuishinka, *"Ijime mondai" to "Jinkenkyōiku,"* foreword. The Tendai denomination newsletter for priests, *Kōhō Tendai,* ran an article on bullying that same year that avoided this rhetoric and focused primarily on studies of bullying and contemporary developments for lowering incidents of bullying including counseling for the bullied and the bullies and sentiment education within families. Ogawa, "Ijime mondai wo kangaeru," 11–13.

67. Tendaishū Sōgōkenkyū senta-, *Kokoro no kyōiku wo kangaeru.*

68. Katō, *Shūkyō to kyōiku,* 121.

69. Tendaishū Sōgōkenkyū senta-, *Kokoro no kyōiku wo kangaeru,* 3–6.

70. Uryūzu, *Bukkyō kara no kokoro no kyōiku wo mezashite,* 31.

71. Ibid., 193.

72. Hōsen Gakuen, *Hōsen no kyōiku,* 7, 11.

73. Hiroaka Hidenobu took over running the Buddhist educational association Seifū Gakuen from his father (Hiraoka Tōhō, 平岡宕峯, 1896–1994), who was the founder. While serving as the leader of Seifū Gakuen, he held many other positions, including as a board member for Kōyasan Gakuen (高野山学園, a Buddhist educational association within the Shingon denomination). Much like his younger brother, he was active in Buddhist education. In his book *Oshieru kokoro, hagukumu kokoro* (教える心育む心, *Teaching Heart, Learning Heart*) he explains what he believes is wrong in Japan and offers solutions to the problems he sees Japan facing. Hiraoka, *Oshieru kokoro, hagukumu kokoro.*

74. Hiraoka, *"Toku, ken, sai" sanfuku shikō no susume,* 8. Hereafter, page numbers for this source are given parenthetically in the text.

75. Hiraoka is not alone in his view that citizens of the world will not take the Japanese seriously if they fail to ground their morals in religion. Yamada Etai (山田恵諦, 1895–1994), head priest of the Tendai denomination from 1974 to 1994, wrote, "The people of the world

take their religion seriously. Why? Because a person of true character cannot be complete without religion. Religion is the norm for how a person should live correctly. If that norm isn't held one cannot be trusted as a human. You become a someone who is blown about at the will of the wind, the place and the time." Yamada, *Jinsei awateru koto wa nai,* 190.

76. Regarding diet, Hiraoka observes that vegetarianism is not required, since "that which you eat becomes a Buddha in your stomach." Hiraoka, *"Toku, ken, sai" sanfuku shikō no susume,* 160.

77. Miyasaka, *Bukkyō ga skū nihon no kyōiku.* Hereafter, page numbers for this source are given parenthetically in the text.

78. He is not alone in this view. Kawamura Kakushō, a past head of the Nihon Bukkyō Kyōiku Gakkai (Nippon Buddhist Educational Research Association), says that there are no examples of other advanced countries that do not teach about religion and that morals should be discussed within the context of religious education. Quoted in *Gekkan Jūshoku,* "Dōtoku no kyōkaka de chūmoku sareru kaku shū seishōnen kyōka katsudō no jisai," 55.

79. Department of Seifū Gakuen and Seifū Nankai Gakuen International Exchange Program, *Seifū,* 11.

80. Seifū Gakuen, "Gakkōhōjin Seifū Gakuen Sōritsusha."

81. Interview with principal of Seifū Gakuen, December 7, 2002.

82. These field trips differ from the typical field trip at a public school in that, in the case of the Buddhist institutions, religious sentiment education is specified as one of the goals of the trip.

83. Hasabe Yūkei sees *aisatsu* as a way to practice courtesy through acts such as bowing. He understands this to be a requirement for a functioning member of society. This practice, in turn, expresses thankfulness. Hasebe, "Bukkyō kyōiku to seikatsu shidō," 11.

84. Interview with principal of Seifū Gakuen, December 7, 2002.

85. Ibid.

86. Ibid.

87. Hōsen Gakuen, *Hōsen no kyōiku,* 61; hereafter, page numbers for this source are given parenthetically in the text. This is a common understanding in Japanese Buddhist temples. Disheveled robes, sandals left scattered in the entryway, and the like all are seen as signs of an unsettled, undisciplined mind.

88. Hōsen Gakuen, "Hōsen Gakuen no Kyōiku."

89. Ibid.

90. See, for example, Reader, *Religion in Contemporary Japan.*

91. Sunada, *Yōji kyōikusha no nozomashii kyōshizō,* 96.

92. Interview with Shiba Gakuen principal, November 13, 2002.

93. At Seifū Gakuen the pattern is similar: junior high school students receive one hour of moral education per week, and senior high school students receive none in their first year, zero or one in their second year (depending on whether they are in the science track or the literature track), and between zero and three in their third year (depending on their track).

94. Fukase, "Seito no 'Shūkyōka' ni taisuru ime-ji," 152–153.

95. Sugawara, "Ima gakkō de shūkyō ha dō oshierareteiru no ka (1)," 71.

96. Bukkyō dokuhon henshūkai, *Bukkyō dokuhon:* vol. 1, *Shason no shōgai to oshie; Bukkyō dokuhon:* vol. 3B, *Honen Shonin goishō;* and *Bukkyō dokuhon:* vol. 2, *Bukkyou wo ikita hitobito;* and Hayashida, *"Watashi" wo mitsumete.*

97. Tsurumi Girls Junior and Senior High School, "Hongaku no kyōiku rinen."

98. Soji Gakuen Tsurumi Joshi Chūgakkō/Kōtōgakkō, *Information,* 1.

99. Ibid., 8.

100. Tsurumi Joshi Chūgakkō/Kōtōgakkō Shutokubu, *Watashitachi no gakuen,* 21.

101. They rotate the sutra that is chanted by school term: the Heart Sūtra in the first term, the Kannon Sūtra in the second, and the Shushōgi (a text by the founder of the Sōtō school) in the third.

102. See Tsurumi Joshi Chūgakkō/Kōtōgakkō Shutokubu, *Watashitachi no gakuen.*

Chapter 5: Learning to Persevere

A version of this chapter previously appeared in the *Japanese Journal of Religious Studies:* Covell, "Learning to Persevere." Epigraph: Hagami, *Kaihōgyō no kokoro,* 85.

1. The *sandaibu* are the major writings of Zhiyi. They are the *Mo ho chih kuan* (Japanese, *makashikan*), the *Fa hua hsüan i* (*hokke gengi*), and the *Fa hua wên chü* (*hokke mongu*).

2. See, for example, the textbook published by the Tendai Denomination Division of Doctrine. Taira, *Tendaishū no kyōgi.*

3. See, for example, the Light Up Your Corner of the World Activities, "Tendaishū no oshie—Ichigū wo terasu undō."

4. See Covell, *Japanese Temple Buddhism,* for more on this movement. It is referred to as the Light Up Your Corner Movement there. A standardized English translation was not yet in use by Tendai. The translation here is the one used by Tendai today.

5. Sakai and Kō, *Ikinukuchikara wo morau,* 99.

6. Conversation at Jindaiji, Tokyo, March 4, 2004.

7. Only three people have successfully completed the *kaihōgyō* twice since the Muromachi period.

8. In English see Rhodes, "The *Kaihōgyō* Practice of Mt. Hiei"; Stevens, *The Marathon Monks of Mount Hiei;* and Ludvik, "In the Service of Kaihōgyō Practitioners of Mt. Hiei."

9. See Nihon Hōsō Kyōkai, "Gyō Hieizan• sennichi kaihōgyō." See also the book written by the director of the NHK special: Wazaki, *Ajari tanjō.* Other documentaries include a French documentary, a sneak preview of which was shown to Tendai priests in the Tokyo area before its debut in Kyoto in 1999: Daniel Moreaeu, dir., *Les mille jours, ou la marche éternelle d'Ajari* (Dia Film Production, 1994). *The Marathon Monks of Mt. Hiei,* directed by Christopher Hayes, was produced by the BBC and later released in a North American version. It is based on John Stevens's book *The Marathon Monks of Mount Hiei.* Regarding the "marathon" image Hagami Shōchō states, "If it were only about walking, the postman would be far greater. Our job is worshipping as we walk." Hagami, *Kaihōgyō no kokoro,* 60.

10. The Tendai denomination held a one-thousand-year anniversary service for Sōō in 2017.

11. See Einami Sogen Tsuitō Shuhensaiinkai, *Einami Sogen Daikashō wo shinobite.*

12. This elongated route takes the practitioners, together with an entourage of supporters, by many of Kyoto's most famous Buddhist temples and Shinto shrines including Sekizanzenin, Yasaka Shrine, Kiyomizudera, and the Kitatenmangu Shrine.

13. Stone, *Original Enlightenment and the Transformation of Medieval Japanese Buddhism,* 125.

14. Shimazono, "Charisma and the Evolution of Religious Consciousness," 156.

15. Miyake, *Shūgendo,* chaps. 3–5.

16. Shimazono, "Charisma and the Evolution of Religious Consciousness," 157.

17. Ludvik, "In the Service of Kaihōgyō Practitioners of Mt. Hiei," 136.

18. Ibid., 136.

19. Shimazono, "Charisma and the Evolution of Religious Consciousness," 160.

20. Hagami, *Kaihōgyō no kokoro,* 79.

21. Unno, "Religions Derive Their Power from Authentic Spiritual Depth," 32.

22. This book was first printed in 1971 under the title *Dōshin—Kaihōgyō no taiken* and was reprinted in 1974. The edition drawn on here was published in 1997 under the title *Kaihōgyō no kokoro—waga dōshin* (回峰行の心—我が道心, *The Spirit of the Kaihōgyō: My Will to Enlightenment*).

23. The practitioner, accompanied by the head priest of Tendai and trailed by a procession of priests, enters the Imperial Palace in Kyoto without removing his sandals to pray for the health of the imperial family.

24. Hagami, *Kaihōgyō no kokoro,* 86.

25. Ibid., 53.

26. Sugitani, "Bukkyōsha to sensō."

27. Hagami, *Kaihōgyō no kokoro,* 173.

28. Ibid., 99. For more on the Meiji debate see Ketelaar, *Of Heretics and Martyrs in Meiji Japan.*

29. *Kaihōgyō* practitioners wear garb that is said to go back to the earliest periods of the practice: white robes, straw sandals, and a lotus-shaped hat.

30. Hagami, *Kaihōgyō no kokoro,* 8. Hereafter, quotations from this work are cited parenthetically in the text.

31. Sōka Gakkai is one of Japan's largest lay Buddhist movements. It is based on the teaching of Nichiren. Unlike many other New Religions and lay Buddhist organizations, which rarely posed a direct threat to Temple Buddhism, Sōka Gakkai refused to allow split affiliation and thus posed a significant threat.

32. Tendaishū Sōhonzan Hieizan Enryakuji, "Enryakuji ni tsuite." A previous iteration of this site had more extensive information under the heading "history" and the subheading "teachers," where there was a list of the founders of the many different Temple Buddhism denominations that had their beginnings on Mt. Hiei. Above the list the following was written: "The founders of the denominations: Trained on Mt. Hiei and opened their denominations." Tendaishū Sōhonzan Hieizan Enryakuji, "Soshi." The reference is also found in the introductory note on Enryakuji's English webpage: see Tendaishū, "Dengyō Daishi's Life and Teachings." This theme of Mt. Hiei as the mother mountain was picked up by scholars of Japan as well. See, for example, Reischauer, *Studies in Japanese Buddhism,* 141. It is also the language used in the online brochure for Hieizan Sakamoto: see Hieizan Sakamoto Tourist Association, "Hieizan Sakamoto," PDF linked under "Hieizan Enryakuji Temple."

33. Shugenhonshū, Washū, and Seikannonshū all broke away from Tendaishū during the postwar period.

34. Hagami, "Hieizan no kokoro," 220.

35. *Mōkorita* appears in Saichō's *Sangegakushōshiki.*

36. Hagami, *Kaihōgyō no kokoro,* 39–40.

37. Lay support groups provide funding for the practitioners, donate material goods, and participate in portions of the practice such as the *Kyoto omawari,* in which they help

direct traffic, plan meetings with local lay believers, and the like. See Ludvik, "In the Service of Kaihōgyō Practitioners of Mt. Hiei."

38. Hagami, *Kaihōgyō no kokoro,* 69.

39. Ibid., 143. That man was from Suntory, which is one of Japan's largest beverage companies (beer, whiskey, soft drinks) and a major sponsor of the Tendai denomination.

40. This is the *gekeshujō* practice noted above.

41. Sakai, *Ichinichi isshō,* 47–49.

42. Sakai and Kō, *Ikinukuchikara wo morau,* 79.

43. Ibid., 68.

44. Nakao, *Sakai Yūsai daiajarai,* 59.

45. Sakai, *Anata ni wa shiawase ni naru chikara ga aru,* 25.

46. Sakai and Kō, *Ikinukuchikara wo morau,* 17.

47. Ibid., 19.

48. Ibid.

49. Ibid., 45.

50. Ibid., 46.

51. Nakao, *Sakai Yūsai daiajarai,* 129.

52. Ibid., 129.

53. Ibid., 130.

54. Sakai and Kō, *Ikinukuchikara wo morau,* 47.

55. Sakai, *Ichinichi isshō,* 16.

56. Sakai and Kō, *Ikinukuchikara wo morau,* 76–77.

57. Ibid., 78.

58. See, for example, the Ministry of Education's 2002 white paper. MEXT, *Monbukagakusho.*

59. Sakai and Kō, *Ikinukuchikara wo morau,* 68–69.

60. Sakai, *Anata ni wa shiawase ni naru chikara ga aru,* 96.

61. Sakai and Kō, *Ikinukuchikara wo morau,* 72. Sakai completed the *jōgyō sanmai* as part of his three-year retreat before beginning the *kaihōgyō. Jōgyō sanmai* is a ninety-day retreat during which the practitioner circumambulates an image of Amida Buddha. He is allowed two hours of rest each day plus bathroom breaks but otherwise must be constantly walking. Sakai describes the practice as a way to unite body (forming a mudra and walking), speech (controlling breathing through the chanting of the *nembutsu*), and mind (keeping in mind/imagining Amida). Sakai, *Kono yo ni inochi wo sazukari mōshite,* 114.

62. Nakao, *Sakai Yūsai daiajarai,* 85.

63. Ibid., 59–60.

64. Sakai and Kō, *Ikinukuchikara wo morau,* 24.

65. Ibid., 22.

66. This call to fight through one's pain and troubles is similar to what one of Holloway's Buddhist informants said about kindergarten: "Living in a strong way is important in Buddhism. By being strong I mean that one should do everything with confidence and determination." Holloway, *Contested Childhood,* 162.

67. Sakai, *Ichinichi isshō,* 18.

68. Nakao, *Sakai Yūsai daiajarai,* 58–59.

69. Sakai, *Ichinichi isshō,* 11.

70. Nakao, *Sakai Yūsai daiajarai,* 67.

71. *Isshin sankan* is drawn from the Chinese T'ien t'ai text *Mo-ho chih-kuan.* See Swanson, *Clear Serenity, Quiet Insight,* for an English translation of this text.

72. Nakao, *Sakai Yūsai daiajarai,* 75.

73. This is a standard idea with Tendai Buddhism. It is found in Zhiyi's *Hsiao chih-kuan,* where he states that one who only studies is stupid, and one who only practices is crazy. Within Tendai, study and practice are seen as the wings of a bird or the two wheels on a cart: both are necessary. Swanson, *Clear Serenity, Quiet Insight,* 1661–1662.

74. Nakao, *Sakai Yūsai daiajarai,* 105.

75. Sakai, *Kono yo ni inochi wo sazukari mōshite,* 27–28.

76. Sakai and Kō, *Ikinukuchikara wo morau,* 99.

77. Ibid., 102.

78. Ibid., 118–119.

79. Ibid., 45, 52.

80. Ibid., 52.

81. Sakai, *Anata ni wa shiawase ni naru chikara ga aru,* 33.

82. Sakai and Kō, *Ikinukuchikara wo morau,* 102.

83. Ibid., 54.

84. Sakai, *Anata ni wa shiawase ni naru chikara ga aru,* 30.

85. Mitsunaga, *Sennichi kaihōgyō,* 51–53.

86. Mitsunaga, *Kaihōgyō,* 84–86. Hereafter, quotations from this work are cited parenthetically in the text.

87. Mitsunaga, *Sennichi kaihōgyō,* 225.

88. Ibid., 127.

89. This can be found in the *Denjutsu isshinkaimon,* a biography of Saichō. Tendai practitioners refer to the line frequently. It was, for example, on a previous iteration of the home page for Mt. Hiei, https://www.tendai.or.jp/journal/kiji.php?nid=203 (accessed December 10, 2023).

90. Mitsunaga, *Sennichi kaihōgyō,* 229.

91. Ibid., 219.

92. Ibid.

93. Ibid., 221.

94. Ibid., 59.

95. Ishihara, *Ima tamashi no kyōiku,* 17.

96. Mukhopadhyaya, "The Brighter Society Movement of Risshō Kōsei-kai," 7.

97. Tendai Shūmuchō, *Tendai zasuki daiyonhen,* 210.

98. The work of Helen Hardacre and others has shown that the New Religions, too, strongly emphasize "traditional" values such as diligence and sincerity—the same values at the heart of Hagami, Mitsunaga, and Sakai's teachings.

99. Befu, *Hegemony of Homogeneity.*

100. Reader, *Religion in Contemporary Japan,* 15–20.

101. Hardacre, *Kurozumikyō and the New Religions of Japan,* 21–28.

102. Tsushima et al., "The Vitalistic Conception of Salvation in Japanese New Religions," 129.

103. Tendaishū, "Tendai ni tsuite."

104. Shimazono, "Charisma and the Evolution of Religious Consciousness," 163–164. The view that linking morals to a higher power is needed can also be seen in the Japanese government's interest in promoting reverential awe, as we saw in chapter 4.

105. This view of the New Religions, especially the lay Buddhist movement Sōka Gakkai, is in no way limited to Hagami and Mitsunaga. Indeed, in 2002 the *Bukkyō Times* ran a series of articles titled "The Basic Problems of Sōka Gakkai." The temple-priest trade journal *Gekkan Jūshoku,* likewise, frequently covers what its editors feel are the dangers of some New Religions and Sōka Gakkai.

BIBLIOGRAPHY

Works in Japanese

Abe Kishi 阿部貴子. "Meiji ni okeru Shingonshū no kyōiku karikyuramu: Futsūgaku no dōnyū wo Megutte" 明治における真言宗の教育カリクラム: 普通学の導入をめぐって. *Gendai Mikkyō* 現代密教 24 (2013): 201–223.

Annaka Naofumi 安中尚史. "Kindai ni okeru nichiren kyōdan no shitei kyōiku" 近代における日蓮教団の師弟教育. In *Bukkyō ni okeru jissen wo tou (II)* *仏教のおける実践を問う(II)*, edited by Nihon Bukkyō Gakkai 日本仏教学会, 129–154. Tokyo: Hōzōkan, 2017.

BSR Tsūshin BSR 通信. "BSR Topikksu: Kumin hiroba de shuchō bukkyō koza!" BSR トピクス: 区民ひろばで出張仏教講座! *BSR Tsūshin BSR 通信,* no. 12 (2015): 4.

———. "BSR toshoshitsu." *BSR Tsūshin BSR 通信,* no. 1 (2014): 3.

———. "Kenkyū no-to: BSR gainen saikō" 研究ノート: BSR 概念再考. *BSR Tsūshin BSR 通信,* no. 14 (2015): 2–3.

———. "Kenkyū no-to: BSR to wa nanika?" 研究ノート: BSR とは何か? *BSR Tsūshin BSR 通信,* no. 1 (2014): 2.

———. "Ōyō bukkyōgaku no kanōsei" 応用仏教学の可能性. *BSR Tsūshin BSR 通信,* no. 14 (2015): 2–3.

———. "Sazaedō dayori" さざえ堂だより. *BSR Tsūshin BSR 通信,* no. 1 (2014): 3.

———. "Sazaedō dayori" さざえ堂だより. *BSR Tsūshin BSR 通信,* no. 2 (2014): 2.

———. "Sazaedō dayori" さざえ堂だより. *BSR Tsūshin BSR 通信,* no. 4 (2014): 2.

———. "Sazaedō dayori" さざえ堂だより. *BSR Tsūshin BSR 通信,* no. 7 (2014): 2.

Bukkyō dokuhon henshūkai 仏教読本編集会, ed. *Bukkyō dokuhon:* vol. 1, *Shason no shōgai to oshie* 仏経読本: vol. 1, *釈尊の生涯と教え*. 2nd ed. Kyoto: Jōdoshū, 1994.

———, ed. *Bukkyō dokuhon:* vol. 2, *Bukkyou wo ikita hitobito* 仏経読本*:* vol. 2, 仏教を生きた人々. 2nd ed. Kyoto: Jōdoshū, 1995.

———, ed. *Bukkyō dokuhon:* vol. 3B, *Hōnen Shōnin goishō* 仏経読本*:* vol. 3B, 法然上人御一生. 2nd ed. Kyoto: Jōdoshū, 1994.

Bukkyō hoiku kyōkai 仏教保育協会. *Heisei 24 nendo jigyo hōkuku* 平成２４年度事業報告. Bukkyō hoiku kyōkai, 2012.

Chūgai Nippō 中外日報. "Rensai Shinsō" 連載新装. 2015. Accessed March 25, 2015. http://www.chugainippoh.co.jp/rensai/shinsou/20150325-001.html.

Chūō Kyōiku Shingikai 中央教育審議会. "Koki chūtōkyōiku no kakujūseibi ni tsuite" 後期中等教育の拡充整備について. 1966. Accessed May 10, 2018. http://www.mext.go.jp/b_menu/shingi/chuuou/toushin/661001.htm#1.

Einami Sogen Tsuitō Shūhensaiinkai 叡南祖賢追悼集編纂委員会, ed. *Einami Sogen Daikashō wo shinobite* 叡南祖賢大和尚を偲びて. Kyoto: Kinseidō, 1971.

Ejima Naotoshi 江島尚俊. "Kindai nihon kōtō kyōiku ni okeru kyōiku to kyōka" 近代日本高等教育における教育と教化. In *Kindai nihon no daigaku to shūkyō* 近代日本の大学と宗教, edited by Naotoshi Ejima 江島尚俊, Miura Shū 三浦周, and Matsuno Tomoaki 松野智章, 3–32. Kyoto: Hōzōkan, 2014.

———. "Sōryo wo sodateru daigaku e" 僧侶を育てる大学へ. In *Kindai bukkyō sutadi-zu* 近代仏教スタディーズ, edited by Ōtani Eiichi 大谷栄一, Yoshinaga Shinichi 吉永進一, and Kondō Shuntarō 近藤俊太郎, 71–74. Tokyo: Hōzōkan, 2016.

Fujidō Okuto 藤堂憶斗. "Shūkyō to kyōiku" 宗教と教育. In *Gendai Bukkyō jōhō jiten* 現代仏教情報辞典, edited by Nihon Bukkyō jōhō jiten henshū iinkai 日本仏教情報辞典編集委員会, 238–242. Kyoto: Hozokan, 2005.

Fukase Shunji 深瀬俊路. "Seito no 'Shūkyōka' ni taisuru ime-ji" 生徒の '宗教科' に対するイメージ. *Nihon bukkyō kyōiku gaku kenkyū* 日本仏教教育学研究 7 (1999): 151–158.

Fuki Yōchien 吹上幼稚園. *Kyōiku rinen* (Educational Ideals), Accessed September 18, 2008. http://www.cc9.ne.jp/~fuki-you/sub4.html.

Gekkan Jūshoku 月刊住職. "Dōtoku no kyōkaka de chūmoku sareru kaku shū seishōnen kyōka katsudō no jissai" 道徳の教化化で注目される各宗青少年教化活動の実際. *Gekkan Jūshoku* 月刊住職 (July 2014): 52–62.

———. "Sengō nijūsannen 'hotoke no ko' wo sodateru yōgofusetsu ni jishin no fukyō no subete wo kakeru jūshoku san ha . . ." 戦後に十三年"ほとけの子"を育てる養護敷設に自信のすべてをかける住職さんは. *Gekkan Jūshoku* 月刊住職 (October 1977): 12–19.

———. "Shūkyō hōjin ritsu yōchien no genjō to mondai" 宗教法人立幼稚園の現状と問題. *Gekkan Jūshoku* 月刊住職 (October 1985): 20–25.

Hagami Shōchō 葉上照澄. "Hieizan no kokoro: Gendai tanka wo tsūjite miru" 比叡山の心: 現代短歌を通じて見る. In *Hieizan II: Sono kokoro to gyō* 比叡山II: その心と行, in Asahi Culture Books, 215–238. Osaka: Osaka Shoseki, 1986.

———. *Kaihōgyō no kokoro: Waga dōshin* 回峰行の心: 我が道心. Tokyo: Shunshūsha, 1997.

Hanazono Daigaku 花園大学. *Heisei 25 nendo Daigaku Kikan betsu ninshō hyōka: Jiko Tenken Hyōka Hōkokusho* 平成２５ 年度大学機関別認証評価: 自己点検評価報告書. Kyoto: Hanazono Daiguku, 2013.

———. "Rekishi hakubutsukan" 歴史博物館. Accessed June 26, 2022. https://www.hanazono.ac.jp/about/museum/.

Harada Katsumi 原田克己. "Taishō shindaigakurei to shūmondaigaku" 大正新大学令と宗門大学. *Nihon bukkyō kyōikugaku kenkyū* 日本仏教教育学研究, no. 8 (2000): 137–140.

Hasabe Yūkei 長谷部幽蹊. "Bukkyō kyōiku to seikatsu shidō" 仏教教育と生活指導 *Nihon bukkyō kyōikugaku kenkyū* 日本仏教教育学研究, no. 6 (1998): 1–19.

Hasegawa Masahiro 長谷川昌弘. "Shūkyōka karikyuramu ni okeru jissenteki kamoku no kōka" 宗教家カリキュラに置ける実践的科目の効果 *Nihon bukkyō kyōikuygaku kenkyū* 日本仏教教育学研究, no. 6 (1998): 106–110.

Hayashida Kōjun 林田康順. *"Watashi" wo mitsumete: Hōnen sama no yasashii oshie* "私"をみつめて法然様の優しい教え. Namu Books, vol. 13. Kyoto: Jōdoshū, 1999.

Hiraoka Hidenobu 平岡英信. *Oshieru kokoro, hagukumu kokoro: Kyōikugenba kara no messe-ji* 教える心育む心: 教育現場からのメッセージ. Tokyo: PHP Kenkyūjo, 1986.

Hiraoka Tatsuto 平岡龍人. *"Toku, ken, sai" sanfuku shikō no susume: Seifū Gakuen no ningen kyōiku* "徳・ケン・財"三福思考の進め: 清風学園の人間教育. Tokyo: Kawade Shōbo Shinsha, 1996.

Hoiku Plus. "Hoiku Hōhō" 保育方法. Accessed June 21, 2022. http://www.hoikuplus.com/post/usefulnurtureinfo/1612.

Hori Ichirō 堀一郎. "Gakusō kyōiku no shisetsu" 学僧 教育の施設. In *Bukkyō kyōiku no sekai* 仏教教育の世界, edited by Akitoshi Saitō 斎藤昭俊, 255–270. Tokyo: Keisuisha, 1993.

Hōsen Gakuen 宝仙学園. "Hōsen Gakuen no Kyōiku" 宝仙学園の教育. Accessed February 10, 2022. ho.hosen.ac.jp/education.php.

———, ed. *Hōsen no kyōiku* 宝仙の教育. Tokyo: Hōsen Gakuen, 2002.

Hoshino Eiki 星野英紀. "Kantōgen" 巻頭言. *BSR Tsūshin BSR 通信,* no. 1 (2014): 1.

Ideno Yukiko 出野由紀子. "Yōchien ni okeru jōsō kyōiku: Bukkyō yōchien no kansatsu kara" 幼稚園における情操教育: 仏教幼稚園の観察から. *Waseda Kyōiku Hyōron* 早稲田教育評論 18, no. 1 (2004): 71–83.

Ieda Ryūgen 家田隆現. "Bukkyō hoiku no genjo to mirai" 仏教保育の現状と未来. In *Bukkyō kyōiku no sekai* 仏教教育の世界, edited by Akitoshi Saitō 斎藤昭俊, 465–487. Tokyo: Keisuisha, 1993.

Ishihara Shintarō 石原慎太郎. *Ima tamashii no kyōiku* 今魂の教育. Tokyo: Kobunsha, 2001.

Isoyama Fukumasa 磯山福正. "Bukkyō hoiku no rekishi" 仏教保育の歴史. In *Bukkyō hoiku kōza: (1) bukkyō hoiku no kihon genri* 仏教保育講座: (1) 仏教保育の基本原理, edited by Masutani Fumio 増谷文雄 and Naka Arata 仲新, 366–380. Tokyo: Suzuki Shuppan Kabushiki Kaisha, 1969.

Itō Tetsuji 伊藤哲司. *Shinrigakusha ga kangaeta "Kokoro no no-to" gyaku katsuyohō* 心理学者が考えた"心のノート"逆活用法. Tokyo: Kōbunken, 2004.

Jimon Kōryū 寺門興隆. "Daigaku zennyū jidai wo mokuzen ni waga shūmondaigaku no genjō: Dentō jyūichi shūmondaigaku ni nyūgaku shita jiin shitei no kazu" 大学全入時代を目前に我が宗門大学の現状: 伝統十一宗門大学に入学した寺院子弟の数. *Jimon Kōryū* 寺門興隆 69, no. 8 (2004): 58–65.

———. "Jiin ya jiinshitei ni totte ima shūmon daigaku to wa nanika wo shiru tokushū" 寺院や寺院子弟にとて今宗門大学とは何かを知る特集 *Jimon Kōryū* 寺門興隆 16, no. 3 (2000): 32–41.

———. "Jiin ya jiinshitei ni totte ima shūmon daigaku to wa nanika wo shiru tokushū 2: Shūmondaigaku no kyodaika wa sōryo ya jiinshitei ga nozondeirukoto ka" 寺院や寺院子弟にとて今宗門大学とは何かを知る特集2: 宗門大学の巨大化は僧侶や寺院子弟が望んでいるこか. *Jimon Kōryū* 寺門興隆 18, no. 5 (2000): 68–75.

———. "Jiin ya jiinshitei ni totte ima shūmon daigaku to wa nanika wo shiru tokushū 3: Shūmonritsudaigaku ni hairitai hito to hairitakunai shitei sono taōsaku" 寺院や寺院子弟にとて今宗門大学とは何かを知る特集3: 宗門立大学に入りたい人と入りたくない子弟その対応策. *Jimon Kōryū* 寺門興隆 19, no. 6 (2000): 58–66.

———. "Jiin ya jiinshitei ni totte ima shūmon daigaku to wa nanika wo shiru tokushū 4: Bukkyōgakubu wo aratameta Taishō Daigaku ni sōryo yōsei no kokorozashi wa ikiteiruka" 寺院や寺院子弟にとて今宗門大学とは何かを知る特集4: 仏教学部を改めた大正大学に僧侶養成の志は生きているか. 寺門興隆 20, no. 7 (2000): 98–104.

———. "Jiin ya jiinshitei ni totte ima shūmon daigaku to wa nanika wo shiru tokushū 5: Shōshika wa mushoro bukkyōkei yosa wo api-ru dekiru jidaika" 寺院や寺院子弟にとて今宗門大学とは何かを知る特集5: 少子化はむしろ仏教系の良さをアピールできる時代か. *Jimon Kōryū* 寺門興隆 21, no. 8 (2000): 78–85.

Kaizuka Shigeki 貝塚茂樹. "Senryōka no shūkyō kyōiku seisaku: 'Shūkyōteki jōsō' kyōiku mondai wo jiku toshite" 占領下の宗教教育政策—「宗教的情操」教育問題を軸として—. *Nihon bukkyō kyōiku gaku kenkyū* 日本仏教教育学研究 10 (2002): 60–81.

Kashiwagi Masahiro 柏木正博. "Daigaku ni okeru sōryo yōsei no kadai" 大学における僧侶養成の課題. In *Bukkyō no ningengaku II: 21 seiki Bukkyō wa dō aru bekki ka?* 仏教の人間学II: 21世紀仏教はどうあるべきか? , edited by Taishō Daigaku 大正大学, 317–329. Tokyo: Michi Shobō, 1997.

Katō Saigō 加藤西郷. *Shūkyō to kyōiku: Kodomo no mirai wo hiraku* 宗教と教育: 子供の未来を開く. Kyoto: Hōzōkan, 1999.

Katō Tsuchimi 加藤地三. *Kyōiku chokugo no jidai* 教育勅語の時代. Tokyo: Sanshusha, 1987.

Koike Takanori 小池孝範. "Kyōka to kyōiku: Futatsu no bukkyō kyōiku wo tsunagumono" 教化と教育: 二つの仏教教育をつなぐ物. In *Bukkyō teki sekai no kyōiku ronri: Bukkyō to kyōiku no setten* 仏教的世界の教育論理: 仏教と教育の接点, edited by Nihon Bukkyō Kyōiku Gakkai 日本仏教教育学会, 89–111. Tokyo: Hōzokan, 2016.

Kōkyōji. "Bukkyō to kokoro" 仏教と心. Accessed September 18, 2013. https://sites.google.com/site/kokyouji/home/bukkyou-to-kokoro/kokoro-no-kyouiku.

Komatsu Makiko 小松万喜子. "Nihon no gendai no seinen no seishikan to shūkyō kyōiku no kadai" 日本の現代の青年の生死観. *Nihon bukkyō kyōikugaku kenkyū* 日本仏教教育学研究 9 (2001): 89–94.

Komazawa Daigaku Zengaku Jiko Tenken Hyōka Hōkokusho Iinkai 駒澤大学全学自己点検評価報告書委員会. *Kyakkashōko: Ashimoto wo tashikanamono toshite zenshin suru: Zengaku Jiko Tenken Hyōka Hōkokusho.* Tokyo: Komazawa Daiguku, 2012.

Komine Ichi'in 小峰一弁. "Bukkyōkyōiku no arikata nitsuite" 仏教教育のあり方について. In *Daigaku ni okeru bukkyōkyōiku—Shakaikyōka kyōiku kenkyūkai no kokoromi* 大学における仏教教育—社会教化教育研究会の試み, edited by Shakaikyōka kyōiku kenkyūkai 社会教化教育研究会, 9–14. Tokyo: Taishō Daigaku, 2006.

Kōrin Yōchien こうりん幼稚園. "Q&A." Accessed June 21, 2022. https://www.ans.co.jp/k/kourin/qa.html.

Kōyasan Daigaku 高野山大学. *Heisei 15 nendo Kōyasan Daigaku ni okeru genjō to kadai: Daigaku kijunkyōkai sōgō hyōka hōkusho* 平成１５ 年度高野山大学における現状と課題: 大学基準協会相互評価報告書. Kōyasan Daigaku. Koyasan: Kōyasan Daigaku, 2003.

———. *Heisei 22 nendo Kōyasan Daigaku ni okeru genjō to kadai: Tenken · hyōka hōkokusho* 平成 22 年度高野山大学における現状と課題: 点検・評価　報告書. Kōyasan Daigaku. Koyasan: Kōyasan Daigaku, 2010.

———. "Heisei 23 Rinen." 2011. Accessed June 26, 2022. http://www.koyasan-u.ac.jp/info/disclosure/pdf/2011/H23rinen.pdf.

Kyoto Joshi Daigaku 京都女子大学. "Hōshin" 方針. Accessed September 8, 2008. http://www.kyoto-wu.ac.jp/daigaku/kyoiku/houshin.html.

Light Up Your Corner of the World Activities. "Tendaishū no oshie—Ichigū wo terasu undō" 天台宗の教え: 一愚を照らす運動. 2016. Accessed June 24, 2022. https://ichigu.net/person/teach.php.

MEXT (Ministry of Education, Culture, Sports, Science, and Technology) 文部科学省. "Atarashii jidai ni fusawahi kyōikukihonhō to kyōiku shinkō kihonkeikaku no arikata ni tsuite (Chūkan hōkoku gaiyō)" 新しい時代にふさわしい教育基本法と教育振興基本計画の在り方について(中間報告 概要). 2002. Accessed August 8, 2019. http://www.mext.go.jp/b_menu/shingi/chukyo/chukyo0/toushin/021102.htm.

———. "Hakusho" 白書. Accessed October 18, 2017. http://mext.go.jp/b_menu/hakusho/html/others/detail/1317591.htm.

———. "Hakusho" 白書. Accessed October 18, 2017. http://www.mext.go.jp/b_menu/hakusho/html/others/details/1317510.htm.

———. "Ministry of Education, Culture, Sports, Science, and Technology Hakusho" 文部科学省 白書. Accessed October 18, 2017. http://www.mext.go.jp/b_menu/hakusho/html/hpab201701/1389013_022.pdf.

———, ed. *Monbukagakusho: 21 seiki no kyōiku kaikaku* 文部科学省: 2 1世紀の教育改革. Tokyo: Monbukagakusho, 2003.

Minagawa Hiroyoshi 皆川廣義. "Bukkyō ni okeru dendō to kyōiku: Bukkyōkeigakkō no kyōiku wo chūshin ni" 仏教における伝導と教育: 仏教系学校の教育を中心に. *Nihon bukkyō kyōikugaku kenkyū* 日本仏教教育学研究 8 (2000): 64–68.

Minori Yōchien みのり幼稚園. "About." Accessed September 18, 2013. http://minorikko.main.jp/about/index.html.

Mitsunaga Kakudō 光永覚道. *Kaihōgyō: Ima hito wa dō ikitara yoi ka* 回峰行: 今人はどう生きたらよいか. Tokyo: Shunshūsha, 1998.

———. *Sennichi kaihōgyō* 千日回峰行. Tokyo: Shunshūsha, 1996.

Miura Shū 三浦周. "'Gakushū' sareru Bukkyō: Taishō/Showa shoki no shūmonkeidaigaku ni okeru karikyuramu no henkan to sono tokushitsu." In *Kindai nihon no daigaku to shūkyō* 近代日本の大学と宗教, edited by Naotoshi Ejima 江島尚俊, Miura Shū 三浦周, and Matsuno Tomoaki 松野智章, 3–32. Kyoto: Hōzōkan, 2014.

Miyasaka Yūkō 宮坂宥洪. *Bukkyō ga skū nihon no kyōiku* 仏教が救う日本の教育. Tokyo: Kakukawa Shoten, 2003.

Mochida Eiichi 持田栄一, ed. *Bukkyō to kyōiku* 仏教と教育. 1979. Reprint, Tokyo: Nihon Hyōronsha, 1998.

Morinaga Shōshin 森永松信. "Bukkyōsha no shakai fukushi katsudō" 仏教者の社会福祉活動. In *Gendai bukkyō wo shiru daijiten* 現代仏教を知る大辞典, edited by Gendai bukkyō wo shiru daijiten henshū iinkai 現代仏教を知る大辞典編集委員会, 371–377. Tokyo: Kinkasha, 1980.

Mori Ryūkichi 森龍吉. "Gendai ni okeru dendō no imi" 現代における伝導の意味. In *Gendai bukkyō wo shiru daijiten* 現代仏教を知る大辞典, 217–220. Tokyo: Kinkasha, 1980.

Murakami Shinzui 村上真瑞. "Jiri rita" 自利利他. 2007. Accessed August 18, 2008. http://www.buppo.com/taisho_hoiku.html.

Myōjōkai 妙常会. "Nursery." Accessed June 26, 2022. http://www.tatibana.ed.jp/nursery/01/004/h-bukkyouhoiku.html.

Naka Arata 仲新. "Hoiku no rekishi" 保育の歴史. In *Bukkyō hoiku kōza: Bukkyō hoiku no kihon genri* 仏教保育講座: 仏教保育の基本原理, edited by Masutani Fumio 増谷文雄 and Naka Arata 仲新, 350–365. Tokyo: Suzuki Shuppan Kabushiki Gaisha, 1969.

Nakai Yoshihiro 中井良宏. "Shūmongakko kyōiku seido no kindaika katei: Meijiki ni okeru jōdoshū sōryo yōseijo kyōiku wo chūshin toshite" 宗門 学校教育制度の近代化課程: 明治期における浄土宗僧侶養成所教育を中心として. In *Bukkyō kyōiku no sekai* 仏教教育の世界, edited by Saitō Akitoshi 斎藤昭俊, 433–450. Tokyo: Keisuisha, 1993.

Nakano Kindergarten. "Naiyō" 内容. Accessed August 6, 2008. http://kosodate-web.com/nakanoy/naiyou/naiyou.html.

Nakao Kiyomitsu 中尾清光. *Sakai Yūsai daiajarai: Chōnin no oshie* 酒井雄哉大阿闍梨: 超人の教え. Tokyo: Chūō Kōronsha, 2000.

Nara Yasuaki 奈良康明. "Daigaku ni okeru Bukkyōkyōiku" 大学における仏教教育. In *Gendai bukkyō wo shiru daijiten* 現代仏教を知る大辞典, 402–408. Tokyo: Kinkasha, 1980.

Narita Hiroshi 成田敬. "Shūkyō kyōiku no gendaiteki igi" 宗教教育の現代的意義. *Nihon bukkyō kyōiku gaku kenkyū* 日本仏教教育学研究 9 (2001): 83–88.

Nihon Bukkyō Hoikukyōkai 日本仏教保育協会. 日本仏教保育協会. *Kodomo no kokoro wo sodateyō: Nyūmon bukkyō hoiku* 子供の心を育てよう: 入門仏教保育. 1984. 2nd ed., Tokyo: Suzuki Shuppan, 2002.

———. "Kyōkai hōshin" 協会方針. Accessed June 22, 2022. http://www.buppo.com/kyoukai_housin.html.

———. "Nihon Bukkyō Hoikukyōkai ni tsuite" 日本仏教保育協会について. Accessed May 13, 2022. http://www.buppo.com/kyoukai_sosiki.html.

Nihon Bukkyō Shakai Fukushi Gakkai 日本仏教社会福祉学会, ed. *Bukkyō Shakai Fukushi Jiten* 仏教社会福祉辞典. Kyoto: Hōzōkan, 2006.

Nihon Hōsō Kyōkai 日本放送協会. "Gyō Hieizan• sennichi kaihōgyō" 行比叡山・千日回峰行. Tokyo: NHK Service Center, 1979.

Ogawa Kōshō 小川晃勝. "Ijime mondai wo kangaeru" いじめ問題を考える. *Kōhō Tendaishū* 広報天台宗 3 (1996): 11–13.

Okamoto Gijō 岡本宜丈. "Kore kara no daigaku no kyōiku to shūmon deshi yōsei ni tsuite" これからの大学の教育と宗門弟子養成について. In *Daigaku ni okeru bukkyōkyōiku—Shakaikyōka kyōiku kenkyūkai no kokoromi* 大学における仏教教育—社会教化教育研究会の試み, edited by Shakaikyōka kyōiku kenkyūkai 社会教化教育研究会, 3–8. Tokyo: Taishō Daigaku, 2006.

Okaya Akio 岡屋昭雄. "'Kokoro no kyōiku' wo kannō ni suru ni ha" 心の教育'を感応にするには. *Nihon bukkyō kyōiku gaku kenkyū* 日本仏教教育学研究 7 (1999): 107–120.

Onishi Kenmei 大西憲明. "Bukkyōhoiku no kongo no kadai ha nanika" 仏教保育の今後の課題は何か. In *Bukkyō kyōiku no sekai* 仏教教育の世界, edited by Akitoshi Saitō 斎藤昭俊, 513–527. Tokyo: Keisuisha, 1993.

Osaka Ohtani University 大阪大谷大学. "Kengaku no seishin" 建学の精神. Accessed September 13, 2013. http://www.osaka-ohtani.ac.jp/about/spiritual.html.

Ozaki Haruki 尾崎春樹. *Kyōikuhō kōgi: Kyōiku seido no kaisetsu to shuyō ronten no seiri* 教育法講義: 教育制度の開設と主要論点の整理. Tokyo: Yōkōdō, 2016.

Saitō Akitoshi 斎藤昭俊. *Kindai Bukkyō kyōikushi* 近代仏教教育史. Tokyo: Kokusho kangyōkai, 1970.

———. "Nihon bukkyō kyōiku" 日本仏教教育. In *Bukkyō kyōiku no sekai* 仏教保育世界, edited by Saitō Akitoshi 斎藤昭俊, 271–316. Tokyo: Keisuisha, 1993.

Sakai Yūsai 酒井雄哉. *Anata ni wa shiawase ni naru chikara ga aru* あなたには幸せになる力がある. Kyoto: PHP Kenkyūjo, 2016.

———. *Ganbaranakute iinn da yo* がんばらなくていいんだよ. Kyoto: PHP Kenkyūjo, 2013.

———. *Ichinichi isshō* 一日一生. Tokyo: Asahi Shinbun Shuppansha, 2008.

———. *Ima dekiru koto wo yareba ii* 今できることをやればいい. Kyoto: PHP Kenkyūjo, 2012.

———. *Inochi kagayaku iyashi no kotoba: Ajari mondōshū* いのち輝く癒しの言葉: 阿闍梨問答集. Tokyo: Nihon Bungeisha, 2011.

———. *Kono yo ni inochi wo sazukari mōshite* この世に命を授かりもうして. Tokyo: Gentosha Renaissance, 2013.

———. *Mudana koto nado hitotsu mo nai* ムダなことなどひとつもない. Kyoto: PHP Kenkyūjo, 2011.

Sakai Yūsai 酒井雄哉 and Kō Ken 孔健. *Ikinukuchikara wo morau* 生き抜き力をもらう. Tokyo: Bijinesusha, 2003.

Sapporo Ōtani Yōchien 札幌大谷幼稚園. "Ōtani Yōchien nitsuite" Accessed December 10, 2023. https://ootani.ac.jp/ohtani/pages/31/.

Satō Benshō 佐藤弁正. "Chiiki shakai to henka" 地域社会と変化. In *Bukkyō hoiku kōza: Bukkyō hoiku no kihon genri* 仏教保育講座: 仏教保育の基本原理, edited by Masutani Fumio 増谷文雄 and Naka Arata 仲新, 129–141. Tokyo: Suzuki Shuppan Kabushiki Gaisha, 1969.

Seifū Gakuen 清風学園. "Gakkōhōjin Seifū Gakuen Sōritsusha" 学校法人清風学園創立者. Accessed February 10, 2022. http://www.seifu.ac.jp/edct/founder.

Seiwa Gakuen Tankidaigaku 聖和学園短期大学. "Hoiku gakka" 保育学科 Accessed September 8, 2008. http://www.seiwa.ac.jp/college/hoiku/.

Shibamoto Emi 柴本 枝美. "Yōchien no kyōikukatei no henkan ni kansuru ichi kosatsu: Shizen ni kakawaru hoiku ni shuten wo atete" 幼稚園の教育課程の変遷に関する一考察：自然にかかわる保育内容に焦点をあてて. *Kyōiku hōhō no tankyū* 教育方法の探究9 (2006): 1–8.

Shingonshū Buzanha Kyōikujigyōdan 真言宗豊山派教育業団, ed. *Buzan kyōikuzaidan shi* 豊山教育財団史. Tokyo: Shingonshū Buzanha Kyōikujigyōdan, 2017.

Shioiri Hōdō 塩入法道. "Taishō Daigaku ni okeru bukkyō kyōiku to NCC" 大正大学における仏教教育と NCC. In *Daigaku ni okeru bukkyōkyōiku—Shakaikyōka kyōiku kenkyūkai no kokoromi* 大学における仏教教育—社会教化教育研究会の試み, edited by Shakaikyōka kyōiku kenkyūkai 社会教化教育研究会, 15–18. Tokyo: Taishō Daigaku, 2006.

Shiroishi Yōchien 白石幼稚園. "Seimei sonchō no hoiku" 生命尊重の保育. Accessed August 6, 2008. http://www.ans.co.jp/k/siroisi/2.html.

Sōji Gakuen Tsurumi Joshi Chūgakkō/Kōtōgakkō 總持学園鶴見女子中学校・高等学校. *2003 Information: Sōji Gakuen Tsurumi Joshi Chūgakkō/Kōtōgakkō 2003 Information:* 總持学園鶴見女子中学校・高等学校. Yokohama: Sōji Gakuen Tsurumi Joshi Chūgakkō/Kōtōgakkō, 2002.

Suemitsu Yoshinobu. "Kyōiku seisaku to Bukkyō: Yōchien kyōiku wo megutte" 教育政策と仏教: 幼稚園教育をめぐって. In *Bukkyō kyōiku no sekai* 仏教教育の世界, edited by Saitō Akitoshi 斎藤昭俊, 489–500. Tokyo: Keisuisha, 1993.

Sugawara Nobuo 菅原信郎. "Ima gakkō de shūkyō ha dō oshierareteiru no ka (1)" 今学校で宗教はどう教えられているのか (1). *Jimon Kōryū* 寺門興隆, no. 61 (December 2003): 64–72.

———. "Ima gakkō de shūkyō ha dō oshierareteiru no ka (2)" 今学校で宗教はどう教えられているのか (2). *Jimon Kōryū* 寺門興隆, no. 62 (January 2004): 100–106.

Sugitani Gijun 杉谷議純. "Bukkyōsha to sensō: Sengo gojūnen ni kangaeru" 仏教者と戦争: 戦後五十年に考える. *Kōhō Tendaishū* 広報天台宗 1 (1995): 4–7.

Sunada Yoshihiro 砂田芳宏. *Yōji kyōikusha no nozomashii kyōshizō* 幼児教育者の望ましい教師像. Tokyo: Hakutsurusha, 2001.

Suzuki Kiyū 鈴木紀裕. "Shūkyō jōsō to shūkyō kyōiku" 宗教情操と宗教教育. *Nihon bukkyō kyōiku gaku kenkyū* 日本仏教教育学研究 6 (1998): 163–168.

Tada Kōshō 多田考正. "Bukkyōkei daigaku ni okeru shōraizō no kōkei (Taishō daigaku no ba'ai)" 仏教系大学における将来像の後継 (大正大学の場合). Sixth International Buddhist Studies Conference, 1991.

Taira Ryōshō 平了照. *Tendaishū no kyōgi* 天台宗の教義. Hieizan Sakamoto Honcho, Shiga: Tendaishū Shūmuchō Kyōgakubu, 1989.

Taishō Daigaku 大正大学. “NCC no senmonkamoku no risshū.” In *Taishō University Curriculum Guide,* edited by Taishō Daigaku 大正大学. Tokyo: Taishō Daigaku, 2005.

———. “Ōdai bondori tokushū [dai 2 kai]” 鴨台盆踊り特集第 2 回. Accessed June 26, 2022. https://www.tais.ac.jp/contribution_society/opc/ohdai_bonodori/p_shioiri/.

———. “Ōdai bondori tokushū [dai 3 kai]” 鴨台盆踊り特集第 3 回. Accessed June 26, 2022. https://www.tais.ac.jp/contribution_society/opc/ohdai_bonodori/p_yumiyama/.

———. “Ōdai bondori tokushū [dai 4 kai]” 鴨台盆踊り特集第 4 回. Accessed June 26, 2022. https://www.tais.ac.jp/contribution_society/opc/ohdai_bonodori/p_kimijima/.

———. “Ōdai bondori tokushū [dai 9 kai]” 鴨台盆踊り特集第 9 回. Accessed June 26, 2022. https://www.tais.ac.jp/contribution_society/opc/ohdai_bonodori/p_hayashi/.

———. “School Philosophy.” Accessed June 26, 2022. https://www.tais.ac.jp/english/philosophy/.

———. *Taishō Daigaku ni taisuru Daigaku Hyōka (Ninshō Hyōka) kekka* 大正大学に対する大学評価（認証評価）結果. Tokyo: Taishō Daiguku, 2013.

———. *Taishō Daigaku Tenken Hyōka Hōkokusho* 大正大学点検評価報告書. Tokyo: Taishō Daiguku, 2013.

———. “Undergraduate.” Accessed June 26, 2022. https://www.tais.ac.jp/english/faculty/.

Taishō Daigaku Gojūnenshi Hensan Iinkai 大正大学五十年史編纂委員会, ed. *Taishō daigaku gojūnen ryakushi* 大正大学五十年略史. Tokyo: Taishō Daigaku Gojūnenshi Hensan Iinkai, 1976.

Takada Shinryo 高田 信良. “Bukkyō (Shinshū) to kindai” kenkyū sosetsu: Shūkyō no keisei, jitsuzon no hakken, kyōgaku no kattō” 〈仏教(真宗)と近代〉研究序説：〈宗教〉の形成、〈実存〉の発見、〈教学〉の葛藤. *Ōtani Daigaku Ronshū* 大谷大学論集(2010): 195–217. http://hdl.handle.net/10519/861.

Tendaishū 天台宗. “Dengyō Daishi’s Life and Teachings.” 2015. Accessed September 5, 2017. https://www.tendai.or.jp/english/.

———. “Tendai ni tsuite” 天台宗について. 2015. Accessed June 24, 2022. https://www.tendai.or.jp/oshie/index.php.

Tendai Shūmuchō 天台宗務庁, ed. *Tendaishū shūkishū* 天台宗宗規集. Ōtsu: Tendaishūmuchō, 1994.

———, ed. *Tendai zasuki daiyonhen* 天台座主記第四編. Ōtsu: Tendaishūmuchō shuppanshitsu, 2001.

Tendai Shūmuchō Dōwasuishinka 天台宗務庁同和推進課. *“Ijime mondai” to “Jinkenkyōiku”* “いじめ問題” と “人権教育.” Otsu, Shiga: Tendaishūmuchō Dōwasuishinka, 1996.

Tendai Shūmuchō Sōmubu 天台宗務庁総務部. “Kuakuka no itto wo tadoru shōnen hanzai” 苦悪化の一途をたどる少年犯罪. *Kōhō Tendaishū* 広報天台宗14 (2000): 24–27.

Tendaishū Sōgō Kenkyū senta- 天台宗総合研究センター. *Kokoro no kyōiku wo kangaeru* 心の教育を考える. Otsu, Shiga: Tendaishū Sōgōkenkyū senta-, 2005.

Tendaishū Sōhonzan Hieizan Enryakuji 天台宗総本山比叡山延暦寺. “Enryakuji ni tsuite” 延暦寺について. 2018. Accessed June 3, 2022. https://www.hieizan.or.jp/about.

———. “Soshi” 祖師. 2018. Accessed August 4, 2014; the contents have since changed. http://www.hieizan.or.jp/about/soshi.html.

Tendaishū Tenhensanjo 天台宗典編纂所. *Kaihōgyō no so: Sōō san* 回峰行の祖: 相応さん. Kyoto: Jinkyūsha, 2017.

Tokuseiji. "Eshin No. 6." 2006. Accessed September 18, 2013. http://www.sanjo.nct9.ne.jp/tokusei/sub6%20eshin%2006.html.

Tsurumi Daigaku 鶴見大学. "Daigaku gakubu—Tandaibu" 大学学部—短大部. Accessed September 8, 2008. http://www.tsurumi-u.ac.jp/departments/junior/childhood.html.

Tsurumi Girls Junior and Senior High School. "Hongaku no kyōiku rinen" 本学の教育理念. 2001. Accessed April 9, 2002. http://www.tsurumijosi.ed.jpto/to_02.html.

Tsurumi Joshi Chūgakkō/Kōtōgakkō Shūtokubu 鶴見女子中学校・高等学校修徳部, ed. *Watashitachi no gakuen: Tsurumi Joshi Chūgakkō/Kōtōgakkō Gyōji Kihan* 私達の学園: 鶴見女子中学校・高等学校行事規範. Yokohama: Tsurumi Joshi Chūgakkō/Kōtōgakkō, 2001.

Uryūzu Ryūshin 瓜生津隆真. *Bukkyō kara no kokoro no kyōiku wo mezashite* 仏教からの心の教育を目指して. Kyoto: Jishōsha shuppan, 2001.

Wakakusa Yōchien 若草幼稚園. "Kōchō no kangae" 校長の考え Accessed June 21, 2022. http://wakakusa.2.pro.tok2.com/main.htm.

———. "Shizen no setsuri wo manabu yōchien toshite" 自然の節理を学ぶ幼稚園として. Accessed June 21, 2022. http://wakakusa.2.pro.tok2.com/sensei/leftomoi.htm.

Ward, Ryan. "Genzai to mirai—kingendai Jōdo Shinshū ni okeru seishikan no mondai nitsuite: Nonomura Naotarō no iannshin jiken wo chūshin ni" 現在と未来—近現代浄土真宗における生死観の問題について: 野々村直太郎の異安心事件を中心に. *Seishigaku Kenkyū* 生死学研究 9 (2008): 145–175.

Watanabe Masumi 渡辺真澄. "Jiin keiei to zaisei mondai" 寺院経営と財政問題. In *Bukkyō hoiku kōza: Bukkyō hoiku no kihon genri* 仏教保育講座: 仏教保育の基本原理, edited by Masutani Fumio 増谷文雄 and Naka Arata 仲新, 142–147. Tokyo: Suzuki Shuppan Kabushiki Gaisha, 1969.

Wazaki Nobuya 和崎信哉. *Ajari tanjō: Hieizan sennichi kaihōgyō—aru gyōja no hansei* 阿闍梨誕生: 比叡山千日回峰行—ある行者の反省. Tokyo: Kōdansha, 1979.

Yamada Etai 山田恵諦. *Jinsei awateru koto wa nai: Kokoro no yutori jūsan seppō* 人生あわてることはない: 心のゆとり１３ 説法. Tokyo: Yamato Shuppan, 1986.

Yasui Akio 安井昭雄. "Yōchien / hoikuen ni okeru bukkyō kyōiku" 幼稚園・保育園における仏教教育. In *Gendai bukkyō wo shiru daijiten* 現代仏教を知る大辞典, edited by Gendai bukkyō wo shiru daijiten henshū iinkai 現代仏教を知る大辞典編集委員会, 389–394. Tokyo: Kinkasha, 1980.

Yoshida Kyūichi 吉田久一. *Nihon kindai bukkyō shakaishi kenkyū* 日本近代仏教社会史研究. Tokyo: Yoshikawa Kōbunkan, 1964.

Zaidan hōjin zen nihon bukkyōkai 財団法人全日本仏教会. "Tekisetsu naru shūkyō kyōiku jitsugen no tame no kyōiku kihonhō daikyūjō kaisei no kansuru onegai" 適切なる宗教教育実現のための教育基本法第九条改正に関するお願い. *Zenbutsu* 全仏 (2005): 4.

Works in English

Aoki, Michiko Y., and Margret B. Dardess. "The Popularization of Samurai Values: A Sermon by Hosoi Heishu." *Monumenta Nipponica* 31, no. 4 (1976): 393–413.

Ban, Tsunenobu, and William K. Cummings. "Moral Orientations of Schoolchildren in the United States and Japan." *Comparative Education Review* 43, no. 1 (1999): 64–85.

Befu, Harumi. *Hegemony of Homogeneity.* Edited by Yoshio Sugimoto. Japanese Society Series. Melbourne: Trans Pacific Press, 2001.

Borup, Jørn. *Japanese Rinzai Zen: Myōshinji, a Living Religion.* Leiden: Brill, 2008.

Covell, Stephen G. *Japanese Temple Buddhism.* Honolulu: University of Hawai'i Press, 2005.

———. "Learning to Persevere: The Popular Teachings of Tendai Ascetics." *Japanese Journal of Religious Studies* 31, no. 2 (2004): 255–287.

Covell, Stephen G., and Mark Rowe. "Round-Table: The Current State of Sectarian Universities." *Japanese Journal of Religious Studies* 31, no. 2 (2004): 429–464.

Daily Yomiuri. "Election '99." March 28, 1999. http://www.yomiuri.co.jp/election-e/pl-ishi.htm.

Davis, Winston. "The Civil Theology of Inoue Tetsujirō." *Japanese Journal of Religious Studies* 3, no. 1 (1976): 5–40.

———. *Japanese Religion and Society: Paradigms of Structure and Change.* Albany: State University of New York Press, 1992.

Department of Seifū Gakuen and Seifū Nankai Gakuen International Exchange Program, ed. *Seifū.* Osaka: Takara Shashin Seiha, 2001.

Frei, Matt. "Japan's New Face of Politics." BBC News, 2001. Accessed December 10, 2023. http://news.bbc.co.uk/1/hi/world/asia-pacific/1399029.stm.

Fujitani, Takashi. *Splendid Monarchy: Power and Pageantry in Modern Japan.* Twentieth-Century Japan: The Emergence of a World Power, edited by Irwin Scheiner. Berkeley: University of California Press, 1996.

Garon, Sheldon. *Molding Japanese Minds: The State in Everyday Life.* Princeton, NJ: Princeton University Press, 1997.

Graf, Timothy. "Buddhist Responses to the 3.11 Disasters in Japan." In *Disasters and Social Crisis in Contemporary Japan,* edited by Mark R. Mullins and Koichi Nakano, 156–181. London: Palgrave Macmillan, 2016.

Hardacre, Helen. *Kurozumikyō and the New Religions of Japan.* Princeton, NJ: Princeton University Press, 1986.

———. *Shintō and the State: 1868–1988.* Princeton, NJ: Princeton University Press, 1989.

Hayashi, Akiko, and Joseph Tobin. "Continuity and Change in Japanese Preschool Education." In *Japanese Education in an Era of Globalization: Culture, Politics, and Equity,* edited by Gary DeCorker and Christopher Bjork, 33–46. New York: Teachers College Press, 2013.

Hayashi, Makoto. "Religious Studies and Religiously Affiliated Universities." In *Modern Buddhism in Japan,* edited by Makoto Hayashi, Eiichi Ōtani, and Paul L. Swanson, 163–193. Nagoya: Nanzan Institute for Religion and Culture, 2014.

Hendry, Joy. *Becoming Japanese: The World of the Pre-school Child.* Honolulu: University of Hawai'i Press, 1989.

———. "Kindergartens and the Transition from Home to School Education." *Comparative Education* 22, no. 1 (1986): 53–58.

Hieizan Sakamoto Tourist Association. "Hieizan Sakamoto." 2015. Accessed June 29, 2022. https://www.hieizansakamoto.jp/foreign/index_en.html.

Holloway, Susan D. *Contested Childhood: Diversity and Change in Japanese Preschools.* New York: Routledge, 2000.

———. "The Role of Religious Beliefs in Early Childhood Education: Christian and Buddhist Preschools in Japan." *Early Childhood Research and Practice* 1, no. 2 (1999): 1–19.

Hosokawa Morihiro. "The True Meaning of Civilization." *Japan Times,* January 1, 2001. https://www.japantimes.co.jp/opinion/2001/01/01/commentary/world-commentary/the-true-meaning-of-civilization/#.WfoCXxRjrzQ.

Hosokawa Ryūichirō. "Only Education Reform Can Save Japan." *Japan Times,* April 6, 2000. https://www.japantimes.co.jp/opinion/2000/04/06/commentary/only-education-reform-can-save-japan/#.WfoFeBRjrzQ.

———. "Regaining the Spirit of Prewar Japan." *Japan Times,* May 3, 2000. https://www.japantimes.co.jp/opinion/2000/05/03/commentary/world-commentary/regaining-the-spirit-of-prewar-japan/#.WfoEXBRjrzQ.

Hur, Nam-Lin. *Prayer and Play in Late Tokugawa Japan: Asakusa Sensōji and Edo Society.* Harvard East Asian Monographs 185. Cambridge, MA: Harvard University Asia Center, 2000.

Imoto, Yuki. "The Japanese Preschool System in Transition." *Research in Comparative and International Education* 2, no. 2 (2007): 88–101.

Inoue, Kyoko. *Individual Dignity in Modern Japanese Thought: The Evolution of the Concept of Jinkaku in Moral and Education Discourse.* Ann Arbor: Center for Japanese Studies, University of Michigan, 2001.

Jaffe, Richard. *Neither Monk nor Layman: Clerical Marriage in Modern Japanese Buddhism.* Princeton, NJ: Princeton University Press, 2001.

Japan Times. "Ozawa Lashes Out with Scathing Remarks on Christianity." November 11, 2009. http://search.japantimes.co.jp/print/nn20091111a2.html.

Jin-ai University. "Department." Accessed September 8, 2008. http://www.jin-ai.ac.jp/static/department/2-2.html.

Josephson-Storm, Jason Ānanda. *The Invention of Religion in Japan.* Chicago: University of Chicago Press, 2012.

Kawahashi, Noriko. "Jizoku (Priests' Wives) in Soto Zen Buddhism: An Ambiguous Category." *Japanese Journal of Religious Studies* 22, nos. 1–2 (1995): 161–183.

Ketelaar, James Edward. *Of Heretics and Martyrs in Meiji Japan: Buddhism and Its Persecution.* Princeton, NJ: Princeton University Press, 1990.

Khan, Yoshimitsu. "The History and Influence of the Imperial Rescript on Education on Moral Education in Contemporary Japan." PhD diss., Pennsylvania State University, 1994.

———. *Japanese Moral Education Past and Present.* Madison, NJ: Fairleigh Dickinson University Press, 1997.

Kisala, Robert. *Prophets of Peace: Pacifism and Cultural Identity in Japan's New Religions.* Honolulu: University of Hawai'i Press, 1999.

Kobayashi, Tetsuya. "Tokugawa Education as a Foundation of Modern Education in Japan." *Comparative Education Review* 9, no. 3 (1965): 288–302.

Kurita, Hidehiko. "The Notion of Shūyō and Conceptualizing the Future of Religion at the Turn of the Twentieth Century." *Religious Studies in Japan* 4 (2018): 65–90.

Lewis, Catherine C. *Educating Hearts and Minds: Reflections on Japanese Preschool and Elementary Education.* Cambridge: Cambridge University Press, 1995.

Ludvik, Catherine. "In the Service of Kaihōgyō Practitioners of Mt. Hiei: The Stopping-Obstacles Confraternity (Sokushō kō) of Kyoto." *Japanese Journal of Religious Studies* 33, no. 1 (2006): 115–142.

Luhmer, Klaus. "Moral Education in Japan." *Journal of Moral Education* 19, no. 3 (1990): 172–182.

McLaughlin, Levi. "In the Wake of the Tsunami: Religious Responses to the Great East Japan Earthquake." *CrossCurrents* 61, no. 3 (2011): 290–297.

McMahan, David L. *The Making of Buddhist Modernism.* New York: Oxford University Press, 2008.

McNeill, David, and Adam Lebowitz. "Hammer Down the Educational Nail: Abe Revises the Fundamental Law of Education." *Asia-Pacific Journal* 5, no. 7 (2007). https://apjjf.org/-David-McNeill/2468/article.html.

Mendes, Eric Teixeira. "Ancient Magic and Modern Accessories: Developments in the Omamori Phenomenon." Master's thesis, Western Michigan University, 2015.

Miyake, Hitoshi. *Shūgendo: Essays on the Structure of Japanese Folk Religion.* Edited by H. Byron Earhart. Ann Arbor: Center for Japanese Studies, University of Michigan, 2001.

Montrose, Victoria Rose. "Making the Modern Scholar-Priest: Buddhist Universities and Clerical Education Reform in Meiji Japan." PhD diss., University of Southern California, 2021.

Moreau, Daniel. *Les mille jours, ou la marche éternelle d'Ajari.* France: Dia Film Production, 1994.

Mukhopadhyaya, Ranjana. "The Brighter Society Movement of Risshō Kōsei-kai: A New Application of the Bodhisattva Way." Paper presented at Asian Studies Conference, Tokyo, June 2000.

Nakakida, Atsushi. "Early Childhood Education and Care Curriculum in Japan." In *Early Childhood Education in Three Cultures: China, Japan, and the United States,* edited by Liyan Huo, Susan B. Neuman, and Atsushi Nanakida, 25–37. Heidelberg: Springer, 2015.

Nakanishi, Teramasu. "Goals for Japan in Its 'Second Postwar Period.'" *Japan Echo,* April 2000, 8–13.

Nelson, John. *Experimental Buddhism: Innovation and Activism in Contemporary Japan.* Honolulu: University of Hawai'i Press, 2015.

Nishida, Yukiyo. "A Chrysanthemum in the Garden: A Christian Kindergarten in the Empire of Japan." *Paedagogica Historica* 51, no. 3 (2015): 280–297.

Nolte, Sharon H. "Individualism in Taisho Japan." *Journal of Asian Studies* 43, no. 4 (1984): 667–684.

Nolte, Sharon H., and Hajime Onishi. "National Morality and Universal Ethics: Onishi Hajime and the Imperial Rescript on Education." *Monumenta Nipponica* 38, no. 3 (1983): 283–294.

Okano, Kaori, and Motonori Tsuchiya. *Education in Contemporary Japan: Inequality and Diversity.* Cambridge: Cambridge University Press, 1999.

Ooms, Emily Groszos. *Women and Millenarian Protest in Meiji Japan: Deguchi Nao and Ōmotokyō.* Cornell East Asia Series. Ithaca, NY: East Asia Program Cornell University, 1993.

Poukka, Päivi. "Moral Education in the Japanese Primary School Curricular Revision at the Turn of the 21st Century: Aiming at a Rich and Beautiful Kokoro." PhD diss., University of Helsinki, 2011.

Prime Minister of Japan and His Cabinet. "The Constitution of Japan." Accessed February 12, 2022. https://japan.kantei.go.jp/constitution_and_government_of_japan/constitution_e.html.

Reader, Ian. *Religion in Contemporary Japan.* Honolulu: University of Hawai'i Press, 1991.

Reischauer, August Karl. *Studies in Japanese Buddhism.* New York: Macmillan, 1917.

Rhodes, Robert F. "The *Kaihōgyō* Practice of Mt. Hiei." *Japanese Journal of Religious Studies* 14, nos. 2–3 (1987): 185–202.

Rissho University. "About Rissho Univ." 2015. Accessed July 31, 2020. https://www.ris.ac.jp/en/about/founding.html.

Rowe, Mark. *Bonds of the Dead: Temples, Burial, and the Transformation of Contemporary Japanese Buddhism.* Chicago: University of Chicago Press, 2011.

Sekicho. "Imperial Rescript on Education." everything2.com, 2002. Accessed May 9, 2018. https://www.everything2.com/index.pl?node_id=1366527.

Shimazono, Susumu. "Charisma and the Evolution of Religious Consciousness: The Rise of the Early New Religions of Japan." *Annual Review of the Social Sciences of Religion* 6 (1982): 153–176.

Starling, Jessie. *Guardians of the Buddha's Home: Domestic Religion in Contemporary Jōdo Shinshū.* Honolulu: University of Hawai'i Press, 2020.

Stevens, John. *The Marathon Monks of Mount Hiei.* Boston: Shambhala, 1988.

Stone, Jacqueline I. *Original Enlightenment and the Transformation of Medieval Japanese Buddhism,* vol. 12: *Kuroda Institute Studies in East Asian Buddhism.* A Kuroda Institute Book. Honolulu: University of Hawai'i Press, 1999.

———. "A Vast and Grave Task: Interwar Buddhist Studies as an Expression of Japan's Envisioned Global Role." In *Culture and Identity: Japanese Intellectuals during the Interwar Years,* edited by J. Thomas Rimer, 217–233. Princeton, NJ: Princeton University Press, 1990.

Swanson, Paul. *Clear Serenity, Quiet Insight: T'ien-t'ai Chih-i's Mo-ho chih-kuan.* Honolulu: University of Hawai'i Press, 2018.

Takeda, Chido. "School Education and Religion in Japan." *Contemporary Religions in Japan* 9, no. 3 (1968): 211–232.

Tanigawa, Yutaka. "The Age of Teaching: Buddhism, the Proselytization of Citizens, the Cultivation of Monks, and the Education of Laypeople during the Formative Period of Modern Japan." In *Modern Buddhism in Japan,* edited by Makoto Hayashi, Eiichi Ōtani, and Paul L. Swanson, 85–111. Nagoya: Nanzan Institute for Religion and Culture, 2014.

Tobin, Joseph J., David Y. H. Wu, and Dana H. Davidson. *Preschool in Three Cultures: Japan, China, and the United States.* New Haven, CT: Yale University Press, 1989.

Tsushima, Michihito, Nishiyama Shigeru, Shimazono Susumu, and Shiramizu Hiroko. "The Vitalistic Conception of Salvation in Japanese New Religions: An Aspect of Modern Religious Consciousness." *Japanese Journal of Religious Studies* 6, nos. 1–2 (1979): 139–161.

Unno, Tetsuo. "Religions Derive Their Power from Authentic Spiritual Depth." *Pacific World* 1 (Fall 1985): 32–33.

Uno, Kathleen. "Civil Society, State, and Institutions for Young Children in Modern Japan: The Initial Years." *History of Higher Education Quarterly* 49, no. 2 (2009): 170–181.

Wollons, Roberta. "The Black Forest in a Bamboo Garden: Missionary Kindergartens in Japan, 1868–1912." *History of Education Quarterly* 33, no. 1 (1993): 1–35.

Wray, Harold J. "A Study in Contrasts: Japanese School Textbooks of 1903 and 1941–5." *Monumenta Nipponica* 28, no. 1 (1973): 69–86.

Yamaguchi, Mari. "Japanese Young Forget Their Manners." *Detroit News,* 2000. Accessed August 15, 2002. http://detnews.com/2000/nation/0004/13/a18-36274.htm.

INDEX

About the Author

Stephen G. Covell is chair of the Department of Comparative Religion and Mary Meader Professor of Comparative Religion at Western Michigan University (WMU). He is the founding director of WMU's Soga Japan Center. A Fulbright Scholar, he has written extensively on modern Japanese Buddhism and teaches Japanese religions and pedagogy. His publications include *Japanese Temple Buddhism: Worldliness in a Religion of Renunciation* (2005).